AESTHETICS OF APPEARING

Cultural Memory
in
the
Present

Mieke Bal and Hent de Vries, Editors

AESTHETICS OF APPEARING

Martin Seel

Translated by John Farrell

STANFORD UNIVERSITY PRESS

STANFORD, CALIFORNIA

2005

Stanford University Press
Stanford, California

Aesthetics of Appearing was originally published in German in 2000
under the title *Ästhetik des Erscheinens* by Carl Hanser Verlag.
© Carl Hanser Verlag München Wien, 2000. Assistance for the
translation was provided by the Goethe-Institut Inter-Nationes, Bonn.

Printed in the United States of America
on acid-free, archival-quality paper.

Library of Congress Cataloging-in-Publication Data

Seel, Martin.
  [Ästhetik des Erscheinens. English]
  Aesthetics of appearing / Martin Seel ; translated by John Farrell.
     p.   cm.—(Cultural memory in the present)
  Includes bibliographical references (p.   ).
  ISBN 0-8047-4380-0 (cloth : alk. paper)—
ISBN 0-8047-4381-9 (pbk. : alk. paper)
1. Aesthetics.   2. Appearance (Philosophy).   I. Title.   II. Series
BH39.S41813   2005
111'85—dc22   2004014234

Original Printing 2005
Last figure below indicates year of this printing:
14   13   12   11   10   09   08   07   06   05

Typeset by Heather Boone in 11/13.5 Garamond

Contents

Preface

This book makes the proposal of having aesthetics begin not with concepts of being-so [*Sosein*] or semblance [*Schein*] but with a concept of appearing [*Erscheinen*]. The appearing of which we shall be speaking is a reality that all aesthetic objects share, however different they may otherwise be. It plays its part everywhere in the aesthetic realm, in all aesthetic activity.

To apprehend things and events in respect to how they appear momentarily and simultaneously to our senses represents a genuine way for human beings to encounter the world. The consciousness that emerges here is an anthropologically central faculty. In perceiving the unfathomable particularity of a sensuously given, we gain insight into the indeterminable presence [*Gegenwart*] of our lives. Attentiveness to what is appearing is therefore at the same time attentiveness to ourselves. This is also the case—indeed, particularly so—when works of art imagine past or future, probable or improbable presences [*Gegenwarten*]. These artworks develop their transgressive energy from their presence as sense-catching [*sinnenfällig*] forms. They bring about a special presence in which a presentation of close or distant presences comes about.

With regard to art in the twentieth century, there could be some doubt about this. It may seem as if modern art had repeatedly taken flight from appearing. One need only recall the object Marcel Duchamp presented in New York in 1915 entitled *In Advance of the Broken Arm*: a completely standard snow shovel suspended from the ceiling of his atelier, which was serving as a gallery. Or recall Walter de Maria's *Vertical Earth Kilometer*, which was erected for *documenta VI* in Kassel, Germany, in 1977: a long, narrow rod extending deep into the earth; nothing of this rod can be seen except a small brass manhole cover in the middle of a sandstone slab measuring two square meters. According to influential commentators, here we encounter objects that, in their artistic rationale, stand above sensuous appearing. The consequence of this is that philosophy would be forced to chase the sins of sensuousness out of the temple of art theory.

I would like to avoid this consequence. Only the *expectation* of a particular appearing, aroused and disappointed by the staging of the object, renders comprehensible the point of that early readymade. In de Maria's installation, it is precisely the withdrawn character of the material art object that constitutes a technique for having something appear. This is because in a subtle and paradoxical manner it makes perceptible the space within which the installation—erected, not by chance, facing a traditional sculpture—extends under the feet of the "beholder." In the context of art, disappearing itself can be a source of appearing.

Even so, not only modern visual art but also literature seems to be able to circumvent appearing—at least wherever it does without rhythm or tone. Here, one might believe, there is no significant sensuous object evident, just a score that, as art, is to be disclosed not by the senses but only by the mind. From the outset, though, this division falls short of literary speech, since without (a sense of) appreciation for their conspicuousness as graphic, rhythmic, and tonal compositions there would not be any literary texts at all.

In these, as in many other points, it is—as ever—the arts that set the decisive test that aesthetics has to stand. But it can stand the test only if it does not turn away from the extra-artistic phenomena of the aesthetic—nature, decoration and design, fashion and sport, as well as all the other occasions of a sensuous alertness that is an end in itself. The particularity of art must after all find expression in art's *aesthetic* particularity, in how its objects differ not only from other things but also from other *aesthetic* objects and events. The philosophy of art is part of general aesthetics; it is only within this framework that it can be developed appropriately. The position of art in the human world is a position in the midst of a plurality of aesthetic opportunities that are themselves not subject to any artistic choreography.

The parts of this book focus on these opportunities in various ways. They all attempt to take plausible steps into aesthetics while proceeding from the central concept of appearing. In this way, they represent "chapters on aesthetics" that, depending on one's preferences, can be read independently of one another or studied as a whole.

The first of these chapters drafts the prehistory of an aesthetics of appearing that primarily serves to make clear to what degree the ensuing observations have already been outlined in traditional aesthetics. From Baumgarten and Kant to Valéry and Adorno, aesthetics has been guided by reflections on "what is indeterminable in things." This anamnesis leads to a determination of aesthetics as an independent and indispensable part of philosophy.

The book's main part, Chapter Two, attempts to develop the concept of appearing as far as is necessary for establishing it as a promising basic concept of aesthetics. Proceeding from a minimal concept of the aesthetic object and of aesthetic perception, a differentiated comprehension of the scope of aesthetic consciousness is developed step by step. This culminates in a thesis on the meaning of aesthetic practice: in the multifarious forms of this practice we are drawn into a play for the intuition of presence.

Chapter Three, on resonating [*Rauschen*], investigates an extreme form of appearing: visual, acoustic, and semantic phenomena that fascinate us as an "occurrence without something occurring" and therefore make perception possible at the limits of our faculty of perception.

Chapter Four comments on the current discussion on the status of pictures. The proposal to understand pictures as a ground of appearance on which something appears as presented leads to the introduction of distinctions vis-à-vis phenomena such as film and cyberspace. It is also the opportunity to reascertain the difference between the reality of the picture and that of the world.

Chapter Five investigates the relationship obtaining between artworks and relations of violence. In metaphorical violence, which art does to its addressees, there lies its ability to articulate processes of literal violence in an undiluted way. Because art has its presentation appear with a special power, it can—like no other medium—allow to appear what is especially violent in violence.

My thanks are due to many people who have on various occasions drawn my attention to the difficulties of my proposal; among them are Gernot Böhme, Karl Heinz Bohrer, Reinhard Brandt, Rüdiger Bubner, Sabine Döring, Christel Fricke, Sebastian Gardner, Lydia Goehr, Ruth and Dieter Groh, Hans Ulrich Gumbrecht, Ted Honderich, Angela Keppler, Bernd Kleimann, Manfred Koch, Sibylle Krämer, Gerhard Kurz, Konrad Paul Liessmann, Karlheinz Lüdeking, Christoph Menke, Anthony O'Hear, Eberhard Ortland, Ulrich Pothast, Klaus Sachs-Hombach, Hannelore and Heinz Schlaffer, Oliver Scholz, Ruth Sonderegger, Hent de Vries, Albrecht Wellmer, and Lambert Wiesing. Renate Kappes, Stefan Deines, Tobias Brodkorb, and Melisande Lauginiger have helped me tirelessly to chase the typographical errors and other reader-unfriendly spirits out of the manuscript. Barbara Klose found all the missing bibliographical details. In joint seminars on the concept of the picture and the mediality of art—and frequently just in passing—I have discussed the topics of this book with Georg Bertram and Jasper Liptow; what is spoken of here thus became a joint concern, though how it is spoken of is my responsibility.

GIEßEN, GERMANY
JANUARY 2000

A Rough History of Modern Aesthetics

This history is rough because it is brief, and brief because it is rough. It is brief since it addresses modern aesthetics—that going back to Baumgarten—only in tiny excerpts. It is rough because it identifies only the points of contact that a long and branching tradition has with the aesthetics of appearing drafted here. On the pages immediately following, therefore, I narrate not *the* history of modern aesthetics, but *a* history. How plausible this philosophical history is depends ultimately on how good the arguments are that support the contours it sketches. These arguments are just hinted at here, however, and not presented; presentation is reserved for the section bearing the title of the study.

The history I put forward here casts light on the background against which the subsequent parts of this book seek plausible steps into—and within—aesthetics. At the same time, it outlines the position that, to my mind, aesthetics assumes within philosophy. Aesthetics is an irreducible part of philosophy because it is an irreducible part of both theoretical and practical philosophy. It is only from the perspective of this dovetailing that the independence (as always in philosophy: the relative independence) of the discipline can be grasped. *Cum grano salis*, this is the response that Kant gave already in the *Critique of Judgment*. Nonetheless, this Kantian line has been followed only infrequently. The subsequent development was not lacking in false trails or confusions, nor, above all, in exaggerated expectations. Aesthetics was to be at one time a better epistemology, at another time a better ethics, and then simply a better way to philosophize. I do not wish to review these illusions once again here. The account in this chapter is rough in its brevity also because it tells a success story of the philosophical discipline called "aesthetics."

1. Eight Short Stories

Baumgarten

It all began with a portentous step. Alexander Gottlieb Baumgarten's *Aesthetica* (1750), which gave the new discipline its name, regards itself as a new and hitherto neglected form of epistemology.[1] It is concerned not solely with the beautiful objects of nature or art but, much more generally, also with a special faculty of perception. Baumgarten gave it the title "sensuous knowledge" (*cognitio sensitiva*). In contrast to clear and distinct conceptual knowledge, sensuous knowledge is a *cognitio confusa*, as Baumgarten says in reference to Leibniz. This is, however, intended as the opposite not of the *clarity* but of the *distinctness* of conceptual-propositional knowledge. Knowing something aesthetically possesses a conciseness completely different from knowing it scientifically. The accomplishments of the former maintain a relation of complementarity with those of the latter. It follows for Baumgarten that "complete" knowledge can be achieved only through scientific *and* aesthetic thinking, since each type of consideration beholds the given in an essentially different manner.[2]

According to Baumgarten, aesthetic knowledge is specialized in perceiving complex phenomena—not in order to analyze them in their composition but to make them present in their intuitive density. Here, something is not determined *as something*; rather, it is apprehended in the repleteness of its features. The goal of this knowledge is not the universal (which is grasped by classification and generalization) but consideration of the particular. To know the particular in its particularity is the real accomplishment of *cognitio sensitiva*, which is something no science will be able to achieve.

In the case of art, this requires a particular capability in presentation; everything art presents is presented with a sense of the particularity both of the presentation itself and of what is presented. In principle, though, the "lower" knowledge faculty—as Baumgarten also calls sensuous knowledge within the scheme of traditional divisions—is not dependent upon the medium of art. It can come into operation at any time and in any place, through a sensuous comprehension that lingers with a thing or a situation in the individuality of its appearing.

Kant

But is it really valid to call this perception in every case a *knowing*? Can aesthetics therefore be grasped correctly as a subspecies of epistemology? "No" is the response that Immanuel Kant gives in the first part of his *Critique of Judgment* (1787). Nevertheless, he attaches great importance to the fact that all the *powers* of knowledge are involved in aesthetic perception. But, he adds, what matters in aesthetic perception is not an acquisition of knowledge. The powers of knowledge are not required here for knowledge—that is the kernel of the numerous paradoxical determinations with which Kant characterizes the aesthetic attitude at the beginning of his aesthetics.

Being capable of epistemic determination, the subject of aesthetic intuition suspends determining epistemically. It does not determine the object of its perception in terms of particular features. Instead, the subject perceives the object in the unrepresentable repleteness of its features. For instance, when intuiting a beautiful flower—at the beginning of his aesthetics Kant considers primarily objects of nature—it is a matter of keeping "the cognitive powers engaged [in their occupation] without any further aim. We *linger* in our contemplation of the beautiful, because this contemplation reinforces and reproduces itself."[3] In contrast to *theoretical* contemplation, *aesthetic* contemplation is not concerned with certain insights that are to be gained by turning toward the object. The object is not to be conceptualized, any more than it is to be directed to a certain practical purpose. Without being reduced to this or that determination, the object is perceived solely in the presence of its appearing.

With this notion we arrive at a plausible initial determination of aesthetics. More resolutely than Baumgarten, Kant ties analysis of the aesthetic object to analysis of the perception of this object (and analysis of this perception to analysis of the judgments that give an account of the exercise of this perception). Aesthetic object and aesthetic perception are recognized as interdependent concepts. The aesthetic object is the object of a genuine form of perception that is concerned not with some of its objects' *appearances* [*Erscheinungen*] but with their process of *appearing* [*Erscheinen*].

Admittedly, this distinction is not drawn by Kant himself. It does, however, capture the core of the difference between theoretical and aesthetic modes of comprehension introduced by Kant in the *Critique of Judgment*. It is above all in the concept of play—a "*free play* of cognitive powers" that triggers a "play of shapes" on the side of the object—that Kant clearly emphasizes the process character of the aesthetic state.[4] The aesthetic appearing we are concerned with here is by no means just a subjective appearing (as, for instance, when I say, "It seems as if there were a cat here") or a purely subjective comprehension (as when I say, "To me the cat looks like a skunk"). Nor are we concerned in general with the phenomenon of a deceptive, or even transparent, collective semblance (as in the case of the illusion that the sun rotates around the earth). Rather, it is a particular *givenness* of phenomena that can be apprehended intersubjectively (just as the "rising" and the "setting" of the sun remain phenomenologically plausible even after Copernicus). Otherwise, Kant argues, aesthetic judgments would not be possible. Aesthetic appearing can be followed by anyone who, first, possesses the appropriate sensuous and cognitive faculties and, second, is willing to be attentive to the full sensuous presence of an object, while forgoing cognitive or practical results.

This theory of aesthetic appearing developed by Kant generates, besides a minimal concept of aesthetic perception, a minimal concept of the aesthetic object. These are minimal determinations because they highlight something that is characteristic for aesthetic objects and modes of comprehension—however radically different they may well be in other respects.[5] The aesthetic object is an object in the process of its appearing; aesthetic perception is attentiveness to this appearing.

Although this is nothing more than a minimal starting point, it is nonetheless a point of intersection at which the domains of aesthetics, epistemology, and ethics—separated initially by Kant—are internally connected. In exercising aesthetic perception, as he shows, we are free in a special way—free from the constraints of conceptual knowing, free from the reckoning of instrumental action, free as well from the conflict between duty and inclination. In the aesthetic state, we are free from the compulsion to determine ourselves and the world. This negative freedom does have a positive side according to Kant. In the play of aesthetic perception, we are free to experience the *determinacy* of ourselves and the world. Wherever the real presents itself in a repleteness and changeability that cannot be grasped but can nonetheless be affirmed, there we experience a scope for the possibilities of knowing and acting that is always already presupposed in all theoretical and practical orientations. For that reason, Kant sees the experience of the beautiful (not to mention the sublime) as an acting out of the highest capabilities of the human being. The richness of the real that is available— indeed, released—in aesthetic contemplation is experienced as a pleasurable confirmation of the extensive determinacy of reality by us human beings.

Hegel

A minimal concept of the aesthetic object such as we find it developed at the beginning of the *Critique of Judgment* can nevertheless be nothing more than the starting point for a plausible aesthetics. The basic concept of appearing does not yet say anything about the specific aesthetic constitution of the objects of *art*. Any aesthetics that deserves the name, however, has to prove itself ultimately in the most complex of all aesthetic phenomena. That is why Georg Wilhelm Friedrich Hegel defined aesthetics in his lectures (held in the 1820s) simply as a "philosophy of art."

That art essentially has to do with appearing is self-evident for Hegel. The work of art is, as he remarks succinctly, "an appearance that means something."[6] In contrast to other signs about which one could say the same, however, the meaning of an artwork is tied to the particular sensuous execution of the individual work. Like the simple object of nature, the work of art appears in its individual form; but in the case of the latter, this is a matter of an articulated (or, even better, an articulating) process of appearing. The *simple* appearing of the minimal aesthetic object is *enunciated* in the appearing of the artwork.

At a number of places, Hegel speaks of an "appearing" of the work of art that must not be equated with its sensuous being so, or with a deceptive apparency [*Anschein*]. The work of art is not exhausted in its sensuous appearance. It does not feign anything. It lets its *content* appear. It is accessible only to an interpretive perception that pursues, in sensuous attentiveness, the constellations and correspondences of the sculptured, gestural, visual, or aural appearance of the work. The content of works is interwoven with the configuration of the artistic material. Thus artworks are not just indescribable events of appearing but also an inexhaustible expression of the human spirit. The work of art presents its own appearing in order to allow forms of human world encounter to appear. In this way, it provides the human being with the possibility of an intuitive self-encounter that points way beyond his or her personal situation.

In Hegel's view, artworks are always media of aesthetic *knowledge*. What Baumgarten claimed for all forms of aesthetic perception applies to the perception of artworks. They can be perceived as artworks only if they are perceived epistemically in a specific manner. According to Hegel, art in classical antiquity was the highest medium of knowledge, only to be surpassed first by religion and then by philosophy.[7] In the present, Hegel says, soberly and correctly (here, little has changed since the beginning of the nineteenth century), art is just one *among other* forms of knowledge—a form of knowledge, moreover, that has increasingly distanced itself from its traditional function of being knowledge of the *absolute*. It is only for the art of his time that Hegel becomes the theorist of an autonomous art in a strict sense. This is no longer the representation of "eternal powers" that determine the lives of all people; it becomes a presentation of historical perspectives and life forms, an exemplary externalization of subjective worlds, closely tied to a heightened self-presentation of artistic material and artistic procedures.[8] Even in modern times, however, art (together with philosophy and religion) remains for Hegel one of the three successors of classical *theoria*, that is, the activity of making present (as an end in itself) the fundamental constitution of the real. But connected to this *theoretical* heritage of aesthetic practice there is also an eminent *ethical* heritage. The "thinking contemplation" of art is for Hegel an indispensable dimension of a life liberated from confinement in everyday life, just as the philosophical *theoria* was for Plato and Aristotle.

Schopenhauer

Arthur Schopenhauer established this connection among aesthetic, theoretical, and ethical practice much more closely. The danger of an *integrative* aesthetics, which assumes not only points of contact and overlap but even a *convergence* of theoretical, ethical, and aesthetic orientations, can be studied here in an exemplary manner. Quite a few theorists of the aesthetic since Kant have been exposed to this danger; after all, aesthetics since Romanticism has been one of the great hopes of a philosophizing fixated on unity, bent on overcoming modern bifurcations. Whereas the other authors I am dealing with here can be read as having ultimately escaped this danger, the possibility of a redeeming interpretation does not apply to Schopenhauer. In his *opus magnum The World as Will and Representation*, first published in 1818, Schopenhauer does indeed support and amplify the view defended by Kant and Hegel that aesthetic perception enables distance both to conceptual knowledge and to teleological action. But his basic thesis is that the subject of aesthetic intuition *abandons* the world of empirical appearances in favor of a contemplation of Platonic "ideas."

According to Schopenhauer, the contemplation of a mountain stream is directed not at the flowing, gushing, sprinkling of this individual stream but at the universal *idea* of a stream: at the unrestrained downward rush of a formless material. Individual appearance is not what aesthetic perception is really concerned with; it is simply the unavoidable external occasion for aesthetic perception. Hence, contemplation of an artwork is devoted not actually to the simultaneously sense-catching and articulating presence of the particular work but to the possibility of transforming oneself during contemplation into a "*pure* will-less, painless, timeless *subject of knowledge*" that exposes the world of everyday life and mundane striving as illusion.[9] For Schopenhauer, the aim of aesthetic perception is not a transformed *encounter* with, but an epistemic *overcoming* of, the empirical world. This is the world in which the principle of causality drafted by human understanding [*Verstand*] prevails; it is also the world in which we are herded about without any prospect of fulfilling our desires. By being able to expose this world in aesthetic contemplation as a semblance—albeit an unavoidable one—the subject of this insight is not only in a privileged epistemic position but also in a privileged ethical position. It experiences moments of a "deliverance from will" and a liberating "resignation" vis-à-vis the striving for worldly goods. The subject succeeds in overcoming all illusions about what is truly real and what is really important.

Aesthetic, theoretical, and ethical attentiveness are thus traced back to one source by Schopenhauer. Aesthetic perception is interpreted as the avenue to optimum knowledge and action, as the acquisition of the correct view of things. Schopenhauer's aesthetics does, though, pay a high price for this reduction. It blinds itself to the individual process of appearing of aesthetic objects. Aesthetic objects of nature and of art are degraded to "means of facilitating"[10] the acquisition of theoretical and ethical insight. Aesthetic respect for the particular is forced to betray individual appearance—to "forget [. . .] all individuality."[11] Instead of offering an alternative access to the phenomenal world, Schopenhauer's aesthetics preaches a radical exit from this world.[12]

Nietzsche

Nonetheless, Schopenhauer must not be excluded if the history of modern aesthetics is to be told with the prospect of a happy end, for without Schopenhauer there would be no Nietzsche (and without at least one bad guy there could not be a good story). In his book on *The Birth of Tragedy out of the Spirit of Music* (1872), Nietzsche puts Schopenhauer's sense-hostile aesthetics on its feet again. For Nietzsche too the experience of art means a radical rupture of the natural attitude. However, it comprises not an ascent to objective spirit or to pure ideas but a descent into a resonating that is devoid of ideas.

Proceeding from the example of music, Nietzsche describes the constitution of artworks as an interplay of Apollonian construction and Dionysian destruction. The work of art creates a complex sensuous and mental order out of the chaotic process of nature; to that extent it is a construct of semblance. In contrast to other cultural artifacts, the work of art discloses its own chaotic origins. In the play of its forms, it lures the observer into the process of an unformed reality. In so doing, the subject of aesthetic perception, as Nietzsche says, "suddenly loses his way amidst the cognitive forms of appearance."[13] The subject encounters a process of appearing that cannot be classified in any order of appearances.[14]

In diametrical opposition to Schopenhauer, the distance to the interpreted world that is torn open by the Dionysian energy of artworks is, for Nietzsche, not a going beyond the world of appearances but rather a radical losing of oneself in this world. Here, the empirical world changes its guise completely. It becomes visible no longer in a continuum of reliable features but in a movement of permanently dwindling forms. Without the construction of an artwork and without the competence of subjects capable of knowledge, though, this state could not come about. Without the presupposition of established culture, it would not be possible to step out of the confines of convention. It is only within a cosmos of meanings, as Nietzsche knows, that we can depart from the cosmos of meanings. It is only within a context of meanings that remain within reach that this departure can be experienced as an abysmal moment of ecstasy.

Nietzsche changes the position of aesthetics reached by Kant and Hegel in three respects. First, he corrects Kant's assumption on the reason for aesthetic delight. It is not the determinacy—and thus the ultimate controllability—but rather the indeterminacy and ultimate uncontrollability of the real that is the source of aesthetic pleasure. In the aesthetic state, we overcome our belief in the possibility and the point of any complete determination of the given. Aesthetic pleasure is guided by an interest in the unknown. Accordingly, playful self-discovery in free aesthetic contemplation has as its complement an ecstatic self-abnegation.

Secondly, Nietzsche provides a reason—one going beyond Kant—as to why aesthetic perception does indeed have a great affinity to knowledge but must not be apprehended from beginning to end as knowledge. In experiencing many artworks—and sublime nature, too—we live through phases of an acoustic or visual resonating, of an occurrence without anything recognizably occurring, something that can be followed sensuously but not cognitively apprehended. Sensuous perception here goes beyond the limits of epistemic consciousness. Outermost consciousness, it turns out, does not have to be epistemic consciousness at the same time; the intensity of perception and that of knowledge can diverge.[15]

From this follows, thirdly, a (vis-à-vis Hegel) changed determination of the constitution of the work of art. The integration of form and content, already fragile in Hegel, is abandoned by Nietzsche. Artworks do continue to be regarded as sign objects that obtain their meaning from their individual form; but now this form is understood as a form-building *process* that continuously switches all meanings back into an asemantic appearing.

Valéry

The first unambiguous apology of appearing comes not from Nietzsche but from Paul Valéry.[16] His *Eupalinos, or The Architect*, published in 1921, has the form of a Platonic dialogue, but only to teach an entirely anti-Platonic—and thus anti-Schopenhauerian—lesson. Phaedrus and Socrates meet in the shadowy world of Hades to talk, proceeding from the example of the architect Eupalinos, about the relationship between architecture and music and between music and poetry, but above all about experiences of the beautiful, which are so different from the orientation toward eternal ideas. "But still, did you never meet among men," Phaedrus asks Socrates, "some whose singular passion for forms and appearances [*la passion singulière pour les formes et les apparences*] surprised you?" "No doubt," Socrates replies. Phaedrus: "And yet whose intelligence and virtues were inferior to none?" Socrates: "To be sure I did!"[17]

In recalling longingly the experience of music and architecture, bodiless souls think of the body as the medium of an incomparable and irretrievable experience. In recalling the pleasures of sensuous perception, Phaedrus goes into raptures: "But I live again, I see once more the ephemeral skies! What is most beautiful finds no place in the eternal!"[18] "All this rings strange in the place where we are," says Socrates, recapitulating these astonishing recollections. "Now that we are deprived of our bodies, we must assuredly bewail it, and consider that life which we have left with the same envious eye with which we formerly looked on the garden of happy shades." To which Phaedrus responds, "These groves are haunted by shades eternally miserable. . . . "[19]

Valéry's theory of aesthetic experience leads into a resolute acclamation of the finiteness and presence of the being of mortals. In aesthetic experience they become aware, in an ecstatic manner, of this, their limitedness. They realize that unlimited possibilities of intuition and form lie in this very limit. Where, on the other hand, everything persists eternally, the experience of the uniqueness and manifoldness of the world is lost. Only a finite being is open to the moment of the here and now.

Within the ironic framework of his dialogue, Valéry develops the first aesthetics that does not just cross the plaza of aesthetic appearing but operates entirely on it. Not only does he speak of "*apparences*" that precisely the intelligent and virtuous can take seriously; he also celebrates the "phantoms" with which an orchestra can fill a concert hall.[20] Art is ascribed the power of generating a unique "edifice of apparitions, of transitions, of conflicts, and of indefinable events."[21] The beholder, listener, or reader can reside in this environment as if in a different reality. Valéry interprets this processuality of the work of art as a sort of *suspended appearing* that generates, in a repeatable manner, the sensations of an otherwise irretrievable presence. By appearing, the work of art creates something that has never existed before in nature.

For Valéry too, art goes beyond the creations of nature—not, however, in order to abandon the human world in favor of a realm of ideas, but to create a new, a second, world of intuitive forms. The artist "takes as the starting point of his act, the very point where the god had left off." The natural order of things serves as "chaos and primitive material" for his production.[22] The ideas and constructions of the artist lead knowledge not out of the phenomenal world but rather into it, in an unforeseeable, novel, and unique manner. Of the work of the painter we read, "He cannot separate color from some being."[23] The being of the work of art remains tied to the play of its appearing.

Where Kant sees aesthetic experience as an affirmation of the *determinacy* of the real, and Nietzsche regards it as an affirmation of its *indeterminacy*, Valéry sees aesthetic practice—above all, the artist's inventive production—as the discovery of a grand *underdeterminacy* of the real.[24] From the perspective of the aesthetic subject, this discovery is once more the revelation of a special human freedom. The acclaimed work of art reveals not an internal order of nature or being but the infinite field of possibilities that is left open by any such order. Everything that is given by nature and culture presents itself for the production and experience of "objects essentially human."[25] If Adorno says, paraphrasing the words of Karl Kraus, that it is the task of art to bring chaos into the order, then it could be said, paraphrasing Valéry's remark cited earlier, that it is the artist's talent to see chaos—an incommensurable repleteness of appearances—in the order of things.

Heidegger

In Martin Heidegger's and Theodor W. Adorno's theories of art—the last two stops in my history—Nietzsche's and Valéry's insight into the irregular processuality of the work of art had far-reaching consequences. Thus, in his article "The Origin of the Work of Art" (written in 1935 but not published in German until 1950) Heidegger sees the work of art caught in an irresolvable "conflict" between meaningful and nonmeaningful elements. The meaning-loaded appearances of the work of art are based on an appearing of the artist's material—"stone, wood, metal, color, language, tone"[26]— that threatens to make all meaning disappear. But the meanings disappear, only to reappear over and over again—as the meaning context of a cultural "world" that is grounded on a resistant, ungraspable, self-secluding "earth."

Heidegger interprets this occurrence as an eminently historical process. The emergence and passing away of cultural horizons of meaning takes place in the work of art. Whoever experiences this in an artwork participates in the changes that are brought about by the artwork; it provides a view of cultural worlds that it itself has opened up. The open-minded beholder steps into the world of works. In this way, there occurs an appearing of meaning contexts that evade any objectivizing appropriation. Thus the work of art makes it possible to experience all determining knowledge and all instrumental disposability [*Verfügen*] as relying upon presuppositions that cannot be determined conceptually or technologically. The work of art in the modern technological world is for Heidegger a display of the a priori nondisposability [*Unverfügbarkeit*] of the human situation.

Like Hegel before him, Heidegger deals severely with an aesthetics that reduces the work of art to a subjective potential for experience. The realm of art, Heidegger counters, must be conceived in terms of its works, but nonetheless under strict inclusion of the "producing," "lingering," and "preserving" attentiveness without which there would be no artistic products. This protest against an exaggerated subjectivization of aesthetics is by no means an objection to the eminence of artistic appearing. Quite the opposite. What is precisely of importance to him is an appropriate concept of this appearing.[27] What matters to him is to distinguish the appearances of the empirical world from the particular sensuous self-presentation of artistic objects. The "setting up of a world" [*Aufstellung einer Welt*] by the work of art, Heidegger says, is possible only by a "setting forth of the earth" [*Herstellen der Erde*].[28] The presentation of a world by art therefore can take place only as the self-presentation of its works. The fathomlessness of historical reality, which is disclosed by the particular work of art, becomes evident in the strangeness of what is set out in its own layout. The material of which a simple use object is made is

all the better and more suitable the less it resists perishing in the equipmental being of the equipment. By contrast the temple-work, in setting up a world, does not cause the material to disappear, but rather causes it to come forth for the very first time and to come into the Open of the work's world. The rock comes to bear and rest and so first becomes rock; metals come to glitter and shimmer, colors to glow, tones to sing, the word to speak. All this comes forth as the work sets itself back into the massiveness and heaviness of stone, into the firmness and pliancy of wood, into the hardness and luster of metal, into the lighting and darkening of color, into the clang of tone, and into the naming power of the word. . . . The earth appears openly cleared as itself only when it is perceived and preserved as that which is by nature undisclosable, that which shrinks from every disclosure. . . . To set forth the earth means to bring it into the Open as the self-secluding.[29]

Adorno

It is not a big step from here to Theodor W. Adorno's incomplete *Aesthetic Theory*, published originally in 1970. For him, the work of art is an object of articulation that is in a permanent state of suspension. As such, it puts up resistance to the petrified living conditions of the present; it tries to bring chaos to a compulsive social order.[30] Doing so, it relies on an irritating appearing that calls for a sensitive interpretation for which it is important "to use concepts to unseal the nonconceptual, without making it their equal."[31] The objects of this intimating interpretation are to be regarded, he says explicitly, "as something that appears, and not as blind appearance."[32]

Adorno does not, however, make terminological use of this distinction. Rather, he loads the concept of "appearance" with connotations that allow the said difference to surface in *one and the same* term. He understands the work of art not as an empirical appearance in the sense of a complex sensory datum but as an appearance in the sense of a reality that remains ungraspable; "Artworks become appearances, in the pregnant sense of the term—that is, as the appearance of an other—when the accent falls on the unreality of their own reality."[33] They relate to the rest of reality as an "apparition," that is, a religious or hallucinogenic vision in which something is suddenly present and then in the same instant is no longer there.[34] In this way, the appearing of an artwork differs radically from all phenomena that can be apprehended in knowledge and action; it is irreal in relation to what is otherwise known and acknowledged as real. Hence Adorno writes, "In each genuine artwork something appears that does not exist."[35]

Since this sounds somewhat mysterious, an example may be helpful. Barnett Newman's painting *Who's Afraid of Red, Yellow and Blue IV* (Nationalgalerie, Berlin) is 274 by 603 centimeters; the huge canvas does not have a frame. On the left we see a large red space, on the right a large yellow one; in the middle there is a much narrower blue strip that is approximately 60 centimeters wide. The paint has been applied homogeneously throughout. Pure colors, symmetrical arrangement—the whole painting rebels against such an apparently well-tempered and well-balanced composition. It is above all the vast color zones that generate a distinct imbalance. Whereas the red stands out aggressively, the yellow recedes from the beholder. This arrangement, which appears askew to a lingering perception, is further shaped by the different demarcations of the two large color spaces to the blue surface in the middle. The blue overlaps the neighboring red just a little, whereas it itself is covered minimally by the yellow surface. The aggressive red is restrained by the blue; the soft yellow, on the other hand, remains unbound. What could act like a balance between the colors' various spatial effects serves only to intensify the boldness of the red and the restraint of the yellow field. Moreover, the large color spaces expand more and more when viewing the painting; they cross the borders of the painting, just as they continually cross the borders to the other colors. The colors illuminate each other. In perception, they let an oscillating continuum evolve, a color space not limited in depth either, a space that gradually enfolds the beholder. In this manner, the painting stages an onslaught of the color fields of which it consists, an onslaught that goes beyond the actual surface of the painting. It is a piece of anticompositional and antipurist painting. It breaks the form in which the beholder encounters it at first glance. It celebrates the ability to go perceptively beyond the order of the visible world.

"In each genuine artwork something appears that does not exist." In this work of art, there appears a rebellion of color against the coercion of balanced design. This cannot be seen in the *natural* attitude. What this attitude sees is just a red, yellow, and blue surface, a piece of technically good painting, nothing more. Nor can an art-remote, *aesthetic* perception—one directed at the *mere* appearing of this object—notice anything of the excesses of this painting; some beholders could for instance stick purely to the glow, interaction, and iridescence of the color surfaces. Other beholders, those concerned not just with the sensuous intensity but with the *decorative* value of the object, could be pleased by its symmetrical surface and regard it as a manifestation of "positive thinking." This apparency disappears only with a deliberate *art-oriented* contemplation of the painting that is in a position to perceive it as a revolt against any decorative, symmetric, balanced style of painting.[36] It is only here that, with compository planning, the "spirit" of the painting becomes noticeable, a spirit that "appears through the appearance."[37] Or, as Adorno circumscribes the status of artworks using one of his pyrotechnic metaphors, "They become eloquent by the force of the kindling of thing and appearance."[38]

The work of art—this is Adorno's plausible contention, which refers back to Baumgarten and Kant no less than to Nietzsche and Heidegger—reveals to its beholder that reality is richer than all of the appearances we can fix in the language of conceptual knowledge. It unfolds the difference between determinable appearance and indeterminable appearing; it underscores the fact that reality is not just given to us as a collection of facts. "Beauty demands, perhaps, the slavish imitation of what is indeterminable in things," Adorno quotes more than once from Paul Valéry's *Autres Rhumbs.*[39] Consideration of this indeterminable is not only of great theoretical importance but also of great ethical significance to Adorno. It opens a "freedom to the object," which is a condition of real freedom among subjects.[40] For Adorno, art thus becomes the hallmark indicating that the world has not been comprehended if it is known only conceptually; that the world has not been appropriated if it is appropriated only technically; that individual and social freedom have not been attained if they are guaranteed merely as a license to make profit; in a word, that we do not really encounter the reality of our lives if we encounter it merely in a spirit of mastery.

2. Aesthetics as Part of Philosophy

That was my history of aesthetics, consisting of eight short stories. Now to the moral of this story. The moral I am concerned with refers to the position of aesthetics in the concert of philosophy. If one looks at the academic organization of philosophy today, then this position is quite marginal. If, on the other hand, one looks at the history of philosophy, at least in the German-speaking world, then this is a very central position. Almost all important philosophers of this tradition—including such authors as Marx, Frege, or Husserl who untypically did not leave behind any classic study on the topic—owe important motifs to aesthetic reflection. I would therefore like to end my historical sketch with a brief systematic synopsis that serves to explain and justify why philosophy has accorded aesthetics such a strong position.

To apprehend something in the process of its appearing for the sake of its appearing is a focal point of all aesthetic perception. Of course, this perception frequently goes way beyond a mere execution-oriented sensing. In particular, the perception of artworks necessarily incorporates interpretive and epistemic attentiveness. However, the aim of this interpretation and knowledge is first and foremost to be with the articulating appearing of their objects. In reference to Hegel, Nietzsche, Heidegger, and Adorno I have said a number of things about the value of this encounter. In conclusion, I would like to focus again on the meaning of aesthetic perception in general.

In aesthetic perception—that is, the unbroken thread in aesthetic theory from Baumgarten to Adorno (and beyond)[41]—there occurs an affirmation of the conceptually and practically indeterminable; it is, as we could say with Valéry, a sensuous consideration of what is indeterminable in things. It wants to leave its objects not as they are under this or that aspect but as they appear individually to our senses here and now. Yet this concentration on the momentary appearing of *things* is always at the same time an attentiveness to the situation of *perception* of their appearing—and thus reflection on the immediate *presence* in which this perception is executed. Aesthetic attentiveness to what happens in the external world is thus an attentiveness to ourselves too: to the moment here and now. In addition, aesthetic attentiveness to the objects of art is frequently an attentiveness to situations in which we do not find ourselves and perhaps never will: to a moment now and never.

Even so, this process of becoming aesthetically aware is in a relation of irresolvable tension to other forms of self-consciousness. As an intuiting consciousness of the actual or possible presence of our being, it differs (in various kinds and degrees) from all consciousness of who we are over an extended period of time, and who we want to be over such a period. In the execution of aesthetic experience, we suspend this knowledge in order to be outside the continuity of our lives for a while. Aesthetic interest—or, if we want to follow Kant's choice of words, particular aesthetic disinterest—is grounded on the desire to be perceptually aware of the presence of one's own being. For epistemic beings, however, the consciously lived present means that indeterminacy flares up in everything that can be theoretically and practically determined. A particular accomplishment of aesthetic intuition is to make present in their nontransparency the unrecognized and unused possibilities that emerge here. No consciousness of one's present is possible without aesthetic consciousness.

Aesthetic attentiveness—in the middle of a city; at the edge of civilization; in the perception, production, and performance of art—would thus be an essential feature of human self-consciousness. But it is essentially a particular feature. It is not so much an awareness of certain facts, desires, duties, or life plans as it is a sense of the here and now of one's own life, as it becomes accessible only in openness to the play of appearance of a given situation. The changeability of these appearances calls to mind the ephemerality of this and every presence of appearing—and the pleasures of this ephemerality hailed by Valéry. Heidegger wanted to show philosophy a way out of its forgetfulness of being [*Seinsvergessenheit*]. Aesthetics—including Heidegger's own philosophy of art—gives a different recommendation. We should not be forgetful of appearance [*erscheinungsvergessen*]. We should not lose a taste for the moment, for it is this aptitude that makes it possible to comprehend uncontrollable presence not as a lack of meaning or being but as an opportunity to get in touch with ourselves in a way that we must leave aside in the course of logical thought and action.

Along this path, aesthetics in the German-speaking world—but not just here, as my chief witness Valéry attests—has developed into an independent and indispensable discipline in philosophy. Aesthetics is an *independent* part of philosophy because it is concerned with a relation to the world that cannot be traced back to theoretical or ethical approaches. Aesthetics is *indispensable* for other philosophical disciplines—and therefore for philosophical thinking itself—because it is concerned with irreducible aspects of world and life. Neither the reality accessible to aesthetic consciousness nor the presence attainable in this consciousness can be treated properly within the framework of other disciplines.

Of course, one could say that aesthetics, as a doctrine of special possibilities of perception and special possibilities of living life, is a part both of a comprehensive theory of perception and of a comprehensive ethics. However, since we are involved not with two parts of aesthetics—one of which would be ascribed to theoretical philosophy and the other to practical philosophy—but with the *selfsame* central pieces of analysis that are relatively independent elements of both an extended ethics and an extended epistemology, aesthetics is thus a discipline in its own right.

From the perspective of *theoretical* philosophy, aesthetics makes an indispensable contribution because it uncovers a dimension of reality that evades epistemic fixation but is nonetheless an aspect of knowable reality.[42] Attending to what is appearing makes it possible to experience reality as being richer than everything that can be known about it by means of propositional determination. Aesthetics lays open a limit to all theoretical world comprehension—a limit to which epistemology and the philosophy of mind should not close their eyes.

From the perspective of *practical* philosophy, aesthetics makes an indispensable contribution because it is concerned with a particular possibility for human life, one that discloses the presence of one's own being as an end in itself. Since aesthetic world encounter represents an excellent possibility for human life, it should not be neglected—neither by an ethics of the good life nor by an ethics of moral respect. It is a part of those life forms that ought to be emulated in one's own interest as well as protected by moral norms.[43]

Nonetheless, there is no reason to elevate aesthetics to the status of the regal discipline of philosophy. Nor is there any reason to declare aesthetic conduct to be the pinnacle of human possibilities. Acts of aesthetic perception can enrich the possibilities of human perception in almost all areas—and that's all. Such acts make possible an affirmation of the momentary present, however fleeting it may be. The fissures they generate can neither outdo nor replace the potential of conceptual knowledge and intervening action, just as this mode of knowledge and action cannot replace or outdo openness to appearing. Encounter with the particular—with the uniqueness of the world, as Adorno and Horkheimer say at one point in their otherwise somber *Dialectic of Enlightenment*[44]—has its meaning in itself. This has been the modest message of aesthetics since the days of Baumgarten and Kant.

II

Aesthetics of Appearing

In aesthetics, as in all areas of philosophy, one can begin almost anywhere—with the objects of nature or those of art; with aesthetic production or reception; with aesthetic judgment or artistic imagination; with concepts of things or concepts of signs; with the existential, cognitive, or ethical meaning of aesthetic states. However one begins aesthetics, the important thing is to examine the *interrelatedness* of these and other phenomena. This also applies when we are concerned predominantly with special phenomena—that is, in aesthetics, with literature or film, ornament or design, monochrome painting or minimal music. One type of aesthetic object enjoys its distinctiveness only in relation to other types, against which it stands out, to which it is related, with which it is in a process of exchange. Ultimately, this holds even for every individual aesthetic object—for this landscape, this building, this installation. Each enjoys its particularity in contrast to other (types of) objects. Theory can support this particularity (and thereby fulfill its most important task) only if it shows in what more general relations this particularity is located. It is only together with a sense of the general that the sense of the particular is there; only together with a concept of this general is it possible to have an understanding of the multiplicity of aesthetic objects and opportunities. No matter how one begins aesthetics, what always matters in the end is to have a sense of the richness of aesthetic states.

Time for the Moment

I shall begin this study with processes of perception. Aesthetic perception is a widespread form of human behavior. We exercise this form in both ordinary and extraordinary life, often without it being particularly conspicuous. Its lofty realizations—attending a concert, a trip into the countryside, suddenly stopping to contemplate something we just don't want to disengage our senses from—unfold in a stream of mundane states. Aesthetic perception is open to us at all times, as long as external or internal pressure does not deny us the latitude necessary for engaging in it. It finds opportunities everywhere. Moreover, it actively seeks opportunities that are particularly suitable for awakening its interest or are specifically created to do so. Also the products of aesthetic production—from decoration to art—are related from the outset to processes of aesthetic perception, just as their production is accompanied by these processes. The situation of aesthetic perception evolves and maintains itself wherever there are opportunities for exercising this perception. The domain of the aesthetic is not a delimited area alongside other areas of life, but one of life's possibilities among others that we can take up from time to time, just as we can be taken up by it from time to time. Also the place at which a particular space is made available for aesthetic practice (a concert hall, theater, cinema, park, museum, atelier, and so on) is there for the specific duration of the aesthetic perception.

Temporal delimitations not only specify the frame of aesthetic activity but also designate what occurs within this frame. It is a basic characteristic of all aesthetic relations that in them we take *time for the moment*, though in entirely different rhythms. In a situation in which aesthetic perception is awakened we relinquish a solely functional orientation. We are no longer preoccupied (or no longer *solely* preoccupied) with what we can *achieve* in this situation through knowledge and action. We encounter what our senses and our imagination happen upon here and now, for the sake of this encounter. This is one reason aesthetic attentiveness represents a form of awareness that is constitutive of the human form of life, for without this possibility of consciousness human beings would have a vastly diminished sense of their life's presence.

A Situation of Perception

To understand this sense of presence we need to analyze the situation of aesthetic perception. As with any other situation of perception, it is characterized by a close relation between what it does and what it refers to. That to which aesthetic perception refers acquires its particular contours through the manner in which this mode of perception relates to it.

The question of the situation of aesthetic perception thus concerns, first, the constitution of this *perception*—its place among other kinds of human comprehension, its specific operation, its specific history. It concerns, second, the constitution of the *objects* of this perception—their place among other kinds of objects, their particular presence, their particular history. Irrespective of whether we inquire into the history or (as we shall do here) into the constitution of this encounter, we always stumble upon an interdependence of the concepts of aesthetic perception and aesthetic object. They designate different aspects of *one* complex, that of the situation of aesthetic perception. The constitution of aesthetic objects is comprehensible only in light of their possible perception, and the constitution of aesthetic perception only in light of its possible objects. An elucidation of one concept must claim to be an elucidation of the other.

This is why we will always speak of the entire situation of aesthetic perception, even though for analytic reasons the exercise of perception or the constitution of its objects will sometimes be in the foreground. In this way, a lot—indeed, everything—has been gained for a theory of aesthetic consciousness if this theory manages to draft a plausible concept of the aesthetic object. In answer to the question of what can be an aesthetic object there is the answer to how—through what mode of perception—something can become an aesthetic object. Aesthetic objects are objects *in* a particular situation of perception or objects *for* such a situation; they are occasions or opportunities to perceive sensuously in a particular way.

In principle, anything that can be perceived sensuously can also be perceived aesthetically. Among possible aesthetic objects there are not only perceivable things and their constellations but also events and their sequences—in short, all states or occurrences of which we can say that we saw, heard, felt, or otherwise sensed them. Nonetheless, the concept of aesthetic object does not coincide with the general concept of an object of

perception, because what is sensuously perceivable and can therefore be
the occasion of aesthetic perception is not for that reason already an aesthetic object. All aesthetic objects are objects of intuition, but not all objects of intuition are aesthetic objects.[1]

The Basic Distinction

Aesthetic objects are objects of appearing. The basic distinction to
which the aesthetics of appearing owes its name points to a difference between *sensuous being-so* and *aesthetic appearing*. Both are ways in which the
empirical *appearance* of an object is accessible. Aesthetic appearing is thus
a mode of the sensuous givenness of something. The relation of perception
and aesthetic perception is determined within the domain of sensuously
accessible *phainomena*. Aesthetic are those objects that in their appearing
stand out more or less radically from their *conceptually determinable* exterior image, sound, or feel. They are given to us in an outstandingly sensuous manner; they are grasped by us in an outstandingly sensuous way. This
applies no less to articles of clothing and locomotives than to symphonies
and novels, no less to grass on the side of the road than to the banal objects
in the domain of modern art.

For a theory of art, this assumption is indeed problematic. Old and
recent philosophy of art is dominated by the view that some artistic genres
and styles are above processes of appearing. For Hegel, it is poetry that de-
parts from the realm of appearances in favor of the world of sensuous
ideas. The idiosyncratic sensuousness of letters and words, the argument
goes, is too marginal for it to be of importance to literary theory. For
Arthur C. Danto, it is modern visual art after Duchamp that has left all the
allurements of appearing behind. If there can be art objects, the argument
goes here, that are phenomenally identical with arbitrary everyday objects,
then the power of this art cannot lie in aesthetic attraction. Just as for
Hegel it is the *idea* awoken by the linguistic artwork that acquires the rank
of deciding artistic quality; for Danto it is the artistic *conception* associated
with the work. Both appear as the distinctive feature of art forms that,
though they have particular appearances as their *presupposition*, are no
longer *fulfilled* in generating processes of appearing. In contrast to this, I
shall attempt to show that appearing is a constitutive element of all forms
of aesthetic production and perception. All relevant *artistic* differences are

also bound to aesthetic differences—differences in appearing. Artworks are not things of appearance with an added intellectual content, but genuine events of appearing processes.

This means aesthetic objects can reveal themselves in appearing processes that are indeed different. The grass at the side of the road, the physiognomy of a locomotive, and the movements of a symphony do not make themselves available to aesthetic perception in the same way. This is why one concept of appearing is not enough. The *mere* appearing of an arbitrary object will have to be distinguished from its *atmospheric* appearing, and this from its *artistic* appearing. It is only then that there is a prospect of actually circumscribing the range of aesthetic objects.

The Course of Things

The course of things has thus been outlined. I begin by developing the basic distinction between sensuous being-so and aesthetic appearing. This distinction provides us with a minimal concept of the aesthetic object and aesthetic perception. This first concept is differentiated step by step and put to the test using primarily examples from art. Finally, I return to the question of the meaning of aesthetic perception. From a restricted to a differentiated concept of appearing—this is the guiding maxim of my presentation.

Using a straightforward example, the first section of this chapter, "What Is Appearing" introduces the general direction of the subsequent study. The succeeding section, "Being-so and Appearing," undertakes a systematic, epistemologically accentuated elaboration of the guiding concept. On the basis of the distinction between being-so and appearing, which attempts to clarify the "being" of perceivable objects, the sections "Appearing and Semblance" and "Appearing and Imagination" discuss the components of an illuminative and imaginative aesthetic "semblance." The section "Situations of Appearing" carries out the internal differentiations just mentioned and explicates the meaning of "presence," which is what is at issue in aesthetic intuition. The section "Constellations of Art" puts to the test in various arts the hitherto obtained understanding of the situation of aesthetic perception. The final section, "A Play for Presence," summarizes the entire reflections in a short deliberation on the meaning of aesthetic practice.

This path touches many phenomena and points out many problems that deserve independent consideration. Completeness, whatever that may be, is not my objective. All I am trying to do is build a sound bridge of sufficient tensile strength to stretch from the chosen minimalist starting point into the heartland of aesthetic consciousness. A prison constituted by a closed system is not what is to be built here, but rather a platform for a theory that is open to (and—if all goes well—is opening to) the phenomena.

1. What Is Appearing

To perceive something in the process of its appearing for the sake of its appearing is the focal point of aesthetic perception, the point at which every exercise of this perception is directed, however it might otherwise unfold. I begin with this attentiveness to what is appearing in order to obtain gradually a differentiated understanding of the situation of aesthetic perception, an understanding that is not reached until the final section of this chapter. Thus, the elaboration of elementary aesthetic attentiveness, whose consideration I start with here, does not yet yield a sufficient conception of the actual latitude of aesthetic perception.

Kinds of Perception

To perceive something in sensuous appearance is how one could characterize the *general* procedure of sensuous perception. Aesthetic perception is a particular mode of this perception. It is distinguished by a specific polarity of seeing, hearing, touching, smelling, and tasting. We should not therefore disconnect aesthetic from other kinds of perception; rather, we have to recognize its particular accentuation.

Here it is of great importance to locate the correct place for distinguishing aesthetic from nonaesthetic perception. Perception is a wide-ranging faculty. In general, it does not necessarily include consciousness or a conceptual consciousness of its objects, and all of its conscious and conceptually articulated states emerge in a context of unconscious and conceptually unfixed perceptions. But human perception is distinguished by the possibility of conscious and conceptualizing experience. It is only where there is propositional, conceptually articulated perception, only where it is at least within reach, that a striking difference between aesthetic and other forms of perception becomes apparent. Here, as the tradition from Baumgarten to Adorno saw very clearly, lies the crucial point of comparison for our project. The issue is how aesthetic perception relates to conceptually articulated perception.[2]

In a simplified sketch, we can distinguish three dimensions of perception. Every living being who can perceive possesses the capacity for the *perceiving of* something. But only beings who can know conceptually have the capacity for *perceiving that*, which is present only in connection with the capacity for *perceiving as.* The dog that chases the cat up the tree sees and smells the cat without perceiving *that* the cat is sitting in the tree. To do so, it would need concepts that allow classifying the object of its desire as a cat and the latter's whereabouts as a tree. It would require a perception of something *as* something and also have the capacity to commit itself to the fact *that* this something is actually thus or not thus. (It would therefore have to have not only opinions but also opinions about opinions.) Human beings have these capacities. But they are not obligated to commit themselves to this or that view *of* a particular object. In their perception they can disengage themselves from any theoretically or practically determined directive as to what their perception is a perception of.

A presupposition of aesthetic perception is the capacity to perceive something that is *conceptually determined.* Whoever can perceive something that is determined can also disregard this determination, or to be more precise can disregard the *fixation* on this determination. The perception of something *as* something is a condition for being able to perceive something in the palpable repleteness of its aspects, something in its unreduced presence. Something that is thus and thus, or appears thus and thus, something that can be determined as this or that is perceived without committing oneself to one of its possible determinations. Kant elucidates this shift of attitude when he says that the aesthetic object is pleasing "without concept." Not that we do not have concepts for the object, not that we cannot perceive the object in its being-so in this or that way; conceptualization is not what matters here, however. We are attentive to the phenomenal presence of the object. We can grasp an object under a certain aspect—or we can encounter it in its appearing.

On reading Eichendorff's poems, Adorno speaks at one point of an ego that "listens instead of localizing."[3] Listening *instead of* localizing can be done, however, only by someone who is in fact *able to* localize. Thus, aesthetic perception generally presupposes a variety of capacities that it makes use of in a way that differs from their use on other occasions (when, for instance, it is a matter of finding one's way out of the forest and back home). But they remain in use even where one abstains from their determining use.

Phenomenal Individuality

A red ball is lying on a green lawn. Everyone who can see and speak and doesn't happen to be color-blind can see *that* it is thus. Not only can they see the ball, they can also see that there is a ball lying on the green lawn. They can see that the ball is red, that it is a leather soccer ball, that it is hand-sewn, that it is Oscar's ball, that it belongs to the boy who lives next door (Oscar is the boy next door), and much more. They can classify this object as a ball and attribute various properties to it. All this is not an accomplishment first of seeing and then of an interpretation of what has been seen; rather, it is an accomplishment of propositional seeing, where something is perceived as something. This kind of seeing takes place from different perspectives and with diverse interests. The interest can be primarily in the location of the ball ("Ah, the red ball is *there!*"); it can be in its composition ("It used to be redder!") or in a fact that is inferred on the basis of its composition ("The red ball is Oscar's ball."). One way or another, perception is exercised here in order to ascertain, en passant or explicitly, something about the object. We ascertain, and perhaps retain, that the ball is like this and that, in this or that visually distinguishable respect.

We can treat a ball in many different ways without treating it aesthetically. The question of the sensuous composition, of the inner constitution, or the appropriate use of a ball or any other perceivable object can be posed and answered without aesthetic intuition. Of principal importance in the aesthetic encounter is not the ascertainment of a visible and an invisible constitution, the investigation of an essence, or optimum use. Frequently, they are of no importance at all. In no way are they necessarily of importance. We do not have to look for the theoretical or practical determinateness and specification of something in order to encounter it in aesthetic attentiveness.

Someone can simply view the ball as it lies here and now in the shade of this garden. Whoever views it in this way beholds it in the repleteness of its sensuously perceivable aspects by directing his or her attention to the momentary and simultaneous givenness of this repleteness. The roundness of the ball is then just as important as its red color in contrast to the green color of the lawn; the scrapes on the surface of the ball (insofar as they are identifiable from where one stands); the kind of lettering on the ball; the decorative element printed on it; the size and wear and tear of the pentagons and hexagons that, sewn together, make up the outside layer of a soccer ball; the distribution of light on the sphere; the various reflections of the leather depending on the incidence of light; how, depending on their dryness and dampness, the blades of grass bend on being touched by the ball; the shadow cast by the ball on the surface of the grass in the penumbra of the tree—and all the other things that can be seen in and around this object. Everything *together* is at the focus of reflection here.

This reflection too is *aspectlike*, for we perceive this or that facet of the ball, thus perceiving the ball *as* this or that; but the reflection is not *aspect-bound*. It goes beyond a perception ascertaining this or that, and not only because it pays attention to qualities that can be discriminated conceptually not at all or only with great difficulty, as is the case with the color nuances of an object, for instance. It also pays attention to a feature diversity of objects that cannot be exhausted conceptually. Not only the conceptual inaccessibility of the *nuances* of the sensuous phenomenon is responsible for this inexhaustibility, nor only the impossibility of a *complete* characterization of all of its sensuously discernible features. Over and above these there is a conceptual incommensurability that follows, first, from a *simultaneous* reception of various aspects of the object and, second, from a consideration of their *momentary* appearance. Aesthetic perception is directed at the concurrent and momentary givenness of its vis-à-vis.

Here it is a matter not of grasping the individual qualities of an object, but of their *interplay* here and now (in this light, from this standpoint, or from this change of perspective). Important for this reflection are contrasts, interferences, and transitions, which defy description since they are given only in the simultaneity and frequently only in the momentariness of the pertinent instants. The reflection of light on the surface of the ball and the brightness of the light on the tips of the blades of grass—blowing lightly in the wind—more or less stand out against each other, more or less harmonize with each other, are in a more or less noticeably tense relation to each other. In this way, the aesthetically perceived object shows itself in a constantly transitory state. In this condition, nothing is simply just what it is; everything appears in the light of relations that, for their part, change with every change in individual appearances. There is enough to see on our ball even for someone who is color-blind.

Attending to the simultaneity and momentariness of sensuous presences is by no means just an issue of seeing. Attention can be paid not only to comparatively stationary things but also to relatively transient events. A noise or a sound is an occurrence that is just momentarily accessible. But it too can be perceived in the concurrence of what is perceivable in it. As soon as we pay attention to the consonance of the particular tones, to the color, the volume, and the rhythm of their resounding, as well as to their relation to the tones that have just faded away and those that are expected presently, we perceive this event in a sensuous repleteness that is in no way inferior to the repleteness of a stationary visual object. Although for sounds the *momentary* character of the sensuously given is immediately evident, for visible things it is the *simultaneity* of their properties. In the presence of *both* kinds of perceptible objects—as well as objects of the other senses—there is always a *relation* of duration (and hence simultaneity) and change (and therefore momentariness). Sounds also have their duration; things also have their time. In his lecture on the temporality of world relations, Heidegger says that "what becomes accessible . . . in the now is the transitional in its transition and the resting in its rest."[4] Aesthetic perception seeks out its objects in the concurrence of these temporal events, even though this is a quite varied—depending on the kind of objects—concomitance of lasting and shifting character. No matter how strongly or weakly the momentariness of perceptible objects may be emphasized, the simultaneity of their enduring or passing appearances is always the focal point of grasping them aesthetically. By steering clear of certain determining aspects, aesthetic perception takes the *phenomenal individuality* of its objects into consideration. It allows something to be present in the repleteness of its appearances.

Not only this repleteness but also its being made present, its being brought to awareness, is a specifically temporal relation. Beholding the play of appearances on an object is possible only if we *linger* in its presence and encounter it with an *end-in-itself* attentiveness.[5] We linger in an act of perception not because of individual perceptions that would be of service to knowledge or action but for the sake of what is perceived in the act. When we perceive in this way, we perceive something in—and on account of—the repleteness of its appearing.

Here as elsewhere, it is quite possible for actions that are ends in themselves to coincide with purposive actions. One need only recall the performance of an inspired musician. His or her recital is an excellent way to experience music for its own sake, by actually playing it; but at the same time it is a highly purposive activity whose aim is an optimal rendition of the written music.[6] But the connection is not always as close as it is here. Aesthetic intuition can accompany other activities that are themselves not aesthetic actions—such as listening to music while driving in heavy traffic. But it is always distinguishable by not being an *exclusively* purposeful activity and by being alert to a dysfunctional presence of phenomena. It is always concerned with *sensing* its objects, even if action itself goes further and takes the path of cognitive or instrumental *appropriation.*

Synaesthesia

Let us suppose that a murder has taken place in the house in whose garden the ball is located. The detective suspects that the injured perpetrator escaped through the garden. The forensic expert searching for clues at the crime scene has therefore the task of examining the red ball for possible traces of blood. He or she examines it in great detail and pays attention to as many elements as possible. The investigator will nonetheless remain blind to the appearing of the ball—if he or she is to do a good job. Such a specialist inspects the ball's surface with a particular intention—to find possible traces of blood. His or her viewing remains an ascertaining viewing, even if it takes a lot into its purview, both sequentially and simultaneously. It is no different when someone scans the forest floor looking for mushrooms: although his or her view is directed at a multitude of appearing things, it is waiting for the moment in which it can grasp the specific form of a mushroom (an edible one). An aesthetic view of the same forest floor is also able, depending on the level of knowledge, to distinguish mushrooms from other flora, but it is not waiting to apprehend this or that. It gives itself over to the multifariousness of what becomes visible, audible, or otherwise sensuously perceivable in the course of its sweep.

Baumgarten had in mind this structure of a perception not fixed on details when he granted aesthetic intuition the lofty ranking of a "confused" knowledge form. It is not aimed at distinctions; it pursues an animated intertwinement of aspects even when it is a matter of a stationary object. It lingers at a process of appearing. To be sure, classifying and determining appearances, which is done according to a particular aspect, is a dimension of sensuous perception central to the human capacity to orient oneself, and therefore central to the capacity to survive. But this, Baumgarten makes clear, is not all human perception can do. It can turn to the objects of its external surroundings without being fixed on a given aspect. In aesthetic encounter we are not determined by the determination of appearances.

This not only relates to theoretical and practical involvement but also concerns sensuous access itself, since no aesthetic perception is restricted solely to one sense. A part of its imaginative constitution—about which we say more in the section "Constellations of Art"—is that the other senses can be involved in the work of one sense, even if they themselves do not actively participate. Even if we just see the red ball on the green ground, we can sensuously imagine what its worn surface would feel like. If we consider the taughtness of the sphere, we can even sense how the ball would sound if it were made to bounce on the lawn or on some other surface. If we see or know that it is a leather ball, an idea of its smell enters into perception, even though the perceiving is done at a distance at which only the neighbor's freshly cut grass can be smelled. The same applies to the other senses because aesthetic perception can of course be executed with *every* sense, or under the *guidance* of every sense, or with many or all senses *concurrently*. Even if we perceive the ball just by touch, this can be accompanied by visions of its worn exterior. A lot of what we hear in aesthetic watchfulness we also imagine in a visual appearing; it often affects us so deeply that the sound experience moves our whole body as if it were a membrane. Even in aesthetic tasting, where it is a question of savoring (and not just consuming) food, the projection of the food's form frequently plays an important part; we could not savor a peach without the visual and haptic projection that it is a peach that we are savoring.

In this way, latent or overt aesthetic *synaesthesia* always revokes the degree of relative perceptive *anesthesia* to which the senses are necessarily subjected in many actions. Nonetheless, it is the interlacing of the senses that is decisive in all perception, be it in a hidden or an explicit manner. One sense does what it can by virtue of its distinction from and support by the other senses. They are coordinated forces of the spatial and temporal orientation of the body without whose cooperation it could not attain any stability—beginning with its sense of balance. But although this interaction of the senses transpires inconspicuously in many situations, it often becomes noticeable in situations of aesthetic perception in one way or another; we *sense* ourselves listening and seeing and feeling. As such, this sensing has not yet anything to do with a *reflexive* self-referentiality, although this is often the case here too, especially in the context of art. It is a sensing self-awareness that accompanies the lingering at the sensuous particularity of something.[7] The special presence of the *object* of perception is thus tied to a special presence of the *exercise* of this perception. We cannot pay attention to the presence of an object without becoming aware of our own presence.

Recalling Presence

Because of this double character, the concept of the *play* of aesthetic perception introduced by Kant is so appropriate. It portrays perception and what is perceived in the same manner. It points to a processuality of both the objects and the beholding of these objects. What reaches perception in aesthetic beholding is an interplay of the latter's sensuous aspects, an interplay with a particular presence in each case. Even so, this play is complemented by an attentiveness that can itself be designated a playing: a perceptive accompanying of the simultaneously and sequentially accessible aspects and interferences that aesthetic intuition observes in its objects. A play of appearances can be seen on the object, a play that can be followed only by a (in this sense) playful perception of the object. In this play of perception there develops a sense of the phenomenal individuality of what comes to perception.

To illustrate the meaning of this sense, Kant called this perception "disinterested." In comparison with theoretical and practical interests (of knowledge and utilization), this is plausible. One condition of aesthetic perception is distance from these interests, or at least from their exclusive pursuit. Still, this distance from interests of ascertainment and determination is itself tied to an eminent interest. This is why every negative determination falls short of the mark here, as it does everywhere in aesthetics. From our reflections so far, it follows that this is an interest in the particular as well as an interest in lingering with the particular. The comparatively "theoretical" motive of perceiving something not comprehensible solely in conceptual terms and the comparatively "practical" motive of considering something otherwise disregarded are joined together here in an interest of a unique type. It is directed at the perception of life possibilities that are as fleeting as they are evident, and it is aimed at the awakening of a heightened "feeling of life," as Kant says in § 1 of the *Critique of Judgment*.[8] This possibility is opened up by an intuiting recourse or rebounding to the momentary situation of those perceiving—by a voluntary or involuntary recalling of the immediate presence of their lives.

The concept of presence is to be understood here—that is to say, prior to the detailed consideration in the section on situations of appearing—first of all in a basic sense. This presence is a continuum of (the states of) things and events as they are perceptibly present in a sensuous manner within the surroundings of a human being. The how of this givenness is important here. The mere being there of objects, including the mere passage of events, does not alone constitute a presence.[9] Presence is an open (that is, an immeasurable, unfathomable, and uncontainable) horizon of *encounter* with what is there—an encounter that senses, acts, and acquires knowledge. This encounter is not as such aesthetic; rather, aesthetic attentiveness represents a *mode* of this encounter. This mode is activated when, in an essentially sensitive encounter, the issue is this—essentially but by no means exclusively—sensitive encounter, that is, when there is an end-in-itself encounter with the given. What is then important above all is how this or that—or all this—here and now, and only here and only now, is perceivable in its phenomenal particularity; what matters is the specific self-presentation of the sensuously given. In this attentiveness to the momentary play of appearances, there emerges an intuiting awareness of presence—an awareness of *a* here and now that also encompasses an awareness of *my* here and now.

Contemplation of presence—as Karl Heinz Bohrer in particular has never tired of emphasizing[10]—is an elementary motive of all aesthetic intuition. The subjects of aesthetic perception are concerned with sensing their own presence while perceiving the presence of something else. In the sensuous presence of the object, we become aware of a moment in our own presence. In this awareness there is also an abstention, a distance from all actions in which we are absorbed by an orientation toward states that we want to create or reach in the future, a distance also from all actions in which we want to commit something to memory once and for all. In aesthetic intuition, we desist from this exclusively determining and affecting orientation. We liberate ourselves from its determinations. We abstain for the sake of presence. We allow ourselves to be abducted to presence. Aesthetic intuition is a radical form of residency in the here and now.

Everything, at All Times

Everything that is—or has—sensuous appearance can be made present in its appearing. Therefore, as we underscored at the outset, aesthetic perception is an extraordinarily common form of behavior. Where their senses are not overcome and their attention is not captivated by something else, the possibility of aesthetic intuition is open to human beings at all times. Nonetheless, not every object of the senses becomes—immediately and concomitantly—an aesthetic object for us. A brief comparison can clarify both: the difference between nonaesthetic and aesthetic states, and the abundant opportunities to enter into these states.

We can look up to the sky to see whether it is going to rain, or to behold the appearing of the heavens. We can watch out for the puddle in order to avoid getting our feet wet, or to observe the buildings' reflection in it. We can stand at the window and listen as to whether the guests are coming, or become engrossed in the sounds of the city. We can look at a person to see what mood she's in today, or linger in beholding her looks. We can listen to the clunk of the automobile door to ascertain whether it has closed, or enjoy the "sated" sound of the door. In a lecture we can pay attention to the lecturer or to the lecturer's language sound, gestures, and facial expressions. We can read a text as a pool of information or as an arrangement of linguistic and other signs. We can attend a conspiratorial meeting in a café, or let the atmosphere of the place act upon us. We can register a visit to the hairdresser as an expensive service, or take it in as a drama of everyday life. We can check the durability of a piece of cloth, or feel the texture of the material. On returning home we can smell what's for dinner, or enjoy the aroma as a prelude to the meal. We can use the *Mona Lisa* as an ironing board or a mug shot, or view it as an artistic picture. We can draw up an index of the characters in *War and Peace*, or succumb imaginatively to the world of the novel. We can use one of Webern's Bagatelles as an automobile horn, or listen to it as a highly dramatic piece of music. We can regard a Beuys bathtub as a cleaning problem or as a piece of sculpture. At a concert we can count the number of times members of the audience sneeze, or follow the sounds of the orchestra. We can read the fine print on a billboard, or let the ad's images act upon us. We can simply endure an appointment at the Public Health Office, or immerse ourselves in the *Gesamtkunstwerk* constituted by a public authority abounding in office suites and corridors, echoing with footsteps and cries, emitting the dissonant odors of hygiene.

Everything is there. We can react aesthetically to anything and everything that is anyway sensuously present—or we need not react thus. There are places where it is difficult *not* to behave aesthetically (depending on one's inclination, in the forest or in the garden, at an auto dealership or in a museum, in a concert hall or in a sports area), just as there are places where it is difficult to do so (in an office of a public authority, in a parking garage, during an examination, at the dentist's, or at Wal-Mart).[11] When we behave aesthetically, we can do so predominantly with one sense or with all of the senses—with eyes or ears, or with body and soul. Frequently, however, there is no actual doing at all required—when what is appearing *suddenly* holds us spellbound, or when the conversion to aesthetic consciousness *befalls* us.

Entry into a state of aesthetic perception can come about actively or passively, as an arbitrary change of attitude or as a nonarbitrary occurrence. Even if great aesthetic moments—in nature, art, or sport—are usually experienced as something that "shakes," "enraptures," "stuns," or "captivates" us,[12] two driving forces are almost always active in the course of aesthetic perceptions: being spellbound by and concentrating on what is appearing. Aesthetic perception is a game that we play and that is played with us.

The alternatives, which I have erected here for the sake of clarity, can of course be turned down too. We can behave aesthetically *and* pragmatically. A practical orientation can be realized alongside the aesthetic one, just as the latter can be realized with the former. The same applies to decidedly theoretical behavior. In general, aesthetic perception excludes neither acquaintance [*Kenntnis*] nor knowledge [*Erkenntnis*], neither instrumental nor social action. In not a few cases, it includes one or the other without reservations. But aesthetic perception includes one or the other when it does and excludes it when it does because it is aimed at processes of appearing. Aesthetic perception wants to take in something in this light, in this movement, in this tone, in this roughness and coldness, in this weather and taste. This is its desire, whatever additional aesthetic and extra-aesthetic ambitions may also be connected.

A Minimal Concept

In this sense, the concept of appearing—as I have sketched it so far and further analyze it in the following section—is a minimal concept of aesthetic encounter. It attempts to formulate the smallest common denominator between the manifold types of aesthetic objects and their perception. It is tenable precisely because of being open to many other specifications. It would be entirely incorrect to say that aesthetic consciousness is *nothing but* attentiveness to what is appearing, in the sense developed so far and proceeding from our first simple example. In the situation of aesthetic perception, there are often many other things present and relevant. The decisive criterion for the appropriateness of the basic concept chosen here is not whether it contains everything that is important to aesthetic intuition; how is a single concept supposed to accomplish this? Rather, what is decisive is whether its elaboration is open to further essential features of the aesthetic situation.

Thus our view is open to the fact that, in perceiving a simple ball, one can make a lot more present than just the appearing of this sensuous object. One could, while beholding the ball and under the inspiration of Rainer Maria Rilke's untitled poem dating from 1922, from which Hans-Georg Gadamer took his motto for *Truth and Method*, speculate about the essence of the ball and the human being.[13] The appearing of the ball would be loaded here with a reflection that goes far beyond the particularity of what is appearing, an appearing at which this reflection nonetheless lingers intuitively. With regard to artworks in particular, exclusive concentration on mere appearing is nothing special; what is required here is an interpretative perception that allows a *different* appearing to emerge. Correspondingly, the thesis of an aesthetic "recourse to the present" does not entail the assumption that reflection on the past and the future does not play a role in aesthetic intuition (not to mention the fact that reference to the present cannot be isolated from the two other temporal dimensions). Aesthetic experience can of course make the past and the future present, be it in recollection, in anticipation, or in simulation—just as many artworks live from recalling the very transience of all things earthly (sometimes including sweeping hopes for the future). My thesis is simply that an aesthetic imagination that moves far away from the historical present of its performance and embarks on a search for past or future times draws its crucial energies from concentration on the present—on the presence of artworks, for instance. In this way, moreover, aesthetic perception can be widely open to acquaintance and knowledge, interpretation and meaning. But it can just as easily refrain from this reach. Lingering at what is appearing is open to both movements, as the example of the ball viewed with or without Rilke's contribution shows; it is essential to lingering to be open to the movements of a speculative or suspenseful awareness—and to the many intermediate states.

Theoretical openness to this aesthetic openness has, of course, its limits. Otherwise it could not be instructive at all. Beginning with appearing entails a nonneutral commitment. To say that it is phenomena of appearing that constitute the be-all and end-all of aesthetic behavior means to say that here, in attentiveness to what is appearing, something can be found and experienced that cannot be found or experienced anywhere else. This is a normative thesis. It reflects on the very potential of aesthetic perception, on its significance to the life of individuals and cultures. An elaboration of the thesis does not just *describe* this value; it *explicates* and *defends* it vis-à-vis other conceptions of the meaning of aesthetic processes. Only in this way can the intrinsic possibility present in the possibilities of aesthetic practice be made evident. This is not an opportunity that is open only to particular people with particular preferences or just to the members of this or that culture. Rather, it is a possibility open to *any* individual capable of perception and knowledge. This general possibility can be analyzed only from the internal perspective of a subject of perception who is capable of knowledge. Reflections on what it *means* for an arbitrary subject of perception to be involved in processes of aesthetic intuition tell us what is *at stake* for this subject in them: what life possibility—on the whole, promising possibility—is opened up by aesthetic behavior. The answer to this is in explicit or implicit conflict with other answers that provide different accounts and thereby ascribe a different individual and cultural significance to aesthetic practice outside and inside art. This has always been the task of philosophical aesthetics: to be an *apology* of aesthetic practice, while drawing on an understanding of its best possibilities.[14] As a direct consequence, but secondarily, philosophical aesthetics formulates a *critique* of theories and states that prevent the unfolding of this potential.

Where apologies are possible and necessary, many things can transpire differently. It is not fixed in the nature of human culture what weight and what place it assigns to aesthetic practices. It is not fixed in the nature of human consciousness to what degree and in what sense it is aesthetic consciousness. It is not fixed in the nature of current civilization whether a great novel or American football—or both, or neither of the two—represents a highlight of our aesthetic practice. Like all other human abilities, the faculty of aesthetic intuition can be employed and developed very differently. But it is probably not by chance that almost all human cultures have a use for this ability. Practically all seem to make use of it, a use that is not exhausted in the celebration of higher powers, compensation for anthropological deficits, the creating of social peace, accumulation of symbolic capital, or distraction from personal concerns. All cultures seem to have a sense of the drama of their own presence.

2. Being-so and Appearing

The object that can at any time become an aesthetic one is an object of perception made present in its phenomenal repleteness. In what follows I further develop this preliminary concept of aesthetic perception and aesthetic object. In doing so it is first a question of the precise status of appearing in comparison to other kinds of sensuous and empirical givenness. Here it is of utmost importance to avoid a false opposition between being and appearing. What is sought is precisely appearing's mode of being. This is to be understood as a dimension of the reality of objects of perception. We can know the phenomenal constitution of an object in its *being-so* or make it present in its *appearing*. The *being* of objects of perception is characterized thus: we can grasp them as something definite or as something special.

A Definition

The aesthetic appearing of an object is a *play of its appearances*. No matter how handy this definition, it is nonetheless quite complex. For this reason I give in what follows a concentrated commentary on this definition. Its three components are at the center of attention: the object, its appearances, and their play.

Objects of Perception

The concept of the object of perception cannot be separated from that of its appearances, since it is an object of perception for the very reason that it can be identified on the basis of its appearances, among other things. By "appearances" I mean here that which, in the correct use of perception predicates, can be determined as a property of the object. What therefore belongs to the appearances of an object is everything that can be determined about it on the basis of sensuous experience and conceptual discrimination: the ball is round, red, moist, cold, scratched, inscribed, and heavy; it smells of leather, and so on. This concept of appearance is much narrower than the concept of the empirical reality of objects as employed, for instance, by Kant in the *Critique of Pure Reason*. What also belongs to the empirical constitution of our ball is the chemical composition of its materials or the atomic and subatomic constellations of its elements, which are specifically not sensuously perceivable. In my language use, by contrast, what counts as the appearance of an object is simply what we can distinguish in it through the medium of our senses.

In identifying an object of perception, though, not all of its appearances are equally important. Usually the enduring properties are more important than the fleeting ones. That it is a round and red object is more important for identifying our ball than the fact that is a wet day today and therefore the ball is heavier than it was yesterday. This latter property disappears as soon as the sun comes out again. Of course, the comparatively enduring perception properties of an object of perception are in principle also fleeting. The form and color of the ball can also change or be lost, but it remains Oscar's ball (or "what's left of it"). It is in principle no different with balls and trees than with that piece of wax with which Descartes demonstrated, in the second of his *Meditations*, the notorious unreliability of the sensuous appearance of objects. No object of perception is simply what it appears to be to our senses here and now or over a longer period of time.[15] The ball *is* not an appearance; appearances *reveal themselves* on it. It is an object of our perceptual discrimination that must not be equated with some of its appearances.

The concept of object stands here for both things and events. What holds for things also holds for sensuously perceivable events, namely, that they cannot be equated with certain of their properties, which we can attribute to them more or less reliably. The ring of my telephone can be perceived as loud or quiet, distorted or undistorted, high- or low-pitched, as a fragment of this or that tune, as melodious or mechanical, as pulsating or halting, as an alarming sound or a chime of joy, and as much more. There is a lot to determine and describe in events and things, but no description can determine them exhaustively. The dictum passed on by Goethe, "*Individuum est ineffabile*," refers to individual entities of all kinds.

Although the concept of an object of perception cannot be separated from that of its appearances, it must not be understood such that it refers to a particular *constellation* of the object's appearances. Rather, it refers to entities that can display quite different constellations of appearances at various times. That is why the identity of objects of perception is essentially tied to their causal history, that is, to a *sequence* or *duration* of states that is characteristic of their passage through space and time. In the case of Oscar's ball, it could be the piece of sports equipment produced by Adidas in Herzogenaurach, Germany, in 1995, bearing production number 23874, and that, via the usual distribution channels, landed in a Hamburg sports store and, after being purchased by Oscar's parents, was subject to a treatment customary for soccer balls, one that rose in vigor with Oscar's increasing age. Sometime in the distant future, when the ball is found in an attic deflated and crumbled, it will still be the same object even though its manifestation has changed dramatically. Only with (approximate, but sufficient) knowledge of the *sequence* of positions and states it has been in can we identify it as *this* ball. As long as we comprehend this entity as a *ball*, however, its individualization remains tied to a form of its visibility; the concept of "ball" is a predicate of shape and refers therefore to a *typical* appearance of the object. Accordingly, we will grasp the lifeless ball in the attic as a *deformed* ball—in any case so long as we classify it in the first place as a ball and not simply as a piece of disused leather that does not belong in the container for recyclable materials.

We address individual objects of this kind by employing singular terms—that is, by resorting to deictic terms, proper names, or characterizations. We can say "this ball," "Oscar's ball," "taw" (that's what Oscar baptized it), "the present that pleased Oscar the most on his second birthday," or, of course, "that piece of sports equipment produced by Adidas in Herzogenaurach, Germany, in 1995, bearing production number 23874." If the sortal predicate "ball" is used, we address the specific object *as* an object of perception; the other expressions also refer to an object of perception, but they do so without characterizing it as such. Nevertheless, all of these expressions make reference to this *one* object *among all* objects of perception, irrespective of whatever its (additional) sensuously perceivable constitution may be. So long as we use here expressions such as "ball," "present," or "sports equipment," we rely on general terms whose use contains specifics about the *kind* of objects in question. But these classifying determinations are anything but completed *descriptions* of the objects under discussion, not to mention a somehow *exhaustive* description of their short-term or long-term constitution. Rather, their function lies in the individuation of objects that in this way become accessible in the first place as being *determinable* objects in many other aspects. This identification makes it possible to follow the spatially moved and unmoved *career* of the chosen object, a career in whose duration the object produces many different and frequently changing appearances.

The particular achievement of *proper names* here is to single out one name among all, without tying it down to one of its attributes. The name "Oscar" refers to the young boy who was baptized by this name, even if it should be discovered that this child is not, as everyone believes, Hubert's son.[16] The expression "taw," used as a name for a ball, refers to the ball that Oscar baptized thus, even if a forgetful neighbor names every ball that flies into his garden thus. Nonetheless, as mentioned, this name or another one could not be employed successfully if there were no predicates, especially of spatiotemporal localization and sortal characterizing, with which we can determine more precisely what *kind* of object is under consideration. Individual reference subsists on the availability of general determinations.[17] Proper names fulfill their function only within the *reach* of a descriptive characterization of the chosen objects, but their reference is not tied to the availability or truth of a *particular* characterization. It could be the case that we are all mistaken, including Oscar. It wasn't his second birthday; it was his third on which the boy got his ball. Nonetheless, the name "taw" refers to the ball that Oscar baptized "taw" at the time (whenever it was), regardless of what Oscar and the others know about the ball's fate or what they think of it.

In this way, deictic expressions and proper names make it possible to address an object *repeatedly*, and to do so *irrespective of* the particular state it is in or we believe it to be in. When using proper names, moreover, this reference can be produced independently of the situation. By means of both forms of address, the object is not characterized expressly but highlighted and made available for all kinds of description, evaluation, and consideration. Characterizations, on the other hand, single out one or just a few properties for identifying an object, without committing themselves with regard to the other attributes. All of these kinds of reference make it possible to address objects in their changing and frequently irreproducible states, and to do so with characterizations and proper names in a manner that can be repeated at any time. The use of singular terms thus creates the *general* possibility of referring to something *individual*. It thereby also creates the possibility of perceiving an object in the plurality, variety, simultaneity, and momentariness of its appearances.

Appearance

Only now does it really become comprehensible why an aesthetic intuition can be exercised solely in the context of a perception equipped with names and general concepts; only within this framework is it possible to confront something in its particularity. Only within this framework is it possible first to highlight something as a *determined*, a particular entity, and second to grasp it such that it comes to perception not in terms of one of its determinations or another but in its *individuality*. Only where concepts are in use can something be highlighted as this object and possibly perceived in its particularity.

I have called the conceptually discriminable sensuous composition of an object of perception its *appearance*. By this I mean not just what, *in each case*, can be distinguished in the object from a particular perspective or with a particular interest, in the way we perceive our ball to be red, round, wet, lying on the green lawn. I also speak of the appearance of an object in a general sense. It is then not only what *is* perceptually distinguished in the object from a particular standpoint under the guidance of one of the senses or another, but everything that *can* be distinguished sensitively and sensibly under any aspect and with any interest. Understood in this way, the concept of appearance comprises everything that can *in principle* be determined by using predicates of perception—entirely irrespective of which of an object's phenomenal properties are relevant and accessible in a *particular* knowledge practice. The sensuous appearance of an object thus comprises all properties that are perceptually determinable in this object.

If, when classifying the sensuous appearance of objects, something is perceived *as* something specific, it is perceived at the same time in such a way *that* it is as it is perceived. The object is perceived as a red ball, and in such a way *that* it is a red ball—not just that it appears as such in the twi-light. The sound is perceived *as* a telephone ring, and thus at the same time *that* the telephone is ringing—not that the boy next door is up to his acoustic tricks again. Here, of course, there can be frequent misapprehen-sions (which are dealt with in greater detail in the section "Appearing and Semblance"). To distinguish it from the concept of "semblance" [*Schein*], however, I would like to reserve the concept of "appearance" for the case of an *actual* incidence of the phenomenal properties of the object. The mere *impression* of an appearance—the mere appearing so—does not con-stitute an appearance in this sense. Rather, appearance in the meaning es-tablished here is only that appearance about which—and with a concep-tual determinateness sufficient for the purpose at hand—we can reliably state that it is so. This being-so, which is ascertainable case by case, is an aspect of the phenomenal *constitution* of objects, an aspect that is in turn a part of their general *empirical* constitution; it is that part accessible to us in the ascription of sensuous qualities.

The question, however, is whether we may speak here of "constitu-tion." In the empirical tradition, the distinction between "primary" and "secondary" qualities, which goes back to Locke, is used to reject this as-sumption. The appearance of an object, in particular its aesthetic appear-ing, would therefore have to be placed in a realm of illusion. The assump-tion that sensuous appearances are part of a constitution of objects that exists independently of our perception would have to be understood as a projection or illusion of common sense—admittedly, an unavoidable one. Thus, a lot depends on whether this doubt concerning the reality of ap-pearance qualities can for its part be challenged, because the question of the objectivity of appearances affects, in its outcome, the question of the objectivity of aesthetic appearing.

However, it is by no means just secondary qualities that become ac-cessible in sensuous perception. Neither the size nor the weight nor the shape of our ball is a quality given solely for our perception, as is the case with the hardness and color of objects (but also with the "tone color" of sounds). The one set of qualities—the primary ones—can be determined without making reference to the impression that they make on our per-ception; the other properties—the secondary ones—can be determined only with reference to how it looks, feels, sounds, and so on, in perception. Quite often, though, both kinds of properties can be phenomenally accessible, that is to say, can be discerned in sensuous perception. But although the concept of secondary properties is tied to a concept of their perceptive presence, this is not the case with primary ones. What a ball is can be established without providing details about the perception of balls. What sounds and colors are, however, cannot be ascertained without talking about listening and seeing.

This is why John McDowell has proposed understanding the distinction between primary and secondary properties as a difference between "essentially phenomenal" and "not essentially phenomenal" qualities. In this way, he avoids the standard statement that only the primary qualities exist "anyway," whereas the secondary ones are given just "for our perception." According to this statement, only the primary properties have an objective status, whereas the secondary ones fall into the realm of the subjective element, projection, or even illusion; aside from their being experienced subjectively by the individual, secondary qualities are not ascribed any reality. Yet, as McDowell submits convincingly, the contrast between the objective and the subjective can be understood in another way. To call a possible object of perception "objective" means here "to say that it is there to be experienced, as opposed to being a mere figment of the subjective state that purports to be an experience of it."[18] Secondary properties too, the argument runs, exist in a certain sense "anyway," that is, independently of their perception. They do not indeed exist independently of the possibility of their perception by appropriately equipped sensuous beings, but they exist independently of the actual *exercise* of this perception. On the basis of a liberal understanding of objectivity, according to which "an experience is an objective reality if its object is independent of the experience itself,"[19] secondary qualities are also objective constituents of objects through which these objects reveal themselves. In a word, how an object of perception looks, sounds, or feels is not a mere impression; it is a matter of perception qualities that are absorbed in sensuous reception.[20]

After all, we can at any time be mistaken about the perceptive qualities of an object. Even though it is red, the ball can look green from a particular perspective or in a particular light. It does not follow from "The ball looks red from this perspective" that "The ball is red" is true. Redness is indeed a matter of how something looks to someone, but this look must be distinguished from opportunities of how something looks to someone *particular*, opportunities in which this person can be mistaken about the color. Moreover, we can distinguish statements about the perception of the ball from statements about how the ball looks. In contrast to the statement "The ball looks out of focus" (because I am not wearing my glasses), which asserts only something about my *perception,* the statement "The ball looks red to me" refers, with a hypothetical restriction, to a *quality* of the ball that can or cannot be ascribed to it.[21] The same applies to the other senses. Talk of the phenomenal constitution of an object is frequently bound to an average perception *ability* and standardized perception *conditions.* The ball is blue even though it appears green in this yellow light. The ball is red even though it appears gray to someone who is color-blind. Whoever is color-blind cannot perceive this property. Creatures that cannot distinguish any colors at all cannot know the properties that all those possessing the possibility of color vision can perceive. Reality reveals itself to them in a different way than to those who have access to the pertinent properties.

That the real can reveal itself in one way or another to perception and knowledge is constitutive of the concept of the real. Following Kant's far-reaching insight, the concept of reality requires that it be *knowable* as reality entirely irrespective of how restrictedly it *is actually* known by epistemic beings.[22] The existence of the "primary" properties of objects can also be understood only in terms of the possibility of their knowability. Just as it was possible to say of secondary qualities that they exist in a certain sense "anyway"—to the extent that they are accessible to any subjects of perception with the relevant perception ability—it can be said of primary qualities that their existence, which is independent of the type of our perception, must also be understood in relation to an epistemological ability that *cannot* be comprehended independently of a receptivity to the phenomenal appearance of things and events. Even so, this requires rejection of the scientistic dogma that there can and must be only *one* description of the constitution of the real—the very description that discredits belief in the reality of the phenomenal world. Peter Strawson drove the point home to every hardliner of this type:

He must . . . accept the consequence that each of us is a sufferer from a persistent and inescapable illusion and that it is fortunate that this is so, since, if it were not, we should be unable to pursue the scientific enterprise itself. Without the illusion of perceiving objects as bearers of sensible qualities, we should not have the illusion of perceiving them as space-occupiers at all; and without that we should have no concept of space and no power to pursue our researches into the nature of its occupants. Science is not only the offspring of common sense; it remains its dependant.[23]

Appearing

The *appearance* of an object is what can be known in it by way of an ascertaining perception. I employ this term as the quintessence of the open multiplicity of properties that can be discriminated by conceptual perception in an object—and thus as the quintessence of the object's *sensuous constitution*.

Still, this constitution can be understood in different ways. It can be epistemically established in aspects or made present in lingering perception; it can be accessible as a connection of facts or as a co-presence of qualities; it can be grasped in a partial *being-so-and-so* or else in states of a given *play* of its appearances. Both kinds of comprehension are modes of encounter with appearance, that is, with the phenomenal being of objects. What comes to light in the difference between these kinds of comprehension I would like to grasp as a difference between *being-so* and *appearing*. The appearance of an object can therefore be grasped either in its being-so or in its appearing.

The phenomenal reality of objects is located in their appearance. This reality can be discerned in various ways. The correlate of these different kinds of comprehension is on the one hand the "being-so" and on the other the "appearing" of phenomenal reality; this is the fundamental distinction in my theory.

I use the expression "being-so" here as an abbreviation for the phenomenal being-so-and-so of an object of perception, a being-so-and-so that can be fixed in propositional knowledge in an aspectlike manner. I reserve, on the other hand, the term "appearing" for the interaction of appearances that is perceivable on the object in a particular present. This interaction is to be understood as a "play" of qualities that are perceivable in an object from a particular perspective and at a particular point in time. The term *play* calls attention to a simultaneity and momentariness of the givenness of qualities whose co-occurrence and interrelationship elude any conceptually determining perception. This play is given as the ease of access to a multitude of an object's sensuously distinguishable aspects; it can be perceptually followed, but it cannot be epistemically fixed.

In every object of perception there is at any time a multitude of phenomenal properties, some of which persist for a long time and some for a short time. Accordingly, the global appearance of an enduring object can be understood as a series of constellations of its individual appearances. To delimit clearly the mode of aesthetic perception from that of theoretical perception, it is necessary to distinguish two kinds of simultaneity for the sensuously given: the factual and the phenomenal simultaneity of the phenomenal properties of an object. It is characteristic of the global sensuous appearance of an object that it *has* many perceivable properties concurrently and that these attributes are knowable from a variety of standpoints. Certain of these properties (and certain constellations of properties) can be cataloged in statements about the object's being-so. But that an object *displays* many perceivable properties concurrently from a particular and therefore limited standpoint (or series of standpoints) is what constitutes its specific appearing. In the concept of appearing, therefore, by no means are all the phenomenal properties addressed that are in fact *attributed* to a given object at a particular point in time. Rather, it is a matter of a simultaneous and momentary *appearing* of appearances. What is important here is not the factual but the phenomenal simultaneity of the aspects sensitively perceivable in an object; what is important is the how of their givenness here and now.

The criminological examination of our ball produces a long list of properties that are concurrently attributed to it twelve hours after the misdeed (but without having been concurrently perceivable then). An aesthetic perception exercised at the same point in time takes in a multitude of aspects that were concurrently perceivable in the object. But even if we assume for the sake of argument that the list drawn up by the investigating detective contained exactly the same properties that were in the play of a purely lingering perception, the perceptions involved and what is perceived by them would still be very different. The one explores the *stock* of qualities present in the object; the other follows the *play* of appearances that come to light simultaneously in the object. This is a difference in the *content* of each particular perception. One beholder sees this and this and this, and holds them to be this and this and this; the other, who also sees this and this and this, sees how this and this and this relate to one another in the period of time in which they are observed.

As soon as we pay attention, from a particular (static or shifting) perception perspective, to the simultaneity of the sensuously given *as* a simultaneity of this given, we encounter the object in a special way in which it encounters us in a special way. Here, a multitude of sensuous contrasts, interferences, and transitions come into play (those already mentioned here);[24] here, an interaction of sensuously perceivable aspects comes into play, aspects that evade ascertaining determination. Appearing is a process of appearances that is not able to come to light as long as an object is under the purview of an epistemic or purposeful treatment. Appearing does not come to perception until we encounter the sensuous presence of an object for the sake of this sensuous presence—not until it is of importance to us to perceive the object in the momentary repleteness of its appearances. Appearing comes to the fore, can be sensed and taken in, so long as we allow an object of perception to have effect without restricting ourselves to specific aspects of its constitution or function.

Objects of perception are objects that can be comprehended in this or that way, (more) in their being-so or (more) in their appearing. But an object that is discerned in its appearing also has the (visual, acoustic, haptic, olfactory, and gustatory) appearances that it simply has. The aesthetically viewed ball is the *same* object as the one examined criminologically or the one that has been kicked about. It has the same sensuous constitution. The proximity of the concepts "appearance" and "appearing" bears witness to this very fact. Through attentiveness to the appearing of a sense object, nothing is added that has not been there already, not one *single* perceivable property that could not be discerned independently of this mode of comprehension. But something particular is revealed in the object through this mode, something that becomes accessible only by virtue of this kind of attentiveness. Aesthetic lingering *lets something be in its repleteness.*[25]

Logical and Phenomenal Order

The sensuous constitution of an object of perception, it has just been argued, is part of its empirical constitution. It is determined by what can be distinguished *to any extent at all* in the object as the amount and composition of its appearances—in contrast to what can be determined *in each case* as the phenomenal being-so of an object. This means that the concept of perception object in my reflections is understood in terms of its "theoretical" determinacy. It is a quintessence of what can be discriminated in the object by seeing, hearing, touching, smelling, and tasting. If an epistemic determination of its sensuous constitution is conducted, a characteristic being-so is ascribed to it. Nevertheless, this comprehension founded on being-so can relate always only to *aspects* of its appearance, without ever being able to give an exhaustive determination of its sensuous perceptibility. Nonetheless, it is this capacity—namely, that it can be characterized phenomenally—that makes an object into an object of perception.

On this concept of the appearance(s) of an object rests the concept of its aesthetic appearing. This logical dependency of the concept of appearing on that of the sensuous constitution or appearance of an object must not lead to false conclusions. The conceptual primacy of the theoretical over the aesthetic constitution of objects of perception does not imply a *phenomenological* disparity, not a ranking in the perceptive *givenness* of these objects. It is by no means the case that an object must first be epistemically fixed in order then to be aesthetically recognizable. After all, the decisive difference that I delineate under the terms "being-so" and "appearing" does not introduce a division between conceptual and nonconceptual perception. Every perception appertaining to one or the other is always already conceptually instrumented. Instead, the decisive difference is located in the existent or nonexistent *fixation* on conceptual knowledge. A perception that is theoretical in the broadest sense carries this fixation through; aesthetic perception, in contrast, desists from it.

These two forms of perceptive comprehension stand open in principle to every object of perception: the form that secures certain facts in the object, and the form that yields to the object's presence. Both take in the object in its phenomenal reality, but each in its own way. This is why, to state it once again, appearing must be conceived of not as being in opposition to the phenomenal *being* of objects but merely in opposition to propositionally fixed aspects of this being—that is, in opposition to their *being-so*, as it is determinable by partial epistemic modes of access. In the case of objects of perception, we are concerned with a being [*Seienden*] of whose being [*Sein*] it is characteristic to be, among other things, absorbed into some or many of its individual appearances or else into its sensuous appearing.

Now, if it was plausible to attribute a specific objectivity to the appearance of an object, then the same must apply to the appearing of the object. Appearances are something that can be perceived in the object: qualities that are ascribed to the object independently of ongoing exercises of perception, even though they can be given, in principle, only from the perspective of an appropriate perception. Aesthetic appearing too can become manifest only by a particular way of perceiving objects. Here, the relationship is reiterated in which sensuous perception and the sensuously perceived object are generally connected to one another. The particular kind of perception to which an object is subject here clears the way to specific states that can be perceived in the object. As is the case with the ascertaining intuition of a being-so, states of appearing exist independently of the particular *exercise* of a corresponding perception. They do not, though, exist independently of the *possibility* of this perception. In every moment of its lying on the green lawn, a play of appearances is perceivable on our red ball, even if no one is there who could linger in their intuition. Thus, if we can say in agreement with McDowell that we can speak of the experience of an objective reality whenever the object of this experience exists independently of the exercise of the experience, then the experience of appearing is also an objective experience. It is a special way of participating in the reality of its objects.

Limits of Knowledge

We may indeed equate the reality of objects of perception with their conceptually and practically *treatable* constitution, but we must not equate it with their conceptually and otherwise *treated* constitution. That the concept of the sensuous constitution of objects and events is logically connected to the concept of their propositional *knowability* does not mean that this constitution can be equated with the *knowledge* available about them at a given time. Otherwise, the disparate historical disclosure of phenomenal (and other) reality, including possible advances and regressions in knowledge of the latter, could not be understood at all.[26] Objects of perception can in many cases be addressed by singular concepts and characterized by general concepts, but they are not exhaustively determined by any conceivable compilation of such characterizations. They are not only what we can grasp them to be in each case; they are also how they can appear to us in each case. Their experiential reality goes beyond what we can epistemically ascertain in them.

In aesthetic perception, the constellation of the appearances of what is perceived is grasped in a process of their simultaneous appearing. A play of appearances is opened up. *One* such play. *The* play of an object's sensuous presence is just as nonexistent as *the* knowledge about the context of its appearances. Neither in the one case nor in the other is there any question of complete access. Conceptual knowledge can establish many aspects of the (momentary or enduring) sensuous constitution of an object, but it is entirely unclear what taking notice, with propositional determinacy, of *all* of these aspects is supposed to mean. One could try to describe ever more precisely a simple object such as our ball, but one would always arrive at only a description that could have been *even* more precisely done (not least by using a magnifying glass, contrasting substances, and other technical methods). Between every pair of successive sentences of a minute description of our ball, an even more minute sentence of description could be inserted; yet this already infinite sequence would describe only the *look* of each of the thirty-two segments of the ball, but not how it feels, how it smells, how it sounds—and all of this in various surroundings, in various weather, and so forth. No human life span would be long enough to describe the appearance of this one ball. No matter how well one can know in our ball, with entirely sufficient precision, what may be important in the various contexts—for instance, its color, size, weight, air pressure, owner— one cannot know *the ball* with descriptive means, just as little as one can know any other sense object.[27]

Yet this lack of knowability is in no relevant respect a deficit. It arises only in comparison with a chimerical completeness that misses the true achievements of knowledge. Hence there are no descriptive deficiencies that would have to be compensated by aesthetic perception. The latter does not compete with a propositional comprehension of its objects. When, in recollection of Kant, I stated in the first part of this study that aesthetic perception is directed toward being attentive to "the full sensuous presence of an object" while forgoing cognitive or practical results,[28] this did not mean that here it is a matter of superior *knowledge* of the momentary constitution of the object. It is precisely not this. It is a matter of a perception of the *presence* of the object, as it is accessible only to a sensing, a discerning that does not resort to cognitive ascertaining. It lingers in a sensuous pursuing.

A lot, of course, is recognized and frequently ascertained in exercising this perception, simply because our senses are to a large degree informed senses. (When my hand senses the scratches on the ball, I know by feel that the ball has scratches; whoever, listening consciously, hears an E flat major chord, will also hear, with the appropriate knowledge, that it is an E flat major chord.) The conceptual instrumentation of all of our senses means that in aesthetic perception too we are open to many aspects of the constitution of the objects of this perception, and thus to an epistemic attitude toward them. Nonetheless, we are interested first and foremost not in this but in an unfettered experience of their sensuous presence.

This presence of an object of perception is not comprehensive either; nor is the ensemble of its appearances. Rather, this presence can be perceived only perspectively, since this perception takes place from a bodily position that can grasp the object only from certain angles (as is the case when using all of the senses).[29] It is constitutive of the experience of the presence of a sense object that it presents itself from various positions, that it displays a changed self-presentation when we change our position. This perceptive encounter is always subject to change. Variability—of perception, no less than of its objects—is its very nature. The aesthetically granted presence of a sense object is not a being-so that is to be registered, but an occurrence that comes to intuition whenever we desist from a purely identifying or discretion-asserting treatment, whenever we free ourselves from the fixation on fixating the object, whenever we let go of assertion. The experience of the "full," unreduced presence of an object is an experience of this event.

In one particular sense, this appearing is richer than everything that can be distinguished in an object through conceptual discrimination. We should not, though, understand this richness in a *quantitative* sense, as if it were somehow possible to discern *more* of the object in aesthetic intuition. The richness of objects accessible in aesthetic intuition should not be understood as a super constitution, as if the true meaning or the inner essence of its objects came to light here. A poor simpleton or a sophisticated conceptual artist who spent his life describing a ball would certainly unearth much more knowledge about the ball than anyone who experienced an intensive aesthetic moment while intuiting it. An emphatic critic, in contrast, who claimed that the "essence of the ball" is expressed in the Rilke poem cited earlier would probably have to concede that not everything essential has thus been said about this kind of thing, not to mention about this one thing here. What is decisive, rather, is the *qualitative* difference that emerges by a sense object's being perceived in the momentary and—

depending on the position of perception—changing play of its appearances. In this way, and only in this way, does it come to consciousness in its individuality: not as a surveyable context but as a source of appearances that can be concurrently discerned in it, but cannot be simultaneously or successively grasped with determinacy.[30]

Indeterminacy

I am now in a position to explicate Paul Valéry's notion of the constitutional "indeterminacy" of aesthetically grasped things and events, which was cited in the first chapter of this book. However, I will comment not on Valéry again but only on the thought that was the leitmotif of my introductory history.[31]

A first meaning of this indeterminacy is the widespread *underdeterminacy* of every object of perception through the relevant determinations that we can discern from its sensuous and other composition. Every determination under which we grasp an object leaves many other aspects of its constitution out of consideration; otherwise it would not be a determination. Even if many appropriate determinations are provided, the situation is not different. Every determination of the being-so of something remains dependent upon the theoretical and practical interests of this determination—dependent upon the manner in which the object becomes significant in each instance. New interests, aspects, or epistemological procedures can be introduced at any time. In this sense, every object of perception remains indeterminable. We can indeed occasionally determine everything that is specifically relevant, but we can never determine everything possible in the object.

A second meaning of indeterminacy is even more important in the context of aesthetics. The aesthetic object is perceived in a simultaneity and a combination of its appearances that defy description. One could speak here paradoxically of an *overdeterminacy* of the object grasped in its unreduced phenomenal presence. The play of appearances renders a cognitive availability of the object impossible—not only because of the huge number of aspects that can be distinguished in it and the multitude of interests that can be directed at it, but because of the simultaneity and momentariness of the facets and nuances in which the object attains attentiveness here. All this together constitutes the *particularity* of its individual appearance.

In the tradition of aesthetics—one need only recall Baumgarten or Nietzsche—it has always been emphasized, and rightly so, that this particularity is not accessible using a conceptually epistemic approach. If an object is characterized by way of general concepts, we have to disregard how it appears here and now. The epistemic process has to ignore the specific and frequently changing sensuous presence of its objects. This does not, of course, mean harm or despoilment; it does not entail any identity coercion, illusion, or semblance, as has been consistently lamented from Schelling and Schopenhauer to Heidegger and Adorno. No knowledge at all of empirical facts would otherwise be possible, and thus no reliable relations (supported by correctable experience) with the circumstances of the human world. Propositional knowledge cannot and must not take the particular into consideration. This ethically altogether unimpeachable inconsiderateness is nothing less than a necessary condition of empirical knowledge. In all knowledge of this kind, we have to disregard the individuality of the object known.

Thus there is no point in playing the supposedly soft empiricism of aesthetic intuition off against the supposedly hard empiricism of conceptual knowledge, since the finitude of all discriminating knowledge is a complement of aesthetic perception. A sense of the particular is a conceptually developed sense that abandons a fixation on conceptual fixation. It must be able to lift its object out of all other objects and set it off against these objects in order to be able to appreciate it in its individuality. For the purposes of this appreciation, a sense of the particular must loosen the connection with conceptual knowledge to a more or less high degree, though without being able to break it completely. Its talent is after all to have something particular, something *determined* (and therefore multiply determinable), appear in its phenomenal *indeterminacy*.

In ascribing predicates of perception—that is, through assertions—we can of course point to this appearing too. We can not only point to moments of the presence of the object (Oh, this red color! Oh, this aroma! Oh, this rhythm!); sometimes we can also try to characterize types of interference that these moments undergo. For instance, we speak of the "iridescent luster" of a colored surface, the "shimmering" of a sun-drenched street, the "roar" of the sea, or the "full" sound of an orchestra. What are characterized in this way are no longer the individual properties of things and events but their *interplay* within a perception and for a perception that

does without an isolating fixation of object qualities. Like complex interpretations of artworks, these assertions function not so much as knowledge
about the object but more as pointers *to* the object, as sort of *deictic* characterizations.[32] They call to memory or raise to consciousness how the object is present when engaging in lingering attentiveness. Here we are concerned with characterizations that in their determinacy present the very
indeterminacy of the aesthetically grasped object.[33]

This dovetailing of determinacy and indeterminacy characterizes all
conduct that is conscious of itself, be it theoretically, aesthetically, or practically oriented.[34] It is the particular *type* of dovetailing that makes the difference. In the aesthetic orientation, objects are perceived, to follow
Valéry's dictum, with greater attentiveness to what is indeterminable in
them. We must not understand elementary aesthetic appearing as Plato
(*Phaidros* 250c–d) and many of his successors do, namely, as the shining
out of a nonsensuous *idea* of the beautiful—and thus as an encounter with
a truth that is above appearing. The basic concept of appearing is not the
appearing *of something*, but appearing, *period.* In regarding this appearing,
there is no step into a preconceptual sphere, no encounter with "raw being," just as there is no getting to know a "chaos" operating behind all
forms. Fundamentalist interpretations of this and other types founder for
the simple reason that a tenable concept of appearing remains dependent
upon the concept of appearance.[35] No appearing without appearances; indeterminacy accompanies determinacy. Only where there is determinacy
can interest in indeterminacy develop. Only where appearances are identifiable is the path to a play of appearances open.

A Different Execution of Perception

Nonaesthetic and aesthetic perception vary by reason of a difference
in focus. The one is directed at what is the case in its objects; the other attends to the simultaneity and momentariness of their phenomenal states.
This difference has nothing to do with the consideration of enduring or
fleeting states of the object, since fleeting states can also be conceptually
fixated in a precise manner under specific aspects, just as the simultaneity
and momentariness of unchanging objects too can be made present. The
said difference relates rather to the specific *process* of perception.

In line with a plausible suggestion of Christoph Menke's, aesthetic consciousness is to be understood not as one *class* alongside others, but as a different *execution* of perception.[36] We perceive, and we sense our perceiving, and we direct attentiveness to relations that otherwise escape perception. A different charging of the poles of perception occurs. The repleteness of linguistic distinctions, in whose perspective we perceive the outer world day by day, leads up to a phenomenal repleteness that cannot be grasped in the medium of these distinctions. This phenomenal repleteness opens the possibility of identifying something in its being-so or of letting it be in its appearing. Access to the appearances of the object of perception *incorporates* access to the object's appearing. The conceptual-epistemic access to the world incorporates access to the aesthetic encounter with it.

It incorporates it as a *possibility* that is always open. By no means is it the case that the one *execution* always incorporates the other. By no means is it the case that all conceptual knowing is an aesthetic perceiving, or is accompanied by it. No aesthetic perceiving aims just at conceptual knowing, however much it might be accompanied by knowing. Aesthetic behavior follows a telos different from the one followed by theoretical behavior. It does not want to explore a constitution of the world; it wants to expose itself to the world's presence.

Abandoning the fixation on theoretical (or practical) determination is the first act here. Perception in the face of not wanting to determine—aesthetic intuition lives from this possibility. We attend here not just to individual appearances of the object, or to an illusionary totality of its appearances, but to what is appearing concurrently and fleetingly from a particular position.

Event Objects

Speaking of "the object" of aesthetic perception is a simplification. We have to give the concept of object a formal meaning if we want to gain an undistorted understanding of the situation of aesthetic perception. It is, after all, not just individual things but quite often constellations of things that come aesthetically to intuition. It is also not just stationary things but equally events—and, in turn, constellations of events—that are occasions of aesthetic perception. One need only think of the performance of an orchestral piece, or of the motion, the aroma, the sound of a city. These are not objects *over against* which perceivers stand; this is a complex occurrence that envelops and embraces them. Even if the aesthetic object is a solid thing, in aesthetic intuition we are never concerned with a static given. Here too, the constellation of appearances, which are recognizable in these things, enters the state of a play, the state of an occurrence *on* the object. By reason of aesthetic sensitivity to the phenomenal simultaneity of objects' givenness, a processuality becomes apparent in them, and through this processuality they acquire the status of aesthetic objects.

In this sense, every object becomes a complex event and every event a complex object in aesthetic perception. An artistic panel painting that is optimally illuminated and in which (unlike objects in the open air) the momentariness of its appearing does not therefore play a dramatic role must also be perceived in the concurrence and interference of its elements in order to become perceivable as an artistic painting—a perception that is in turn possible only in the sequential viewing of the painting's sections. In this sense, all art is temporal art. In a temporal art form such as music, nonetheless, the space in which the music unfolds plays a special role, as do the changing simultaneities that it imparts in the sequence of its tones. This is in principle no different in the space of nature or the city, or when one is absorbed in a natural or artificial entity. The gerund *appearing* serves to express exactly this: aesthetic perception is attentiveness to the *occurrence* of its objects.

The concept of the object of this perception is formal insofar as it encompasses not only individual things and events but also randomly complex sequences and constellations of sensuously perceivable processes and states. This formal concept is broad enough to support the project of an initially minimal view that concentrates on the few features of the aesthetic relation that are evident in all of its manifestations. The expression "aesthetic object" stands here for everything we can encounter in aesthetic attentiveness. The *analysis* of these objects I am conducting here, however, always relates to a specific type of perceptive *encounter* with these objects, that is, with the *situation* of aesthetic perception—just to call this to mind once again here. Aesthetics, one could say laconically, has to do with situations in which something or everything becomes a special (objective) event of perception by reason of there being a special (subjective) event of perception.

So far we have gotten to know the aesthetic object only as an occasion of intensive sensuous perception that is accessible to any subjects of perception who possess an appropriate sensitivity. The aesthetic object reveals itself in this perception in an objective presence that differs significantly from the objectivity of a knowledge that concentrates on the being-so of reality. But this is not everything that can occur on and in aesthetic objects. Apparency [*Anschein*], manifestation [*Vorschein*], independent semblance [*Schein*], as well as imagination and representation—all frequently characterize aesthetic objects to a great degree, and often exactly in that situation where we are particularly enraptured by aesthetic events. But nothing of this is necessary for an object to assume the status of an aesthetic object. What is necessary is only that we come to a play of its appearances.

So far I have concentrated on this minimal necessity. But now it is time to open this initial concept of the aesthetic to an understanding of the complexity of aesthetic situations.

3. Appearing and Semblance

The conception developed so far makes it possible to understand why aesthetic perception is often attributed a heightened sense of the real. It is not indeed a higher reality, simply an otherwise obstructed dimension of reality that we enjoy by virtue of our attentiveness to appearing. Nonetheless, something becomes real here; to be more precise, something becomes present in its reality, something that remains closed to the theoretical and practical appropriation of the world. In a modified manner, the reflections so far have thus corresponded to the classic intuition that aesthetic experience can yield revelation about the world.

There is another, diametrical intuition that is equally well anchored in the tradition, and the reflections so far have not yet done justice to it. For this intuition, the power of aesthetic experience consists in opening a way out of the facticity of reality, by entering a sphere of semblance. This conforms to the trajectory of our findings, insofar as a concentration on appearing is possible only by forgoing a securing of the facts that are perceivable in this appearing. But an aesthetics of semblance—whether inspired by Schiller, Nietzsche, or Bloch—defends a much stronger view, namely, that the telos of aesthetic perception lies not at all in a *turning toward* but in a *transcending of* the real.

This intuition also contains an important insight. But it too must be corrected if we want to express its truth, since the contrast between an "aesthetics of being" and an "aesthetics of semblance" is misleading. This conflict between two figures of thought has dominated reflection on art and the beautiful since Plato certified painting and poetry as offering only a semblable presentation of reality. In countermoves against Plato, there have been regular reevaluations of this evaluation in which semblance itself has been recognized as the aesthetically central accomplishment.[37] It is not until this contrast has been annulled that the truth of both positions can be formulated. By beginning with appearing, we have so far been led to a reformulation of one position. On the basis of this reformulation, though, we can do justice to the other one too. My thesis in this and the following section ("Appearing and Imagination") is that the forms of aesthetic semblance must be understood as modes of aesthetic appearing. The power of aesthetic semblance emerges from an alliance with the processes of appearing. It is founded on the presence of what is appearing and yet goes way beyond presence and reality.

Two Concepts, Two Steps

The concept of aesthetic semblance cannot be analyzed in one step. It is in actual fact two concepts that are frequently brought together in aesthetics under the tile of "semblance." One could speak of an illuminative semblance and an imaginative semblance. By aesthetic semblance we can understand sensuous *simulation*, to which no phenomenal reality corresponds in the situation of perception; or else sensuous *imagination*, which refers to real or fictitious worlds (way) beyond the situation of aesthetic perception. In one case, something is present in a manner phenomenally different from how it actually is—for instance, thunder sound effects generated in a theater or natural scenery that "looks like a painting." In the other case, a present is made present that is different from the one that is present—for instance, reading a novel or watching a movie.

Closely tied though these two cases can be—on stage, for instance—they are clearly different cases of transcending situative reality, and they can just as easily present themselves independently of each other. If their relation is to be rendered transparent, then they will have to be held apart. For this reason, I distinguish them terminologically quite clearly. I speak of phenomena of *semblance* only where something is present sensuously in a manner different from how it actually is. Of states of the *imagination*, in contrast, I speak wherever something is made present that goes beyond the perceivable present. Neither semblance nor imagination is an aesthetic state as such. They are aesthetic states only when they enter a relation with what is appearing.

I begin this section with a discussion of aesthetic semblance and then turn to aesthetic imagination, which is of significantly greater importance to aesthetic consciousness. In the previous section I argued for the comprehension of appearing as something that is actually real here and now; what is now important is to understand how aesthetic openness to a dimension of the real can include being open to dimensions of the partly or wholly unreal.

Deceptive or Supportive Semblance

With regard to all objects of perception, we can deceive ourselves in various ways. We can falsely identify them or characterize them incorrectly or in a confusing manner. If this occurs in the situation in which the pertinent objects are present, then we are the victims not only of a *mistake* (caused by erroneous memory or misinformation) but also of a *semblance*. Something appears to us as it is not in reality. Some of the things we ascertain in the course of perception are incorrect. Because attentiveness to the appearing of an object has a peculiar relation to the possibility of generating ascertainments about the object (ascertainments are within its reach, but attentiveness does not reach for any), a question arises here: How does appearing relate to this kind of semblance?

The ball we believe we see at some distance is not a ball at all but a bicycle helmet in tall grass. The hamburger on the garden table, which the hungry Oscar is about to snatch, is not a hamburger at all but a plastic toy for dogs designed in the spirit of Claes Oldenburg. The muffled cry for help is coming from the garden and not from the basement, where the detective is going. The telephone ring is from the television and not from the apparatus I am about to grasp. "Our senses deceived us," those involved could say in all of these cases. From their viewpoint, the appearances in question looked or sounded different from what they actually were; they had a different sensuous constitution or location from the one ascribed to them. Those perceiving deceived themselves about these appearances in one way or another. The helmet looked like a ball, the toy like something edible, the cry sounded as if it came from the basement, the ringing was deceptively similar to the sound of my phone.

These are misconstruals in knowledge and performance. They are registered as a faulty determination of the object. This can be painful (I kick the helmet), fatal (the murderer is in the garden), or comical (I rush to the phone). Whatever the case, discovering the deception brings about a correction in all of these instances. The preceding perception is immediately invalidated and replaced by the purportedly correct view. Where it is a matter of ascertaining how something is, or of establishing how something ought to be, it is rational to take one's orientation from how things actually are. In aesthetic perception, by contrast, the discovery of a sense deception does not necessarily bring about a correction of this perception; the otherwise *deceptive* semblance can *support* a positively valued perception here.

"Oh, I see, it's a helmet," an observer of our supposed ball could say, "but from this perspective it looks like a ball." "Oh, I see, that's a sound installation," a visitor could say, "I thought it was the rustling of the forest." Regardless of how disappointing this might be in the one instance or the other, the discovery of what is in truth the case does not, in the aesthetic context, necessarily bring about a devaluation of the preceding perception. It can be registered as an expansion. In this case, the sensuous impression retains value not as a purported *fact* nor as a deceptive *apparency* (which could be of interest to a psychologist of perception) but as an aspect of the presence of the object that is remarkable in itself—as an additional element of its *appearing*.

An object seems to have this or that appearance even though it does not do so in reality. There is no empirical being [*Sein*] here corresponding to sensuous apparency. For the stable formation of an *aesthetic* semblance, there must first be an *affirmation* of this apparency. In aesthetic positivization, this otherwise deceptive appearance enters the play of phenomenal appearing as a desirable element. It enriches the play of appearances that are perceivable in the object. This is even the case precisely when those perceiving *know* that it is not so. "But it looks (sounds, feels, smells) *like . . . ,*" they can say to one another.[38] The bicycle helmet looks like a ball, the street looks like a scene from a crime film, the mountain formation looks like a skyline (or vice versa), the traffic noise sounds like a resonating of nature, the moss feels like velvet, the subway tunnel smells like elderberry.

Of course, in these simple cases it depends entirely on the perceivers whether these forms of apparency awake an independent interest in them, just as it generally depends on their reactions whether the appearance of a particular object occasions them to make present its appearing. But if, while regarding such a transparent apparency, they sense an independent stimulus, the perceivers give themselves over to moments of an aesthetic semblance. They execute free "perceiving as" that is not only not *directed* at "ascertaining that" but also does not *contain* any such ascertaining whatsoever.

Accordingly, I wish to define aesthetic semblance as follows. We perceive something given in a situation *as something*—having a particular sensuously discoverable constitution or disposition. About this something we know (or can know) that *it is not* as we perceive it to be, and we enter into a lingering with the object that is appearing thus (at least partially). In other words, aesthetic semblance consists in appearances that, in *transparent contradiction* to the actual being-so of objects, can be perceived and welcomed as such. It is to be distinguished from the conditions of a *factual* semblance, where something appears differently from what it is; its perception is a mistake when seen through and a deception when not.

However, this affirmed semblance can only be one more or less strong *element* in a play of appearances, since it is only from this that the positivization of an otherwise mistaken perception can follow. Aesthetic semblance enriches aesthetic appearing with additional aspects. If this were not the case, *simulations* would also have to be understood generally as phenomena of aesthetic semblance. Here too there is an irreal givenness of something that retains its value despite knowledge of its irreality and, what is more, acquires its practical value precisely because of this. Whether we think of a flight simulator, a three-dimensional presentation of nonexistent compounds, or a room of a virtual library, perception is always presented with numerous appearances to which no material reality corresponds. We do not fly through any airspace, no material object is moved, there are no books that can be grasped in the usual sense (not even if a perfect illusion of their being graspable could be generated). The successful mastery of these simulation techniques is based entirely on transparent semblance. This relation alone, though, is not sufficient to constitute a case of *aesthetic* semblance. The latter comes to light first as an aspect of an abundance of appearances, one that is taken up for its own sake. Of course, the same can happen with respect to the said simulations; yet it is not the simulation as such that generates an aesthetic semblance, but a perception that is not so much concerned with its practical achievements as with the play of its (in part illusionary) appearances.

Aesthetic semblance understood in this way is therefore a mode of appearing, not an opponent thereof. In respect also of its perception we are attentive to the simultaneous and momentary phenomenal givenness of objects, only that here, in addition to the aspects already considered, there are also those to which no appearances in the object correspond. The emergence or admittance of an aesthetic semblance intensifies the aesthetic play of appearances, though without dominating it.

Here there is something important to be learned about aesthetic interest. It is characterized by a potential *indifference* vis-à-vis being-so. Up to now it has been said that aesthetic perception has a *telos* different from that of the determination of being. It becomes clear that this orientation can include an indifference toward the being-so of its objects. But this indifference is a matter of degree. No sensuous perception, not even an aesthetic one, could take its orientation from pure semblance formations; there would be nothing existent that could be perceived in its being-so or in apparency, and there would be nothing there that could be grasped in the play of its real and purported appearances. The object of aesthetic perception is never a mere illusion. There *is* a thing, there *is* a tone, there *is* a movement, there *is* a scene, which in some aspects appear differently from what they really are, and for that reason, among others, they awaken our interest. It is only in real objects that irreal aspects come to appearance.

James Turrell: Slow Dissolve

Before investigating the status of this irreality, I would like to view a more complex example. It has to become clearer what it means to say that aesthetic semblance is a state about which we know *or can know* that no actual appearance corresponds to it, because sense deceptions are not always (immediately) transparent in aesthetic relations either; and it depends by no means always on the disposition of the perceivers whether an aesthetic semblance is formed. Precisely in the context of art, the creation of a semblance can work explicitly with effects that are not transparent at first sight. The deceptive and the supportive semblance appear, then, together; deceptive appearance proves to be a phase of supportive semblance.

In 1992 in the Sprengel Museum in Hanover, Germany, the U.S. artist James Turrell designed a room that he entitled *Slow Dissolve*. This work is part of a series of space installations that the artist calls *Space Di-*

vision Constructions; it belongs to the group *Sensing Space* in this series. Through a dark passageway, the beholder enters a large, dimly lit space at the front of which a rectangular violet picture surface can be seen. Anyone relying on his or her sense of seeing first has the impression that a monochrome *painting* is to be seen here. The closer one gets to the luminous segment on the wall, the greater are the irritations with respect to the appearance of the painting. The color area displays an unusual spatiality that, from a distance, is reminiscent of the colored spatial pictures of Gotthard Graubner. At the same time, it displays a mysterious immateriality, as if the canvas had dissolved behind the paint. What this actually is cannot be discerned until one stands directly in front of the picturelike artifact. Some beholders do not want to believe what they see until they have stretched their hand through the "painting," for there is no painting there. What first looks like a painting is in fact a lighting effect, generated by neon lights that are concealed in a recess in the wall. The side borders of this space in the space, in front of which the painting effect emerges, clearly exceed the bounds of the picturelike opening. What looks like a painting *surface* from the perspective of a typical art-museum viewing is thus in reality a light and color *space* into which one could actually enter. It is the illumination of an image—an illumination, however, that wants to be seen through and can be seen through.

Here is not the place for a detailed interpretation of this work of art.[39] This interpretation would have to discuss how the work stages a reflection on pictoriality by drawing attention, in a paradoxical way, to situations of picture experience. (Because the central appearance of the installation is not a real picture, it acquires a literal transparency and depth that are frequently ascribed metaphorically to real pictures.) In this way, there evolves a subtle experiment with the spatial and affective relations, the ontological certainties, and the metaphysical needs on the basis of which we encounter pictures of art.

What is of primary importance in our context is that here there is a semblance that is as inevitable as it is inescapable. At the first encounter, everyone has the impression of a painting, though doubts may soon arise. But even after someone has seen through the construction of the work, he or she will see the illuminated detail on the wall again and again *as* a painting. This semblance "survives" its being seen through. It is fascinating despite and because of knowledge of its seeming character [*Scheinhaftigkeit*].

No matter how often we might enter the space of this installation, we see first of all a surface that from a distance displays all the characteristics of an unframed monochrome canvas. No matter how much we were deceived the first time, the discovery of the deception does not make this appearance of a painting disappear. Just as Hegel emphatically pointed out, aesthetic semblance is something categorically different from an illusion of perception.

Semblance Is Real

I perceive the bicycle helmet as if it were a ball. I view the colored surface in Turrell's installation as if it were a painting. I hear the sound of a pneumatic hammer as a beat. I listen to the bark of a desperate dog as if it were a saxophone improvisation by Anthony Braxton. These visual and aural discernments could be the outcome of a purely idiosyncratic reaction; *to me*, they look or sound like this. This is not enough in order to speak of a semblance, not to mention an aesthetic semblance. In contrast to mere idiosyncrasies and hallucinations, semblance is an appearance sensorially *shareable* with others. It is not simply a matter of a purely subjective impression. Rather, it can be *asserted* with a claim to intersubjective validity that, from this or that position, something appears as something that it is not (just as I have asserted in my description of Turrell's installation). There can be disputes about the existence or nonexistence of a semblance—for instance, about whether the apparency of a painting in Turrell's installation is really "inescapable," and that means whether the apparency is really "there." Aesthetic semblance is a perception possibility that is openly available on the particular objects and can be recognized or overlooked, grasped or waived.

But how is this possible? Haven't we just spoken of the irreality of aesthetic semblance? How else could we speak of a semblance? How is a semblance supposed to be real?

Let us think of a mirage. It is a hot-air reflection whereby a distant object appears in proximate distance. This proximity is a semblance. The appearances, however, that simulate this proximity are not a semblance; they are actual appearances that can be perceived by someone in the appropriate location. Even simpler is the example of a rod in water. The rod is straight, but it appears under water as if it were bent. This bend of the rod is a semblance. Nevertheless, the *apparency* of this bend is actually there—anyone with eyes in his or her head can see that a rod submerged partly in water assumes a bent look. However irreal the appearance in question is, the *self-presentation* of this appearance is a universally accessible reality.

We encounter here once again the problem of the objectivity of appearances. Appearances, it was stated above, are the discriminable sensuous *compositions* of objects of perception. In the previous section, these appearances were discussed only in terms of the significance of the qualities actually ascribed to particular objects. In the case of a semblance, we are concerned with qualities that are not ascribed to the objects in question even though they present themselves to perception as if they were ascribed to them. This self-presentation of objects can nonetheless be real even if what presents itself does not have any reality as that which presents itself in that manner.

The colored surface created by Turrell *really* does look as if it were the surface of a painting that it is not. This is a statement about how this object encounters our vision at a certain distance. In this encounter, the seeming phenomenon acquires a relative reality that is tied to the type of encounter this is. To that extent, this phenomenon is part of the appearances whose play is perceivable on the object. It does not follow simply from a private perspective but applies to *any* beholder whosoever. The illuminated space is ascribed the property of being (again and again) the *apparency of a painting*, independently of the reactions of particular museum visitors. This apparency thus satisfies the accepted liberal criterion of an objectively given fact. The apparency is universally accessible, and in this sense real.

Yet, there is no pictorial being [*Bild-Sein*] corresponding to pictorial semblance [*Bild-Schein*]. Unlike, for instance, the color of the light zone, its status as a painting (understood as the presence of paint on canvas or another paint-bearing surface) is a property that it does not really have. Rather, the illuminated space is arranged with artistic planning in such a way that it appears for a time to all viewers as a painting. It is given to them phenomenally in this manner. This *self-presentation* has reality, without the *appearance* that presents itself for recurring moments having reality.

The situation of aesthetic perception often experiences an enormous enrichment in this way. Even the sight of a rod bent in water is well worth viewing. What is important for aesthetic intuition is not so much the being-so of something as the how of its appearing. Here, the reality of perceivable appearances can be of secondary importance without the reality of the encounter with them being of secondary importance. "I don't believe in vampires," says a dubious screen hero of our day after he had literally worked his way through hundreds of them at the side of the obligatory maiden, "but I believe in what I see."[40] This fine maxim, delivered in a somewhat mediocre film, expresses clearly a fundamental ontological reservation of aesthetic perception. What is not always, and never solely, important in aesthetic perception is how things *are* independent of their particular phenomenal self-presentation, but what is always important is how they *appear* in a given situation of perception, with the possibility here of an aesthetic *semblance* forming.

Not Everything Is Semblance

Supportive sensuous semblance is an important element of aesthetic perception, but nothing more than this. There does not have to be an aesthetic semblance involved when some object or other is made present for the sake of its sensuous presence; nor does there have to be an aesthetic semblance involved so that artworks of a particular kind can be created. The world of art is open to the realm of semblance, but it is not in general a domain of semblance.

These statements are not so radical when one bears in mind that I am operating with a highly limited concept of aesthetic semblance. This concept refers solely to a sensuous semblance in which real objects are perceived differently from what they actually are; it does not refer to an imagination semblance, to which I will turn in the next section. Although a systematic treatment of art is reserved for the sections "Situations of Appearing" and "Constellations of Art," some comments on the role of semblance in the arts are helpful here in order to further clarify the contours of this concept.

It is only on real sensory objects that a sensuous semblance can evolve. What was established in our first mundane examples applies also to the objects of art. Barnett Newman's painting *Who's Afraid of Red, Yellow and Blue IV* (1969–70, Nationalgalerie, Berlin), which has already been discussed in Chapter One,[41] seems at first glance to have the very symmetrical and balanced construction that it negates with great artistic force. This semblance is constitutive of the movement of the entire work, but it rests on an arrangement of the three color zones that is literally a symmetrical arrangement in a specific sense, namely, when we disregard the minimal, initially invisible overlapping of the painted areas and their different space effects. In this way, the work transforms an aspect of its being-so into an artistic semblance. Turrell's illumination of a painting in *Slow Dissolve*, by contrast, evolves in the context of an installation that generates an irreal painting appearance through an arrangement of space and light. This arrangement is eminently real in every respect. The space-in-space, at whose front boundary the illusion of a painting emerges, is no more a semblance than is the lighting devices employed in various locations to generate it. In addition to this material facticity, it is above all the medial facticity that is decisive. The space designed by the artist is a *presentation* of its central effect. It presents the semblance of a painting; herein lies its artistic being.

In general, works of art cannot be semblance formations because they are presentations that can make use of seeming operations without themselves being seeming operations.[42] This—the fact that artworks are genuine presentations even if they present irreal appearances—could appear trivial, but its consequence is not; art semblance too is possible only within an aesthetic play of real appearances.

If in a movie theater we see vampires "coming toward us," we are faced not with a seeming encounter with a fictional being but with the presentation of their movement in virtual space. The appearances on the screen that we grasp as the activities of vampires are precisely this: a romping around of vampires presented through lighting effects. There *are* no vampires there, and there do not *seem* to be any either. We see a *presentation* of vampires. We speak of this presentation when we say that in the movie *From Dusk Till Dawn* there are "heaps of vampires to be seen." These *figures* can actually be seen even though no actual vampires are seen. Within the pictorial world of film, there can perhaps be hidden and transparent illusions, but this world of pictures is not itself an illusionary world.[43]

When the members of the audience got a fright at the legendary screenings of *L'arrivée d'un train en gare de La Ciotat* by the Lumière brothers at the end of the nineteenth century because it looked to them as if a locomotive would drive directly into them, this was not an aesthetic semblance but a factual one. Perceived as a "transparent contradiction," this would have probably been an occasion for astonishment but not fright.[44] Of course, today's action cinema also operates with the ambivalence of astonishment and fright, as when the dinosaurs in Steven Spielberg's *Lost*

World (USA 1997), conveyed by sound effects, seem to sneak up "from be-hind" through the high grass. Here, for a moment, the illusion is created that the fictional events in the movie are happening in the reality of the movie theater, which can indeed produce a real fright. Nonetheless, this time it is less a factual than an aesthetic semblance. Here the surprising oc-currence is part of an evidently aesthetic play of perception. In the movie theater no one—except for sensitive souls—will be concerned about pro-tecting himself or herself against cinematic shocks; on the contrary, it is all about experiencing them.

There are many cinematographic procedures available to generate an aesthetic semblance. The Bronx can be filmed as if it were an idyllic spot, or a poker game as if it were a feverish activity. Here is an extraordinary ex-ample. In the movie *Face/Off* by John Woo (USA 1997) the real good guy (played by John Travolta) gets the face and the body of the actual bad guy (played by Nicolas Cage) in order to solve an otherwise unsolvable case, which is, however, made more difficult by the fact that, in a countermove, the real bad guy assumes the face and the body of the actual good guy and covers all the traces of this metamorphosis. For most of the movie, the good guy—now played by Cage—is on the move with the face of the bad guy, in the desperate attempt (which as usual succeeds after many false leads and much confusion) to save his face in the struggle with the bad guy—now played by Travolta—who bears the face of the good guy. Strangely enough, it works. The moviegoer imagines that Travolta is now in Cage's body, and Cage in Travolta's, as if the operation had actually taken place with the *actors*. (One sees here how much imagination is sometimes needed to develop an aesthetic semblance or to let oneself become entan-gled in it.) The audience is suitably relieved when in the end Travolta, the real good guy, gets "his" face back again—although there is a shudder at how little the face of a person vouches for his or her personality. Illusory feats of this kind are not to be discounted, but no movie can be reduced to them, whatever Hollywood might say or do.

What I have spelled out a little for cinema can be said analogously about theater. The stage is often *also* a world of semblance, but first and foremost it is the location of a play within whose framework more or less meaningful occurrences are actually performed and actually presented. When Hamlet kills his stepfather, it might seem to the audience—depend-ing on the production—*as if* the latter were really murdered. In any case, within the framework of the acting on stage Hamlet kills him. For this, the sensuous *apparency* of a killing act is not needed necessarily; a scenic suggestion suffices. The events of narrative theater are, for long stretches, meaning occurrences. As such they are not seeming occurrences. When Hamlet speaks his monologue "To be or not to be," and the performance succeeds to some degree, he does not *seem* to be moved by these questions, he *is* moved. Hamlet, the figure, procrastinates and quarrels *in actual fact.* The actor who plays Hamlet should not do one or the other. We will certainly be dissatisfied with his performance if he merely *seems* to be moved. He is not supposed to appear to us somehow as a human being; he is supposed to give us Hamlet. Hamlet and the other figures of classic theater are first of all creations of aesthetic imagination, not figures of aesthetic semblance.[45]

The simultaneity of aesthetic appearing, we can conclude for now, is not tied to processes of a sensuous semblance, not in cinema or in theater, not in sculpture or in painting, not in music and certainly not in literature. The appearing of irreal appearances is an important form of aesthetic appearing, but it is not a constitutive factor of the aesthetic situation.

4. Appearing and Imagination

Irrespective of whether or not the perception of appearing is open to elements of a semblance, it is always concerned with events that are given to our senses here and now. It is always directed at the current self-presentation of its objects. This means, however, that in our investigation of illuminative semblance we still have not found a way to avoid taking our orientation from situative reality. To be sure, the apparency that there is a painting on the wall does not correspond to any reality in the space of Turrell's installation. But at the same time the fact of this apparency continues to be an important truth about the situation created by the artist. The apparency is really there, and it is only here that it is there.

Thus, if we want to understand why it is said of aesthetic experience that it opens not only a special access to reality but also a special way out of it, we have to take a further dimension of the aesthetic into consideration. This dimension has its roots in the power of the imagination [*Vorstellung*] to go way beyond the particular situation and even beyond any real situation whatsoever. This is not, however, a solely aesthetic faculty. In thought and planning, excursions into the past and the future or into possible and impossible relations are quite common. Moreover, the sensuous projections of the imagination involved here are not aesthetic as such; rather, aesthetic projections represent a variety of sensuous ones. Yet these aesthetic projections of the imagination are for their part not *perceptions* in the sense covered so far since they refer not to a presence that is present but to one that is absent.

This chapter is concerned with how the two, aesthetic imagination and aesthetic perception, become closely connected. On the objects on which this connection comes about, we have both: an intensified turning toward presence, as well as an increased turning away from presence. Wherever this connection is created in one way or another, I speak of *objects of imagination* [*Objekte der Imagination*]. These are objects that, as special objects of perception, are also special objects of the imagination. This eminent possibility, as it is generated above all by objects of art, has not been mentioned so far. Only an analysis of aesthetic *imagination* will lead us to a sufficiently differentiated concept of aesthetic *perception* and its objects.

Imagination

We can not only perceive sensuous objects; we can also imagine them. Sensuous perception requires that its objects be present; sensuous imagination does not. In what follows I employ the concept of imagination in this sense, as a concept contrasting to the concept of perception.[46] Perceptions refer to objects and states that reside within the reach of the execution of these perceptions; sensuous imagination refers to objects and states that are not within the reach of perception—to the extent that they exist at all. In imaginative consciousness we keep present, in a more or less clear or complex sensuous condition, objects and situations that are absent.[47]

Just as aesthetic perception is a mode of sensuous perception, aesthetic imagination is a mode of sensuous imagination. Aesthetic imagination differs from nonaesthetic by the fact that sensuous objects are presented in it *in their appearing*.

Before commenting on this new relation I would like to point out a consequence that concerns us later. Just as sensuous consciousness reaches significantly further than the consciousness of sensuous perception—namely, to include the use of sensuous imagination—aesthetic consciousness also reaches significantly further than the consciousness of aesthetic perception in the sense covered so far, that is, in the simultaneous reception of real and present appearances, however seemingly configured they may be. Even if we restrict ourselves to waking, imagining consciousness—not paying specific attention to dream imagination—it is evident here that the domain of the aesthetic is by no means exhausted in states of perception. These states of perception, however, have been the focal point of the investigation so far, and they will remain so as the study progresses, the reason being that I argue that perception and its objects do indeed constitute the central sphere of aesthetics, even if the aesthetic imagination often likes to leave this domain behind. Yet before being able to formulate the argument, we have to expand our horizons once again.

Objects of Sensuous Consciousness

Among the objects of sensuous consciousness are, first, not only *present* but also *past* and *future* objects; and second, not only *real* but also *irreal* objects. We have to keep this spectrum of possibilities in mind when distinguishing between sensuous perception and sensuous imagination.

By *real sense objects* I mean empirical objects that were, are, or could be within the reach of our perception. These real objects can be present in perception (like this ball here), or were able to be present (like my breakfast yesterday), or will be able to be present (like my breakfast tomorrow). What is decisive is the *possibility* of real presence. Real objects, it follows, can indeed be temporally or spatially unreachable (just as John Travolta's breakfast today is out of reach for me, or spring on a delightful planet in a distant galaxy is unreachable for present-day humanity). They are real because they are or were *in principle* accessible to perceptual encounter.

Irreal sense objects, by contrast, are objects that are not (at least in principle) within the reach of our perception. They cannot be present to us as empirical givens, as things stand to the best of our knowledge. This means that irreal objects are "objects" of a special kind. They are "given" only in conjunction with projections of them. They lack the self-sufficiency of real objects. We cannot *encounter* them. They do not have a presence of their own.

Nevertheless we are entirely familiar with many irreal objects—with Rosinante, Don Quixote's donkey; with unicorns and vampires of various ancestries; with Italo Calvino's *Invisible Cities*, with a certain Danish prince, or with the sonata by Vinteuil in Proust's *Remembrance of Things Past*. But in all of these cases there is a (literary or cinematic) *playscript* (or a series of such scripts) that makes them imaginable or visualizable to us. These sources of a fantasy guided by literature or cinema are for their part *real* objects that are there, among other things, to provide our fantasy with nourishment. The acquaintance with the essence and worlds of fantasy is always at the same time an encounter with literary or cinematic *works*. The irreal objects presented in these works are not simply given in conjunction with the particular subjective projections of these objects. The history of Rosinante and its owner can be read in every edition of the novel written by Cervantes. Although we can discuss these scripts extensively ("Isn't Rosinante actually a mule?" "Doesn't Rosinante secretly symbolize the inadequacy of language?"), we can scarcely debate objects purely of my imagination. At best we could talk about the feebleness of my *accounts*; but the projections of the imagination of which I give an account are not themselves accessible to public evaluation. Collective fantasies are dependent upon public media (oral transmission, literature, cinema, and so on); projections of the imagination exist only as constructs of an individual fantasy.

The distinction between real and irreal objects of sensuous consciousness does not relate symmetrically to the distinction between perception and imagination. Real objects can be objects of the imagination in various ways. While sitting at my writing desk I imagine James Turrell's installation; I view the color patch on the wall as if it were a monochrome painting by Yves Klein. The decisive difference between sensuous perception and sensuous imagination (in the meaning intended here) lies rather in the kind of *presence* their objects enjoy. Perception relates to currently *present* objects, imagination to objects that are *absent* (at the moment or as a matter of principle).

Objects of perception in this sense are objects that are given—or could be given—within the environs of sensuous comprehension. They are phenomenally reachable objects. Objects of sensuous imagination, by contrast, are objects that are not present at the moment of their apprehension but are made present in a remembering, anticipating, or fantasizing appropriation. They are phenomenally characterizable objects, but (at present or in principle) unreachable ones. The possibilities of a consciousness imagining in this manner are extraordinarily complex. We can, in the imaginative mode, relate to real or irreal objects—to absent balls or creatures that have never existed. We do it in the anamnestic or the anticipatory mode, thinking of the apples that were lying on the lawn last fall or will be lying there again soon. We can do it in the constative or the fantasy mode, in memory of how something really was; or in an imaginative metamorphosis, how it could have been in this or another world. We can be more or less subject to all of these imaginative projections, or we are able to more or less steer them. We can also let the sensuously imagined be present in its being-so or in its appearing.

When I recall the red ball in the garden that has now been in the attic for some time, then this is an object of the imagination; this is also the case when I go into the garden again and expect the ball to be still lying there (irrespective of whether it is or not). If, however, this time instead of a ball there is a red bicycle helmet lying there, this helmet (which at first I think is a ball) is an object of perception, and it remains so when I notice the mistake. If, however, believing a red helmet to be lying there (although in truth it is a ball) I imagine that a ball is there, then the object of my sensuous consciousness is a real *and* an irreal object—and in both cases a ball. But if, recalling Rilke, I imagine a ball *like this one* as the object of a cosmic game, then it is transformed into an object of the imagination. If, on the other hand, I linger in considering *this* ball and while doing so think about Rilke's poem, then this ball is an object of *both* my perception *and* my imagination. Here it is not a matter of a real ball and an imagined one, as was the case in my mistaken projection of the shape of a ball onto a supposed helmet, which was in truth a ball. Rather, the *real* ball present becomes the *object* of aesthetic imagination (which is stimulated by the poem); perception lingers with a given object and in this lingering goes way beyond everything immediately given.

Aesthetic Imagination

These modulations characterize an expanse of sensuous consciousness that aesthetic imagination frequently makes use of, up to and including extensive ontological intermixtures.[48] It is constitutive of the scope of aesthetic consciousness that in its duration we do not always remain (only) with really *present* objects, nor always (only) with the making present of *real* objects. But the aesthetic imagination is always characterized by an imagined sensuous *presence* of what is envisaged.

Sensuous projections of the imagination refer to objects that are not within the scope of bodily perception. These projections become *aesthetic* projections as soon as the objects are imagined in their appearing. Speaking of "objects" of imagination here is always to be understood in the *formal* sense elaborated at the end of the earlier section "Being-so and Appearing." Imagining something aesthetically [*ästhetisches Vorstellen*]—an individual thing or event, or a constellation of things and events—I will also call *imag-ination* [*Imagination*] for brevity. Just like aesthetic perception, this imagi-nation can be set in motion at any time or place. Like the former, it is not a matter just of visual consciousness; it encompasses the sensitivity of all senses. Like the former, it is also synaesthetically disposed where the per-spective of *one* sense is in the foreground. Imagination in this sense means to recall or imagine a visible, audible, tangible, gustatory, olfactory object *in its appearing*. Aesthetic imagination understood in this manner is thus also always a making present of events of appearing—events, however, that are not present in the (bodily centered) location of this imagining.

An important medium of imagination is memory. But remembering is also situated in the polarity of a more nonaesthetic or aesthetic reference. I can remember what something was and where it was, or else how it was there. "The ball was lying in the middle of the lawn" is a statement a wit-ness could make in a murder trial. This would be a purely factual recollec-tion. "The red ball on the green lawn!" is a statement that, on the other hand, could evoke an aesthetic memory. This is often the case when we re-flect on something past. We can recall the time and place of an occurrence or else, going far beyond this, *how it was* to be in that place at that time: we can recall the sensuous presence, the atmosphere, the experience of the place. I can think about when and where I last went to the North Sea as a child, or I can anamnestically make present how it was for me, in my ex-perience, to be there then. In the case of biographical recollections, the one can be seldom separated from the other. These times and places of the past are saturated with imaginations of their *past present*. They present them-selves in light of their appearing. I make present the smell and taste of the sea, the light of the countryside, the dampness of the clothes, the coldness of the wind, the action and inaction of my playmates, and much more— not one after the other but as an oscillating happening that frequently dis-solves into diffuseness. These imaginative reminiscences are connected to a recollection of the expectations and disappointments, the hopes and fears, the mix and change of feelings and moods that dominated me at the time. This reexperiencing of the past is never disengaged from an imaginative projection of its face and smell, its sound and taste. There is no anamnestic emotionality without anamnestic sensuality.

Analogously, the same applies to the other temporal modes of free aesthetic imagination. I can imagine how it would have been at the North Sea if I had returned there once again; using all of my senses I can "paint a picture" of what it would be like to pursue a decent profession as a New York stock broker, or of what it would be like to start a new life on a distant, hospitable planet. Likewise I can imagine the life situation of others—not what it would be like *for me* to be the proprietor of my regular pub, but what it might be like *for him*, the actual proprietor, to see the pub fill up and empty day in and day out. In each of these cases, the projection of the presence of these situations is connected to sensuous projections of a simultaneity of states and events, just as it is the case with the aesthetic intuition of present presences [*präsente Gegenwarten*]. There is no imaginative projection of an experienced presence without the imaginative projection of its appearing.

Imagination and Semblance

Nonetheless, we can also make objects that are *present* the object of an imaginative perception. We see someone and imagine how it would be to spend a night or an entire life with him or her; we see a ball and imagine it to be an enigmatic sculpture; we hear alarm sirens and imagine them to be a composition by Cage. Here, the imagination operates in more or less close proximity to the perception of an aesthetic semblance—and yet differently, since the imagination is not tied to any semblance of perception. It can take liberties that are not available to the turn toward an efflorescing [*Aufscheinen*] of irreal appearances. Something does not have to look or sound like something else for us to be able to imagine that it is just so, namely, something different.

Aesthetic semblance, it was said, exists when we can perceive something that appears so and so *as* something, without believing *that* it is so. But it has to *actually* appear thus—the bicycle helmet as a ball, the rod bent, the light space as the surface of a picture. Free imagination can emancipate itself from this peculiar reality of semblance. A seascape that I appreciate and discuss as I would a Gerhard Richter painting does not have to appear at all like a *picture* by Richter. The siren concert *cannot* appear at all like a Cage composition since there are no comparable compositions by him. Nonetheless we can imagine it as a concert à la Cage. Even if it has its starting point in sensuous states, the power of the aesthetic imagination can emancipate itself at any time from all concrete sensuous apparency and appearing. I see shapes in mountain formations and imagine the countryside as the home of fabulous beings—while excluding all traces of civilization, which this countryside has in abundance. I see Potsdamer Platz in Berlin in 1996 and imagine it were an installation by Ilja Kabakov—with sovereign disregard for the planning to which it actually owes its condition. I perceive a weathered wall as if it were a relief and decide to make a relief of this kind—while strictly separating this wall from its functions and surroundings. Free imagination is capable of unlimited modulation that can exceed everything that is given and is possible in real situations. Moreover, it does not always need external prompting in order to enter the land of its dreams. It satisfies our need for semblance way beyond the boundaries of all empirical being and semblance.

An Asymmetry

Aesthetic imagination has a much longer (and yet also much shorter) range than aesthetic perception. It can dispose of its objects in a completely different manner, but it can spark off only a much more limited play of appearances on its objects. This becomes evident as soon as we consider a serious asymmetry between aesthetic perception and aesthetic imagination.

Whereas aesthetic perception takes up something in *its* appearing, aesthetic imagination makes something present in *an* appearing. The objects of free aesthetic fantasy do not have the kind of stubborn appearing that the objects of aesthetic perception always enjoy. Of course, they too can be perceived only from a limited perspective; to sense something in its appearing does not mean to grasp it in all of its appearances. Still, the objects of aesthetic perception are in constant interplay with their being perceived. Imagined objects, on the other hand, display a much more limited variety in their appearing. Whereas an object of perception continuously offers different impressions when we move in its presence, the objects of aesthetic imagination are constantly under the *direction* of this imagination. Because aesthetic projections of the imagination (unicorns, aliens, vacation resorts) are frequently conventionalized, it would be nonetheless incorrect to say that what is imagined is generally under the direction of those who *make* these projections; rather, this depends entirely on the intensity and creativity of the imaginative process. But what is imagined here is determined much more by the act of imagination than by what is experienced in the aesthetic perception of any real object. The object of the imagination *follows* the (collective or creative) directions of our imagination in a manner in which no object satisfies the expectations of an act-oriented perception. What the unfettered imagination gains in latitude with respect to unreachable spaces, times, and forms, it loses on the side of the particularity of its objects. The anamnestic, anticipating, and fantasizing projection of sensuously given objects diminishes their phenomenal repleteness. Nonetheless, once it is made imaginatively present in an appearing, each absent object also unfolds, to a certain extent, *its* appearing, *like* an object within the range of perception. Our fantasy *projects* a certain phenomenal autonomy onto the merely imagined object. These objects are also imagined *as* objects of perception in a manner that is *analogous* to the intuition of real objects. But this remains a borrowed autonomy, one that cannot match the vital indeterminacy of real sense objects.

This also means that the *content* of perceptions and imaginative projections is not the same, even if the perceptions and projections refer to the same object—and most certainly not when it is a matter of the *appearing* of this object. My perception of this ball here in the garden, my *recollection* of it tomorrow, and my free imaginative projection of such a ball in such a garden do not have the same content. When I see it here and now, I take up aspects that will already have been erased in my recollection; when I imagine it, aspects are excluded or added that could never correspond precisely to this view of the ball lying here in the garden.[49] In short, it does make a difference whether I perceive an object *in* a given situation or whether I imagine it *from out of* a given situation. The sensuous *encounter* with the object becomes an imagining *making present*, one that is not dependent upon a presence of what is imagined and therefore meets with less resistance from it.

Objects of Imagination

The aesthetic imagination frees itself of the present—and thus seems to be in contradiction to aesthetic perception's emphatic relation to the present, which has been asserted thus far. The aesthetic imagination is directed toward objects of appearing that are not objects of perception—and thus seems to contradict the maxim claimed at the outset, namely, that all aesthetic objects are objects of intuition. My response, however, is that here, on the one hand, it is a matter of a *borrowed* present and a *borrowed* sensuousness; on the other, the aesthetic imagination finds its way, in the form of a *bounded* imagination, back to a heightened consciousness of the present. We have to examine this possibility of *imaginative* aesthetic perception more closely before we can redetermine the pivotal role of perception in aesthetic consciousness as a whole.

Like all perception, aesthetic imagining is also a subjective act. In perception, however, something becomes accessible that exists independently of the acts of the perception. Even if sensuous projections frequently make reference to existing states—to holiday resorts at the North Sea, or the ambience of Wall Street—their actual objects, which have often been modified by the imagination, are not accessible to others. Much as I can share with others my memories of the North Sea or my fantasies of life as a stockbroker, I cannot share with anyone what is imagined in the projection of these situations—no matter how much I might speak about them, no matter how much others can (as they believe they do) "relive" my fantasies. *Imagined objects* have no objectivity.

With respect to *objects of imagination*, however, it is another matter. Recall mention of the literary and cinematic "playscripts" of an aesthetic imagination—*Don Quixote, Remembrance of Things Past*; or *Nosferatu*, or the episodes of *Star Wars*. However imaginative the perception of these objects may be, the acts of perception are subjective too. But *what* is perceived here is not subjective. It possesses the objectivity of aesthetic objects described in the earlier section "Being-so and Appearing." We are concerned here with *formed* imaginative projections that are objects of aesthetic perception, which for their part call for imaginative *affiliation*.

This is the arena in which the two opposing movements of aesthetic consciousness encounter each other. This is the arena for probing deeper into the reality of what is momentarily appearing as well as the arena for going beyond all immediate reality. Here are objects that unleash a play of appearances that carries the imagination way beyond the play of those appearances present. Here is a perception that takes its objects in their particularity seriously by allowing them to lead it into another present. Here is an imagination that ties itself to a choreography of real processes of appearing and through them establishes contact to situations of extended or unreachable existence.

A simple example is a sentence taken from Raymond Chandler's 1959 novel *The Long Goodbye,* a sentence that Peter Handke cited as the motto for his meta-detective novel *Der Hausierer*: " . . . nothing ever looks emptier than an empty swimming pool."[50] This is a brilliant aphorism; it maintains an elegant balance between vividness and meaninglessness. We imagine a swimming pool and wonder why it of all things is supposed to represent optimal emptiness. (In the detective novel in which it appears, other connotations are of course present.) At the same time, the sentence *has* something of the condition of which it speaks. The double use (one comparative) of the term "empty" presents a range of sounds that produces something like a sound pattern of the state in question. In this way, the imagination, set in motion by the sentence, is not simply produced or nudged by the sentence, as could indeed be done by an empty swimming pool; rather, the imagination is tied to the contemplation of this sentence. The metaphysical emptiness of the pool is reflected in the artificial emptiness of the sentence.

Whoever considers this an overinterpretation should read the full statement in the original. "Off to my left there was an empty swimming pool, and nothing ever looks emptier than an empty swimming pool," Chandler writes.[51] With respect to the whole sentence, it is not just the twofold flat "empty" that is in the foreground but the contrast between, on the one hand, the word and the presented state of "emptiness," on whose side the energetic "ever" falls, and, on the other, the sonorous "O" sounds promising sensuous and other fulfillment and bundled effectively again at the end ("off" "pool" "looks" "pool"). The image of absent fullness (this also means the absent interchange of warm and cold, tension and release, that is, an absent life that has become lifeless, in Chandler's California) is carried here by the conflict between the phonetics of "empty" and those of "pool" and thus held in a multiply ambivalent balance, one that is therefore incidentally humorous. The intensity of the image that the sentence can awaken depends on the suggestiveness of the formulation it employs to do so. Attentiveness to the *imagination* of this sentence is synonymous with reading or listening attentiveness to the imagination of this *sentence.* It triggers an imaginative making present that is led from the semantic, rhythmic, and acoustic arrangement of precisely these words to a succinct image of the matter.[52] The appearing of the linguistic object allows an absent presence to appear.

This one sentence itself is a true object of imagination, as is of course the novel in which it appears. Many other novels and stories that allow a nonexistent world to evolve in the rhythm of their sentences are also true objects of imagination. It is the case for many forms of music too that in the sequence of their tones they do not (just) generate mental states but characterize the latter as they could be dominating not in the present situation but in *possible* situations. Analogously, the movements of dance often present an imaginary reality that is supported from beginning to end by the visible and audible events on stage. The actor playing Hamlet must not be Hamlet, nor seem to be Hamlet; he just has to give us a surprising and rich performance of Hamlet. Most presentations in the theater are *imaginative projections* precisely in the sense that they allow a space of the imagination to evolve within the time-space of their staging. Similarly, but nonetheless differently, pictures of art and the movement pictures of the cinema often project images of a present, images from which the beholders are safe in the presence of these objects, for better or for worse.

Imagination, Interpretation, Reflection

Many works of art proceed in this manner. But not all. Newman's *Who's Afraid of Red, Yellow and Blue IV*—which accompanies us through this book not least of all for this reason—dispenses with imagining a situation fundamentally different from the one it produces for the beholder. Nonetheless, it can be regarded as an object of the imagination since it is the vivid dramatization of an artistic dynamic and a cultural dynamic that are operative far beyond the situation of perception of this picture. Here, the work of art itself is part of a more general situation that it uncovers. The object present to the beholder becomes the sign of a presence that reaches far beyond the situation of its perception. The imagination set in motion by the picture relates in this case not to a world relation *different* from the one that evolves in the act of perceiving the picture; rather, this imagination grasps the picture as an *exemplification* of a general relation given, among other places, in the situation prior to the picture.[53] The real art object refers here not to irreal or currently inaccessible objects and situations; rather, it uncovers a general state that can be experienced through an interpretative lingering in *its* presence.

This interpreting is also an imagining, for here too (as was mentioned at the beginning of the section "Appearing and Semblance") "something is made present that goes beyond the perceivable present."[54] But now it becomes evident that the imaginative relation to a *different* present—the relation that has been the topic up to now—can be fulfilled in a relation to a present that is *expanded* in comparison to the concrete situation of perception. Absent objects are not imaginatively projected here; instead, an artistic object is presented, one that elevates itself to the arena of the vivid making present of a general situation that is not tied to the object's presence. Here, going beyond the given situation lies in the artistically arranged situation itself—in demonstrating a meaning process that reaches beyond this situation but is nonetheless operative in it.

The fact that objects of art envision a situation in which they themselves participate is by no means limited to so-called "abstract" modern art. For instance, Christian painting and sculpture, which was in the service of ritual functions, always had this sense too: not only a *sign* [*Zeichen*] but over and above this a *symbol* [*Anzeichen*] of the meaning embodied in them. Nonetheless, there are certain developments in modern art in which the arousing of human *presences* is *isolated* from the presentation of things and events *in* these presences. There is an aesthetic imagination operative here that is fulfilled not in consciousness of the appearing of absent events but solely in making processes of meaning present vividly. In contexts of "figurative" art, by contrast, we are usually concerned with *both* forms of imagination: something (a swimming pool) is presented in such a way that general relations (the heightened emptiness of an empty location of heightened pleasure) become apparent in the presentation of this thing. Irrespective of whether the meaning imagination initiated by works of art is directed at reachable or unreachable, real or irreal, present or absent presences, it always lingers at the appearing of these works and it always prompts the intuition of a world relation that goes beyond the momentary situation of perception.

This artistic admixture of perception and imagination too can be rejected by artistic means. Some of Marcel Duchamp's readymades, for instance, do without presenting a meaning that reaches beyond their mere appearing. Nonetheless, they too stage a situation of perception in which

general possibilities of a fulfilled aesthetic imagination are reduced to ab-
surdity. But even in this rejection itself, there is a reference to the imaginative potential of art. Otherwise, artistic paradox, the cunning and in-
tractability of these objects would not be discernible at all. I return to this
in the section "Constellations of Art," where I deal expressly with art objects' constitution, which is necessarily a factor in the analysis of aesthetic
semblance and aesthetic imagination. For the time being, the following
rule of thumb can apply: all works of art generate a particular presence but
not all of them present the intuition of a *different* presence.

Yet all of them must be followed and understood in their modus
operandi or construction so that they can come to perception as artistic
objects. To this end, intuition and imagination are necessary, but often
enough reflection is too. This aesthetic reflection is woven into the process
of the interpretative and imaginative perception of artworks. Again, we are
concerned with an admixture of mental energies. The lingering consideration of a painting by Newman *propels* us toward a contemplation of the
relativity of artistic and cultural orders; but the more intensive it is, the
more emphatically it will actually *be* such a reflection. Relishing Chandler's sentence does not so much *occasion* the reader to engage in exemplary reflection; rather, it *consists of* astonishment at the deep relatedness of
fullness and emptiness. Accordingly, the picture semblance arranged by
Turrell can lead further to the imagination of a walk-in picture, and this
imagination develops into a reflection on the spatiality of two-dimensional
objects and the pictoriality of many three-dimensional objects. These reflections do not stand alongside aesthetic perception; they are an essential
form of executing the intuition of art objects. They are also the ones operative when thoughts of one kind or another first lead into the world of a
work—as can happen when reading Musil's *The Man Without Qualities*;
Proust's *Remembrance of Things Past*; or Beckett's trilogy *Molloy, Malone
Dies*, and *The Unnamable*. For the process of art-related perception, it is
not decisive which of these forces—sensuous sensing, imaginative projection, or reflective contemplation—takes the lead; rather, what is decisive is
that they come together one way or another and enter into *one* movement
sooner or later.

After all, we should not forget that, in the sphere of art, aesthetic perception has to rely on multifarious *knowledge* too. Just as rich conceptual
knowledge is involved in sensuous perception—knowledge without which

nothing could be experienced in its particularity, a particularity that nonetheless goes beyond all that is knowable—the perception of artworks takes up a rich historical and theoretical as well as practical knowledge without which these works could not be experienced in *their* particularity. Here too it is impossible to separate aesthetic from epistemic intuition. Here too the notion of a complete cognitive comprehension of the entities under consideration remains empty. Here too what is important in the aesthetic encounter is not to measure a being-so but to be close to an appearing.

In the case of art, it is necessary to know a number of things that are not needed for enjoying a moment in the garden. I have to know the elements of the components of the saints' legends to be able to gain access to Christian painting; it is helpful to know about Newman's opposition to Mondrian's painting in order to understand the operations of his *Who's Afraid of Red, Yellow and Blue* series. Frequently, it is a comprehension supported by historical and art-historical knowledge that first puts us in a position to allow ourselves to be captivated by certain objects of art. Frequently, it is only through such an interpretative basis that we can be secure that our imagination, directed at artworks, is carried away by *their* imaginative projections. No matter how much it is a launching pad for reflections and imaginative projections that can lead far beyond the composition of its works,[55] art is this expedition into the unforeseeable only because it paves the way to an otherwise unreachable (intuition of) presence.

Facultative and Constitutive Objects of Imagination

However self-evident it is to elucidate this object-bound imagination using works of art, it can be operative also outside the presence of artworks. Objects of imagination can have their status in a *constitutive* or *facultative* sense. They have it in a constitutive sense when they are made expressly for imaginative perceiving (and are suitable for it). They acquire the status in a facultative sense when they are a constellation of appearances that makes an imaginative play of perception possible for the people inspired even though they are neither made expressly for this purpose nor suitable for it. Any empty swimming pool can awaken reminiscences of Chandler's melancholic image. Similarly, the huge construction site at Potsdamer Platz between 1994 and 1997, perceived as if it were an unusual Kabakov installation, could acquire the status of a facultative object of the imagination. By contrast, Kabakov's installation *Der Lesesaal* from 1996, which filled the southern Deichtorhalle in Hamburg, had a constitutive status for the period of its existence: it was made to be explored as an object of the imagination, and it was highly suitable for this.

Frequently, it is not an *unequivocal* art-analogous perception through which certain places become facultative objects of the imagination. One need only think of Manhattan or the Forum Romanum, which offer constant opportunity for this without certain paintings or movies dominating the perception, however much their aura is permeated by a multitude of paintings and movies. One need only think of landscapes that look like backdrops of an imaginative stage production without having to think of a particular theatrical style. One need only think of places of one's own past, which can be experienced like a personal Combray (three church steeples and a hawthorn hedge can be found almost anywhere) without there being a concordance between the fictional place of Marcel's childhood and the real place of one's own place of origin. Close or remote, unequivocal or equivocal, the relation to real or imagined artworks is in the perception of a facultative object of imagination; analogies to art are always involved here, though not always in a conscious manner. Works of art are the central model of the bound imagination—a model that is influential far beyond the intuition of artworks. They are the model for the *theory* of the bound imagination because they are the model for its *practice*. In our dealing with objects of art we have learned to raise things and events of the human world to the status of objects of the imagination.[56]

Hence, this means that the imagination *bound to* the perception of real objects makes important models available to the free imagination, which is not linked to the perception of existent sense objects and is therefore *unbound.* Anyone who reads works by Marcel Proust or Claude Simon gives his or her biographical memories a different beat and a different sound. Whoever is familiar with movie series such as *Star Trek* imagines the distant future in a manner inspired by the pictorial world of these movies. For listeners of classical music, the imaginative projection of pleasant and unpleasant situations is coded acoustically differently from the admirers of jazz (where for the one Chopin is needed, the other listens to the blues, and a third to the diatribes of rap). Anyone fixed on doctors' series on TV will view a threatening sanatorium stay with imaginative projections different from those of a reader of *The Magic Mountain.* And so forth. Not just in the "media age" is human fantasy lavishly furnished with formats of elite and popular aesthetic production, but it certainly is all the more so today. It is so much so that the *unbound* imaginative projections accompanying our lives have to be understood as variations of the *bound* aesthetic imagination that finds its models everywhere. The free imagination is free in the sense that it can choose the times and junctures at which it comes into play; it is free also in the sense of being open to variations and combinations of the models on which it relies for the most part implicitly. But it remains steered by the predominantly acoustic, visual, and narrative patterns that we owe to the *artistic* imagination of artists or advertising people.

The imagined objects merely presented in their appearing are, in a word, offsprings of the objects of the imagination. They originate in real objects of appearing, which are occasions for making present far-reaching or unreachable situations. They draw their sustenance from the intuition of the real objects. They have their roots not in the mere power of the *imagination* but in processes of aesthetic *perception*.

A Primacy of Perception

This is most probably true not only of aesthetic but also of all sensuous imaginative projections. They have been formed from the arsenal of perceivable appearances. The beetle in Kafka's *Metamorphosis* is created in the image of a beetle even if it is a specimen unknown in nature and one about which the author gives no further information. The fantastically shaped aliens in movies such as *Men in Black* (Barry Sonnenfeld, USA 1997) are still recognizable from this world even if they crop up in jumbled, twisted, stretched, and otherwise corrupted forms of known species. If artistic imagination were to take complete leave of the world of human perception, it could no longer captivate people's imagination.

Moreover, the faculty of the imagination is connected to that of perception for internal reasons, because what we imagine sensuously, although it is not concurrently given to the senses, are objects *as they would be perceivable* at times and places at which we are not or cannot be. Hence, the concept of sensuous imagination is in principle dependent upon the concept of sensuous perception. Accordingly, the concept of aesthetic imagination we are concerned with here is a descendant of the previously developed concept of aesthetic perception. Nonetheless, we have to consider retrospectively how this current concept of aesthetic perception relates to the concept of aesthetic imagination.

The most important outcome is that aesthetic perception can include processes of "bound" aesthetic imagination. The constitutive and facultative "objects of imagination" are objects of *perception* that at the same time permit or call for *imaginative* reception. Aesthetic perception is in principle open to imaginative implementation, continuation, or expansion.

It is simultaneously an imaginative *implementation* wherever the perception of an object as an *aesthetic* occurrence calls from the outset for our being imaginatively carried away; as at a performance of *Hamlet*, at the screening of a narrative movie, when viewing many artistic pictures, while listening to very expressive music. Without an imagination of the presence of what is presented—an imagination that is projected in the presence of the presentation—the particular presentation could not be perceived as an *artistic* one. It is also an imaginatively accomplished perception, however, in the case of the concurrent accomplishment [*Mitvollzug*] of abstract world relations that become vivid in the form of objectless artwork (like Newman's triptych). It is an imaginative *continuation* of aesthetic perception wherever objects that are already aesthetically eye-catching are also treated as objects of the imagination; one need only think of our ball perceived "à la Rilke." It is, finally, an imaginative *expansion* of aesthetic perception wherever the latter becomes the starting point of an imaginative activity that no longer sticks (close) to the intuition of the initial object. Here, proceeding from an aesthetic object, aesthetic perception can change into an unbound fantasizing that has been merely *occasioned* by this object.

Even though aesthetic imagining can be embedded in or linked up with aesthetic perception in all of these ways, aesthetic *consciousness* goes clearly beyond the scope of perception. Despite the logical dependence of the concept of imagination on the concept of perception, the process of imagining can be performed independently of processes of perception. In periods of aesthetic consciousness we make present something in its appearing, be it a spatiotemporally reachable or unreachable object, a real or an irreal one—and that means whether it is or not a sensuously presented object of perception. The situation of aesthetic perception at the center of my reflections is therefore indeed a general aesthetic situation, but nonetheless a limited one.

Still, it is the *paradigmatic* situation for all aesthetic relations. It is with respect to this situation that the context of aesthetic object and aesthetic perception must be elaborated, a context on which the context of aesthetic imagination and its objects also exist, despite characteristic differences. Only with respect to this situation are we concerned—on the part of aesthetic objects—with intersubjectively accessible things, events, and situations, that is, with instances of an *objectivity* of aesthetic objects that are not at the discretion of our sensuous comprehension. Much as processes of free aesthetic imagination represent a serious modification of this situation, since there is no objectivity and no phenomenal autonomy of intentional objects here, it is nonetheless a *modification* of the fundamental aesthetic situation. For this reason I continue to reserve the concept of *aesthetic object* for those objects that come to intuition in this situation, the situation paradigmatic for all aesthetic consciousness. Thus understood, not all aesthetically *imagined* objects are at the same time aesthetic *objects*.

Together with the aesthetic objects of perception, however, we must understand the modifications to which these objects can be subjected in imaginative consciousness, since it has become evident in the objects of the imagination that the concept of aesthetic perception, *of its own accord*, calls for analysis of aesthetic imagination if we are not to miss those outstanding objects that are there precisely for imaginative aesthetic perception. Aesthetic perception is as a matter of principle open to aesthetic imagination. This is a decisive feature of its constitution. It is why the *reversion* to the present that it enacts is often at the same time a *going beyond* this present. The occurrence of aesthetic perception can satisfy the need for being, the desire for the here and now, just as it can satisfy the need for semblance, the desire for a different here and a different now. Often enough, the two come together in the longing for an intuition of real and irreal presence, which is perhaps the strongest driving force of aesthetic perception.

5. Situations of Appearing

We have in the meantime secured a concept of aesthetic perception that is much more differentiated and richer than the minimal one drafted in the first section and explicated in the second section of this chapter. But this expanded view also highlights general features of the aesthetic situation without specifically thematizing the variability of these situations. Discussing this enlarged perspective did indeed require consideration of the breadth of aesthetic practice, but it was not yet able to do justice to it theoretically. The plurality of aesthetic situations has been represented so far solely through the diversity of examples. It has not yet been possible to deal with it systematically. On the path from minimal to comprehensive concept of the situation of aesthetic perception, therefore, there is still a decisive step to be taken.

This step is not as big as it might perhaps seem; the related concepts of aesthetic object and aesthetic perception, at which we have arrived, already bear the necessary differentiations. Depending on whether, and in what way, attentiveness to what is appearing is also open to the sensations of a sensuous or an imaginative semblance and to the concurrent execution [*Mitvollzug*] of presentations that operate in the medium of appearing, this attentiveness encounters different kinds of aesthetic objects. I present three fundamental dimensions of this appearing in this section. It is only with their differentiation that we reach a comprehensive understanding of the situation of aesthetic perception. It is only with consciousness of the diversity of possible objects of appearing that the scope of aesthetic consciousness can be measured. It is only with knowledge of this scope that aesthetic perception's emphatic relation to the present can be clarified.

Interim Results

I begin with a brief recapitulation that serves to recall what has been secured in the analysis so far. Aesthetic perception is perception of something in its appearing, for the sake of this appearing. Aesthetic objects are the objects of this perception. It is crucial for the plausibility of this minimal characterization that the constitutive *openness* of aesthetic perception is emphasized and observed in it. The most important aspects are as follows.

First, aesthetic perception is open to the simultaneous and momentary play of appearances on its objects; it is open to the specific phenomenal particularity of its objects and therefore to what remains underdetermined in any determination (and in any number of determinations) of an object of perception.

Second, in this respect it is at the same time open to an interaction of sensuous sensing even where it is predominantly *one* sense with which the presence of the object in question is sensed. It is essentially a synaesthetic sensing.

Third, in this latent or manifest synaesthetic attentiveness to what is appearing, aesthetic perception delineates an openness to the immediate presence of the situation of its execution, understood as the particular momentary constellation of things and events in whose surroundings the aesthetic perception occurs (or, in the individual case, understood as the sense-catching particularity of the individual thing and event on which the perception concentrates).

Fourth, aesthetic perception is open to phenomena of a nonillusionary semblance (which is maintained despite transparency), phenomena that this perception recognizes as additional aspects of the encounter with the object and thus as an intensification of the courses it takes.

Fifth, this perception is open at all times to imaginative implementation, continuation, and expansion—to a sensuous imagining that loads the presence of the real and present object of intuition with a making present of relations that are more general, or more irreal, or spatially and temporally more unreachable (and through this loading enriches the presence).

Sixth, as an irreducible sensuous perception, aesthetic perception is richly equipped not just with concepts that it retains in its play, it is also open to reflective movements with which it ascertains the strategy and construction of the objects of appearing. In doing so, it employs and produces a lot of (historical, art-historical, and theoretical) knowledge that serves, in the process of perception, to elucidate complex processes in the object of this perception.

Understood in this manner, aesthetic perception does not form an alternative to sensuous perception. It is a specific execution of this perception. It is sensuous perception that in the course of its executions *opens itself* to some or all (but at least to the first three) of the aspects and relations mentioned.

To be *open* to some or all of these aspects could also be said, in principle, of sensuous perception *in general.* Precisely for this reason, aesthetic perception is always close at hand wherever we perceive per se. But what applies to all perception only in principle applies to aesthetic perception at all times. This is what constitutes its special place. In one way or another, it realizes the modifications mentioned. It is characterized by an *active* openness to (some or all of) the aspects listed. It goes beyond fixation on a theoretical or practical treatment of its objects. It perceives its objects in their phenomenal presence, independently of such functionalizations. It is open here and now to the play of appearances accessible to it.

Three Dimensions

This perception can encounter a completely different appearing in its objects; this too is part of its openness to what is appearing. If we restrict ourselves completely to something's being sensuously present, it comes to perception in its *mere* appearing. As soon as the phenomenal presence of an object or a situation is grasped as the reflection of a life situation, *atmospheric* appearing comes to the fore in attentiveness. When, on the other hand, objects of perception are understood as (usually imaginative) presentations of a particular kind, we are concerned with forms of *artistic* appearing.

The sensuous constitution of perception objects can thus enter an aesthetic presence in three ways.[57] The distinction between three kinds of appearing is not a purely analytical distinction. We can view Oscar's ball in its mere appearing, disregarding the atmospheric relations in which it is located. Or we can perceive it in the repleteness of these relations, say, in a glimmering of the silence in which the garden has been enveloped ever since the children's game came to an end. (This situation changes completely if the ball is still lying on the grass long after the child has left home, or when it exists temporarily behind a police line as an object of evidence in a criminal investigation.) Finally we can view the (visibly deflated) ball as if it were a sculpture by Oldenburg, through which it would be transformed, among other things, into a *humorous* object that could also unfold its lackadaisical charm in a place completely *different* from this garden. Even so, much as aesthetic objects can acquire one aesthetic status independently of the others the boundaries between them are usually fluid, especially since the significant objects of artistic appearing are usually also outstanding objects of atmospheric and mere appearing. The various dimensions of the aesthetic can pass into one another; they can coexist, but they can also have tense relations with one another. *One* object of perception can be a multidimensional object of *aesthetic* perception. Analogously, the same holds for those dimensions of the *present* that we become aware of in aesthetic intuition. The mere, the atmospheric, and the artistic presence of sense objects issue a different "time for the moment" and thus time for a different moment in each particular case. But these moments can also replace, overlap, or interchange with one another, or—especially in the perception of art—transpire in *one* tense period of time.

Mere Appearing

We attend to the mere appearing of an object when we pay attention to nothing other than the repleteness of its momentary and simultaneous givenness, including the effects of a supportive sensuous semblance that might thereby arise. One could say that we let the object be, purely in its sensuous appearing. We allow ourselves to be captivated by the mere presence of the appearances interfering and coexisting on it. I refer to this form of sensitive encounter also as *contemplative* aesthetic perception.

This is a *special* form of aesthetic perception, not its basic form, for the fact that, in the course of aesthetic intuition, *nothing other* than the pure phenomenality of its objects comes to perception is a *particular* mode of the intuition's realization. The *simultaneity* of appearances discernible on the object is perceived here in a strict *momentariness.* The perception of objects stays at this radical making present; staying here constitutes its specific meaning. The minimal comprehension developed in the first two sections of this chapter elaborated a *general* feature of aesthetic perception, but here it is a matter of one mode of aesthetic encounter *among other* modes. Focusing on what is appearing is all that contemplative aesthetic perception is concerned with, and it shares this with the richer forms of aesthetic intuition.

Being concerned with what is appearing does, however, imply great sensitiveness to the attractions of aesthetic semblance. The potential "ontological indifference" of aesthetic perception is carried to extremes here. While being spellbound by mere appearing, we accept everything just as it appears now, irrespective of its actual sensuous constitution. With respect to the scope of the minimal characterization of the aesthetic situation, elements of semblance can therefore come into play at any time; this again shows that this first characterization did not yet apply to any *particular* form of aesthetic perception. But the components of semblance can come and go or be completely absent; mere appearing *is* no semblance, much as it might *contain* elements of a supportive semblance.

Aesthetic contemplation lingers at the phenomena, without imagination and without reflection. In no way does it go beyond the present; it does not pass into the exemplary or the general; it neither seeks nor finds meaning; it stays at a bodily perception of the sensuous presence of its objects. This includes an intensive sensuous self-sensing on the part of the subjects of this perception—without ambitions of a comprehension going beyond the moment, without ambitions of transcending the here and now. Only in making present mere appearing can we apply ourselves so *exclusively* to an intuition of what is present. What counts here is nothing but perceiving the momentary simultaneity of what is sensuously perceivable. This is nonetheless just *one* concept of aesthetic presence. The other two dimensions are covered by two further concepts of the aesthetic sense of the moment.

Atmospheric Appearing

Something reveals itself in atmospheric appearing when it becomes intuitable in its existential significance to the perceivers. The ball thus reminds us of the sound of children who are long gone; an apartment's furnishing portrays a standard of living that can be seen to be bogus. Atmosphere is a sensuously and affectionally perceptible (and, in this respect, existentially significant) articulation of realized or nonrealized life possibilities. In the form that they *have*, the objects of this appearing *give* the respective situation a characteristic form, in such a way that this character of the situation—a character co-created by them—becomes intuitable in these objects. One need only think of how a particular piece of music can change the atmosphere in a room; how a particular article of clothing can alter the impression a person makes; how a certain architecture can modify the expression of a city. Through these objects and styles, the surroundings and relations of life assume a character that does not just *come* to appearance in them; rather, it is a character they *possess* solely in the repleteness of their appearing. *Mere* appearing transforms itself here into an atmospherically *articulated* appearing.

Of course, atmospheres are also given even if no one is paying attention specifically to them. We are surrounded by the atmosphere of a room and sense it even if we do not know anything about it. On account of this omnifariousness, Gernot Böhme has proposed raising the concept of atmosphere to the status of a basic concept of aesthetics.[58] Aesthetics as a whole should, he argues, become a doctrine of atmospheres, a theory of one dimension of perception that has always accompanied us in all other processes of intuition, knowledge, and action; an analysis of aesthetic sensing that gives us orientation independently of the degrees of its awareness. This is an exciting proposal, though one that results in considerable limitations. From this position, mere appearing cannot come into view at all; art's particular appearing can find articulation only in a limited form. Anyone setting up aesthetics in a manner as general as Böhme's has difficulties doing justice to the internal hiatuses of aesthetic practice.

This is why I work with a narrower concept of aesthetic perception, for which it is a criterion that something become *noticeable* in its appearing. The atmospheric appearing I am speaking of here is thus not to be equated with the general perceptibility of atmospheres; rather, it is to be understood as a sensuous-emotional *awareness* of existential correspondences. This explicitness of the atmospheric arises when it is expressly perceived in its primordial domain: in the synaesthetic play of appearances from which it is formed. Atmospheres are not ominous "demi-objects," as Böhme says with reference to Hermann Schmitz; they are a situation's appearing, consisting of temperatures, smells, sounds, visuals, gestures, and symbols; an appearing that touches and concerns in one way or another those who find themselves in this situation. As soon as the latter are exposed to this play of emotionally significant appearances, not simply positively or negatively but actually becoming attentive to it, they perceive their surroundings in atmospheric appearing.

That something reveals itself in *an* atmospheric appearing can well mean that something reveals itself in *its* atmospheric appearing; it can mean that an atmosphere that is already *operative* becomes noticeable. But it can also mean that the atmosphere abruptly changes on account of aesthetic attentiveness. I linger at the sight of the ball and lapse into melancholy with the memory of the children long gone. Here, the atmospheric always reveals itself or arises from a correspondence between (long-term or momentary) imaginative projections and expectations of life on the one hand, and how a situation (in the long run or momentarily) appears in the light of these dispositions on the other. For this reason, it is possible to speak here of *corresponsive* aesthetic perception. This too, however, is an objective relation in the sense that it can be understood by someone who has or is familiar with the pertinent existential affinities.[59]

Unlike the perception of mere appearing, which concentrates on the sensuous givenness of its objects and consequently establishes *distance* to all meaning allocation, the perception of atmospheric correspondences is always a *meaningful* perception. Here, aspects of biographical and historical knowledge frequently play an important part. The employment of ritual objects in a religious ceremony does not communicate anything to me if I do not know what kind of objects they are and what they represent; the superior aura of a piece of expensive designer furniture in contrast to a piece of coarse Ikea furniture will not dawn on me if I have no knowledge of such fine distinctions. Awareness for atmospheres activates a knowledge of cultural references in which the perception of these atmospheres is situated. In addition, it often includes acts of the imagination in which a *different* present is fantasized or recalled (the time when this ball was at the center of Oscar's life; the time when my grandchildren will once again fill the garden with life). Here, aspects of the present situation can also come to perception as facultative objects of the imagination (for instance, when a landscape is perceived simultaneously as a landscape painting, or an urban scene as stage scenery). Even so, what remains decisive for the awareness of atmospheric appearing in all of these forms is that the making present of a present situation is in the foreground. At the center of this awareness is the perceptive sensing of how something *in* this situation—or of how this *situation*—corresponds or could correspond (positively or negatively) with my weal and woe.[60]

This sense-catching interweaving of perception situation and life situation distinguishes corresponsive aesthetic intuition's orientation toward the present from contemplative aesthetic intuition's orientation. The life situation of human beings goes beyond their spatiotemporal location: into the past of their history up to now (and of this history's embeddedment in general history), into a future colored by their intentions, hopes, and fears.[61] Facets of this life situation become perceptible to corresponsive aesthetic consciousness. While perceiving, we look into how it is, or how it was, or how it could be to exist here and now, or to have existed there and then. With an alert sense of atmospheric appearing, we perceive our particular concrete, sensuously discoverable situation as a temporary *form of our life*.

Reflection on presence, which also takes place here, has a character clearly different from its character in mere appearing. Here, concentration is not exclusively on the here and now; corresponsive consciousness is open to all—beautiful as well as terrible—reverberations of past and future times. Much as these two kinds of aesthetic situation can supersede each other, they cannot achieve congruency. The exclusive and the inclusive aesthetic reflection on the moment are a countermovement of aesthetic attentiveness.

Artistic Appearing

Works of art are objects not solely of *mere* appearing, nor just of *atmospheric* appearing, even though frequently they are *also* both—and both to an eminent degree. They have an even different appearing from the kinds of aesthetic objects dealt with so far. No art at all nor any reference to art is needed for us to be able to perceive a mere (or an atmospheric) play of appearances. Even if facultative and constitutive objects of the imagination frequently play a part in the atmosphere of a place, the *concept* of aesthetic correspondence is nevertheless not to be formulated in terms of such art references. The noticeability of atmospheres is not as such an artistic relation. This means conversely that the status of artworks cannot be grasped adequately by the concepts of aesthetic contemplation and correspondence.[62]

Artworks differ in principle from other objects of appearing by virtue of their being *presentations* [*Darbietungen*]. Following Arthur Danto's convincing proposal, objects of art must be equated neither with "mere real things" nor with "mere representations."[63] They are objects of the senses that differ from other sense objects by being presentations; they are presentations that differ from other presentations by being (to use my formulation, not Danto's) presentations *in the medium of appearing.* It is not enough to demarcate the objects of art from other nonaesthetic things and presentations; they have to be demarcated from other kinds of *aesthetic* objects too, that is, from objects of mere and atmospheric appearing; or, to be more precise, from those objects that are *merely* objects of mere and atmospheric appearing.

Since the next section deals explicitly with art, I only intimate the difference here. Works of art are *constellational presentations.* Presentations are constellational when their meaning is tied to a nonsubstitutable rendering of their material—nonsubstitutable in the sense of not being replaceable by any other combination of elements. The decisive difference from other forms of linguistic presentation or other presentation is that what is important here is a precise, individual sequence of sign elements— in contradistinction to (nonliterary) writing, the spoken word, press photos, traffic lights, pictograms, and so on.[64] Under this aspect of the individuality of their sign formation, artworks are also objects of appearing. The configurations from which they acquire their meaning are accessible only to lingering sensuous perception. In contrast to objects of *mere* appearing or atmospherically *articulated* appearing, they are formations of an *articulating* appearing.

This is why a special concurrent execution is necessary here. Artworks are objects that need to be *understood* in their performative intent. This understanding does not have to be executed verbally; it can also unfold in bodily movement, as in dancing to music or in exploring a spatial installation with all of one's senses. Nevertheless, it generally unfolds in the context of an interpretative, an imaginative, and occasionally a reflective disclosure of artistic objects. In this dependence on implicit or explicit understanding, there is a further important difference from the aesthetic objects of contemplation and correspondence. In the latter, there is often nothing to be understood. "I don't understand this ball," uttered in the course of a lingering viewing, would be a rather peculiar statement. In the case of a lamp that disrupts the atmosphere of a room, we would hardly say, "I don't understand this lamp." We would probably say, "I don't understand how someone can put such a lamp there." Of course, atmospheric awareness ordinarily includes a complex understanding of ourselves and the world too; existential understanding *reveals* itself in its sensitivity. Knowledge and understanding can also be involved here at any time, though without the situations that appear in a certain atmosphere becoming *objects* of a particular understanding as a result.

By contrast, those objects to which we ascribe the status of artworks are from the outset interpreted objects and objects created for interpretation. Frequently, they are accessible only to those who possess specific historical and art-historical knowledge. Whoever does not know that Walter de Maria's huge sculpture *Vertical Earth Kilometer*, which was erected in front of the Fridericianum in Kassel, Germany, in 1977 consists of a long rod extending into the earth, will not notice that he or she is in the midst of an artwork, even when standing directly upon it. Whoever is unable to read Thomas Bernhard's novel *Correction* as a parody on Hegel and Heidegger misses an important dimension of the work. All knowledge and all reflection, all interpretation and all imagination that an artwork calls for on the part of the perceiver has the aim here of bringing the artistic appearing of the work to life. It is only on or in this appearing that real or irreal presences of the human world can come to presentation. It is only through attentiveness to the constellations of this *presentation* that we can participate in the constellations *presented* by the artistic work.

Here lies the double presence of the objects of art. They produce a special presence and present a special presence. To be sure, not all objects of art unclose the intuition of a presence different from the one in which they themselves come to perception. Not all are in this sense "objects of imagination." But all (this will become clear in the following section) can be understood as presentations of presence that make use of various techniques of the *production* of a special presence. The produced and presented presence can be quite different situations, but also one and the same situation. The encounter with a well-executed object of art does not just put us into a moment of time, as is the case with the perception of mere appearing; it does not just emphasize dispositions and relations of actual or potential life situations, as happens in the consciousness of atmospheric appearing. The encounter makes the presences of human life present *independently* of the particular life situation of their beholders, readers, or listeners. It releases real and irreal presences of general experience. In the encounter with works of art, we *encounter* presences of human life.

Presences

The relation of presence that is decisive here must itself be understood as a form of human encounter. The presence radiating in aesthetic perception, it was said at the outset,[65] is not simply a temporary constellation of things and events but a kind of experiential encounter with this constellation; it is a *relation* of human beings to their life surroundings. In agreement with Heidegger, we can speak of an *ecstatic* presence, of position *in the midst of* extensive spatial, temporal, and meaningful relations.[66] The efflorescing of this presence—as consideration of the three dimensions of the aesthetic has shown (and the passage through the arts in the next section confirms) can have very different manifestations. In mere appearing, a situation leaves its meaningful ascriptions for one moment; in atmospheric appearing, a situation reveals itself as an accommodating or rejective location of life; in artistic appearing, an encounter with presented presences takes place. In attentiveness to this appearing, though, there always occurs the radiance of something that is present here and now. However semblancelike appearing might be and however much it exceeds the present imaginatively, it is always an appearing of real presence; it is a process to which we cannot attend without attending to the presence of our existence with sensuous intensity.[67]

Every present of human action and experience is a dovetailing of space and time: a space in which action and experience are conducted, and a time in which they extend sequentially. Each of these spaces of time, big or small though it might be,[68] is located within the horizons of a greater space and a greater time that has already passed or is yet to come. From the perspective of people who find themselves in these spaces of time, these horizons are constantly present as horizons of meaning, that is, as a range of accessible or inaccessible, certain or uncertain, proven or imagined, gained or lost, promising or hopeless *possibilities* of action and understanding. In terms of the near and the remote, the feared and the desired, the important and the unimportant, the possibilities are graded according to positive and negative, increasing and decreasing relevance. The spaces of time within which we move in action are the time spaces of the world as it concerns us or could concern us.

Here, the role of the indeterminable in our reflections becomes clear again from another side. Every present consists of numerous seized and missed possibilities of commission and omission that are to be found in it. Most of the possibilities seized in it are seized unnoticeably, and most of the opportunities missed in it are lost unnoticeably. Heidegger expressed this in *Being and Time* using the term "thrownness" [*Geworfenheit*], which is the counterpart of all "projecting" [*entwerfend*] conduct.[69] According to this, all searching for orientation is conducted within the horizons of indeterminate relations, which actually remain for the most part indeterminable. The present within which we move as acting beings is always equipped with an abundance of unexhausted epistemic possibilities and unrealized action opportunities. In this dovetailing of reality and possibility—in the fact that every present of action consists of existent and nonexistent, seized and missed possibilities of knowledge and action—there is a common root of the two contrary driving forces of aesthetic perception: to lose oneself in the real or to go beyond everything that is (so far) real. It is part of the basic constitution of every reality experienced as presence to be an open diversity of available and unavailable opportunities to act—a variety of theoretically and practically realized (or perhaps realizable) possibilities as well as a diversity of possibilities that go (largely far) beyond current cognitive and practical capabilities. It is thus an elementary characteristic of human life reality that all those situated in it with unclouded consciousness always see themselves simultaneously in past and future referred to probable, improbable, and merely imagined states.[70] For this reason, aesthetic sense can also be understood as a sense of the potentiality of those realities that we experience or imagine as presences of our lives.

Nonetheless we still have to clarify in what sense this sense is directed at real and irreal presences. The time spaces that form the presence of human existence can be grasped on the one hand as *enduring* spectrums of action. "Morning at school" is reality five times a week for schoolchildren. For those who attend the elementary school in Greenland Street, this is always a morning that is organized in repeated actions and events, even if each of these mornings unfolds differently in its specifics for each child. No school—and no other institution—could exist if it did not erect and maintain spatial and temporal regularities of conduct (along with its habitual practices and traditions). These too change little by little, just as they evolved little by little; nonetheless, we can speak here of an enduring present that becomes reality for pupils and teachers every morning.

This concept of a present that maintains itself for a long period of time contrasts with the concept of a present that *passes* all the time. This is the *moment* that we wish might linger or pass. In this understanding, no morning in the school or elsewhere is the same; each morning unfolds in different external and internal rhythms, against the background of different horizons of hope and fear, of being curious and being satiated. These presents are not enduring but passing because they are unrepeatable and irretrievable. This morning, this night, this hour will never be repeated in *this* way; not in precisely these external surroundings, not in precisely this mood, not at precisely this point in one's own history or the world's. Just like the concept of an *enduring* present, this concept of a *passing* present also captures a central aspect of the reality of human life. We are often in the same situation even though we are never in the same situation; both are true of the circumstances of our lives.

In addition, we can speak of these enduring or passing situations in an *abstract* or a *concrete* sense. When we hear in the news talk of the "present state of German universities" or the "present state of global pollution," highly abstract conditions are being addressed. They refer not to individual situations of action in the areas mentioned but to general aspects of a totality of concrete situations. On account of this generality, one can find oneself—as a member of the university or an inhabitant of the earth—permanently in the said circumstance, no matter how many different concrete situations one may pass through during the period of its existence. We constantly find ourselves in many general circumstances, but in each case we find ourselves only in one concrete situation (which, like everything else, can of course be determined and described very differently). Whereas the present "situation in the Greenland Street School" represents an enduring abstract present, daily life in this school unfolds in changing concrete situations. Accordingly, episodes of a *concrete* present is what I call situations of current experiencing and acting, whose arena can be specified in the use of perception predicates; it is a matter of perception situations that are themselves perceivable—like a break in the school yard or a math lesson in a classroom. They are existential situations within an overarching, meaningfully tiered spatial and temporal horizon. On the other hand, time spaces of an *abstract* present are what I call currently existing situations whose determination results from an isolation of general aspects of concrete presents; it is a matter of life situations that are not perceivable as such, no matter how much their determination might relate to diverse perceptions in concrete situations.

Abstract and concrete presents can for their part be more or less enduring or passing. The examples I gave for abstract presents were instances of enduring states. The "present of aesthetic moments," by contrast, is an abstraction that refers to passing states. Concrete presents are enduring situations as long as they occur at the same kind of location in the execution of the same kind of actions. In a certain sense, the mornings at the school in Greenland Street are always the same: a perpetual sameness that is then often heavily criticized by some children (while others secretly love it). However, the same mornings can, as we have seen, also be understood as episodes of passing presents. It is clear here that even the enduring concrete presents can be grasped as *abstractions* of passing concrete presents. We should not of course make the mistake of regarding only the passing presents as real; the general aspects of a situation that continues to endure beyond the passing present are also real. Likewise, the passing present is real only because it can be experienced as a passing within parameters that remain constant. Without the experience of passing, nothing could be recognized as being temporarily enduring; without the experience of at least a transitory enduring, nothing could be experienced as temporary; without the interchange between relative enduring and relative passing, no experience at all would be possible. Only in the coexistence of comparatively enduring and comparatively passing states is a present of ephemeral existence given.

Modes of Acquaintance

We can assure ourselves of the enduring situations of our lives in many ways. We can look for them purposely, reassemble them through appropriate actions, or explore them through intentional changes. Even where these practical explorations are not possible (because the particular situations are irretrievably past or no longer accessible for other reasons), we can represent the enduring situations in one way or another in language or images (or call them to memory on the basis of such representations) and analyze them in the medium of concepts. In these ways they are to a certain degree recognizable and controllable; we can thereby acquire a heightened awareness of current or past presents. In today's world, electronic media play a role here that can scarcely be overestimated. By making universally accessible events public, these media create in modern societies a present that transcends local life practices but is at the same time anchored in local orientations.[71]

None of these kinds of acquaintance with enduring presents presupposes a decided aesthetic consciousness. In order to know where I am, what is the case with this or that at a given time, or which situation is mine and which a general one, aesthetic intuition is not necessary (much as aesthetic perception and imagination might be enlightening here). The constant *differentness* of presents that are always *passing* in these enduring relations does not lend itself to primarily theoretical or practical, constructive or reconstructive processing. Making present these special situations, which emerge and pass within more general relations, is the domain of aesthetic perception. It applies itself to concrete presents in their irreproducibility, potentiality, and momentariness. It activates a sensitivity to the unmistakable color and hue, the unmistakable sound and mood, the unmistakable taste, and the unmistakable feel of a situation. Consciousness of presence in this sense—the consciousness of *particular* presents—is aesthetic consciousness.

The diverse kinds of aesthetic perception make these presents present in various ways. In attentiveness to *mere* appearing we become aware of a present while temporarily suspending its meaningfulness. What appears thus is unrepeatable in the strictest of senses: a concrete situation in the momentariness of (one or all of) its simultaneous appearances. Of course, the ball's lying there remains a meaningful state, even in view of its mere lying there; it is, as I still know, Oscar's ball that is lying there. But this knowledge and the being-so associated with it are bracketed here. In the course of aesthetic contemplation it does not count; what counts is the moment of a radically dysfunctional appearing that is removed from meaning. This bracketing of the meaningfulness of its objects, which is executed by contemplative perception, is also an abstract achievement. But the bracketing can be done only amid the situation of concrete and passing presents. This abstraction, which is achieved by all of the senses, does not lead out of the concreteness and ephemerality of the here and now but rather leads into them in an extreme manner.

In openness to *atmospheric* appearing, by contrast, it is precisely dimensions of the existential meaningfulness of concrete conditions that come to consciousness. These can be repeatable or unrepeatable situations; but even where it is a matter of a conscious apprehension of *enduring* existential correspondences, they are always experienced in a momentary play of their forms. The atmosphere of the Greenland Street School might be the same for years, but the *experience* of this atmosphere always relates to an unmistakable *impression*. (Today, and only today, snow is melting from the shoes left outside the classrooms, while workmen are hammering away trying to repair a burst water pipe.) Here too the momentariness of appearing is always a decisive ingredient in which the dovetailing of passing and lasting life situations can be picked up by the senses.

In the perception of *artistic* appearing, finally, there occurs a presentation of particular presents. These presentations frequently create a concrete and enduring present that can be revisited again and again. Nonetheless, wherever they come to appearance solely through *performances*—an appearance that is made possible not simply by playing recorded media (film rolls, cassettes, CDs)—artistic presentation is for its part accessible only for the duration of a passing present. Whatever kind of present the artistic presentation might produce, however, it is a presentation of passing time—even if it tells of the joys of eternal life.[72] Even the artistic creation of an incapacitatingly or menacingly *monotonous* present—as found in Ivan A. Goncharov's *Oblomov*, Alain Robbe-Grillet's *La Jalousie*, or Aleksander Tisma's *The Book of Blam*—is always the presentation of a present that is *passing* second by second, day by day, month by month, or year by year—a present that, in its oppressive traits, will just not pass away. The artistic creation of enduring and abstract presents, as found in Tolstoy's *War and Peace* or in our Newman painting, portrays their meaning in a wealth of concrete scenes or in the repleteness of the scenes created by the work. It is probably a law of artistic presentation that it can present abstract and enduring presents only by virtue of a presentation of *passing* presents, and achieve this only through the staging of *its* (enduring or even passing) appearing. From this limitation come all of its marvels; here lies what artistic presentation, in contrast to all kinds of representation, is capable of doing.

Aesthetic Consciousness

The next section deals with this contrast in detail. First I would like to sketch the contours of the situation of aesthetic perception that follow from the distinctions that have just been introduced.

The most important finding is that we are not dealing with three perception situations that could be sought out independently of one another; rather, we are dealing with three dimensions of the *one* situation, dimensions that are more or less strongly to the fore in the situation. This is a final aspect of the aforementioned transcendences of aesthetic perception: every type of aesthetic perception is in principle open to a transition to another type.[73] This does not, of course, mean that the various kinds of perception merge completely into one another. They are and will continue to be different modes of aesthetic consciousness, modes that can nonetheless trigger and sharpen one another. Thus, though art produces performative aesthetic objects that bring something to presentation, it frequently creates objects of an intensive mere and atmospheric appearing. Hence, the objects of mere appearing are often the starting point for becoming aware of the atmosphere that surrounds them or of art-related or artistic projections of the imagination. Therefore the locations of efflorescing existential correspondences are frequently also occasions of a contemplative liberation from one's passions, or occasions of an imaginative expansion of the scope of one's existence. In the situation of aesthetic perception, the phenomena of a mere, an atmospheric, and an artistic appearing intersect.

Aesthetic *consciousness*, as we saw in the previous section, reaches much further; it includes not only the sphere of aesthetic perception but also the sphere of aesthetic imagination, irrespective of whether it is tied to perceptions or not. Wherever the ability to perceive or imagine something in its appearing is realized, aesthetic consciousness emerges. For this to come about, an encounter with attending objects of perception is not necessary; what is necessary is an *imaginative projection* of their presence. In this sense, the theory of the situation of aesthetic perception drafted here is not indeed a comprehensive analysis of the processes of aesthetic consciousness, but it is nonetheless an essential one since analysis of aesthetic imagination is logically subordinate to analysis of aesthetic perception.

A further question can be answered already at this point. It has to do with the *permanence* of aesthetic consciousness. If aesthetic consciousness has such a broad spectrum, is it then not necessary to say that consciousness is essentially always aesthetic consciousness too? Isn't it obvious to conclude that this is a constantly attending *dimension* of consciousness, just as the three aforementioned forms are constantly attending dimensions of aesthetic consciousness? Couldn't it be said that we always react *aesthetically* to the world, though to very different degrees and in very different ways?

Nonetheless I would like to stay with the claim that aesthetic watchfulness is indeed an ever-present possibility but not a permanent state of the conscious existence of human beings. They do not have the time or energy for this, nor therefore the permanent irritability generated by occurrences of appearing. Quite a few acts of reflection and accomplishment rule out an accompanying aesthetic attentiveness insofar as they can succeed definitely only if there is no distraction from their goal-oriented execution. One thinks of converting a penalty in soccer, solving a difficult arithmetical problem, defusing a bomb, answering an examination question. It always depends on the kind of demand made on the actors as to whether they are responsive to aesthetic sensations in concrete situations (with the score at four to zero, a penalty can be lightheartedly celebrated). Just as often as aesthetic consciousness can accompany any nonaesthetic action—from driving an automobile to holding a lecture on logic—such a consciousness can be ruled out because of the great demands made by acts of determining and directing. The atmosphere in which the action is performed (and under whose influence it is) comes as little to consciousness as the other dimensions of appearing. The present in which the action is located, in which it intensifies and loses itself with regard to an end, is not accessible to a lingering viewing. The action occurs in immeasurable constellations at which it cannot look, and to which it does not listen. As a result, it does not *have* less presence than conduct that is open to these constellations, but it has a diminished (or no) *sensitivity* to the concrete present in which it is directly involved. Without this temporary withdrawal of aesthetic consciousness, the latter would have much less attraction.

On the other hand, the observations in this section have again made clear how much and how often our consciousness is in fact aesthetic or aesthetically colored. Memories, imaginative projections, and dreams frequently have an aesthetic trait, if they are not in fact already performed *as* acts of the aesthetic imagination; many everyday perceptions—whether they relate to today's weather, a strolling passer-by, the newest automobiles, or the oldest cities—frequently have aesthetic components, if they are not in fact already realized momentarily *as* aesthetic perceptions; biographical reminiscences, ethical reflections, and theoretical meditations frequently take their orientation from models and examples in art, if they don't in fact come about through the perception of objects of art. This is not a chance composition of this or that historical culture, but an inner necessity of human individuals' mental orientation. Aesthetic consciousness is part of their self-consciousness as beings living in limited time, beings who do not always have the time and space for perceiving their special present.

6. Constellations of Art

In this section, it is just a single thesis that I wish to elaborate and defend against a frequently raised objection. The thesis is that artworks are objects of a *different appearing*. They require a perception different from all other objects of perception. The objection opposing this view argues that this may well apply to many works of art, but belief in an exclusive appearing on the part of art has been unequivocally refuted by a central tradition of twentieth-century art, the one going back to Marcel Duchamp. Not types of sensuous presence but rather types of conception and interpretation are decisive for the art status of objects. Those art objects (greatly multiplied by Danto's theoretical fantasy) that do not look or sound any different from any other nonartistic objects are said to prove that appearance and appearing do indeed represent fundamental concepts for aesthetics, but not for art theory. In opposition to this, I would like to make clear that it is precisely the objects of art that have to be cognized in terms of the concept of appearing. I would like to show that the sensuality and the intellectuality of artworks are *one* thing.[74]

The Material and Medium of the Arts

Most objects of art originate in the specific employment of a sensuous material. Genres of art can be distinguished according to, among other things, the material that is their starting point or the way this material is worked. The sensuousness of the material, which an art object can share with any other object, undergoes a metamorphosis into a state that it does not share with any other kinds of objects. I wish to retrace some of the steps of this transformation.

The constitutive *material* of an art form is a presupposition without which there can be no work of this art—its employment is a *conditio sine qua non* for this art form. "Material" does not stand for "matter" here but for that which has to be worked and with which one has to work so that we can speak of the art of a particular genre. For instance, the relatively solid (from stone through steel to textiles) could be regarded as the material of architecture; sculpture also relies on this material (different arts can share the same starting material). The material of music would be sounds and tones; that of painting would be a surface, paint, and line. For recent arts, the options are much less obvious. The material of installations would have to include the space within which their choreographies unfold. The inescapable material of literature is probably the word (but sometimes just the letter), in its graphical and tonal form as well as in its conventional meaning. Drama uses this material, along with the human body and its movements, which it shares with dance as a starting point.

This artistic material is often already contaminated with meanings and ideas, particularly of course in the sphere of language; nor in other arts is the starting material a neutral mass that is first ascribed meaning solely by the artist. In the historical, in the cultural, and above all in the specifically artistic context, certain materials *have always had* a more or less fixed significance or symbolism; the artist reacts to and operates with it. The objects of art are made from one or many such precharged materials; without their perceptive accessibility, most of them could not appear as artworks.[75]

No art form, of course, can be understood solely in terms of its material. The contours of particular genres first emerge from the kind of *use* to which the basic materials are put. Thus, architecture's fundamental operation could be determined as *dividing space*, as an establishing of internal and external differences; in the case of music, one would have to think of the production of rhythms and tonal relations (one could say that it works with intervals of time and tones); a basic operation of painting is certainly the production of a difference between picture surface and picture appearance. Regarding installations, one could say that they generate a difference between the space *in which* they present themselves and the space *as which* they present themselves. Arranging letters and words into graphically visible texts could be understood as the basic operation of literature; one could say that it works with the difference between ephemeral and enduring sequences of linguistic constituents.

These differences, which follow from a specific use of a basic material, can be understood as the primary *medium* of an artistic creation.[76] It sets up a wide spectrum of possibilities for combining elements, a spectrum from which something can be put into the form of a particular artifact. In the manner in which these basic operations can be realized in the specific handling of different materials (that is, in the use of different media), they do not of course in themselves lead to a concept of *artistic* genres. With the exception of the installation example, the uses sketched so far do indeed constitute a particular semiotic, aesthetic, or other *genre* of artifacts (buildings, paintings, texts) but are still not objects of art. Nonetheless, the employment of different creation media is an important step in artistic production. One cannot simply perceive the results of all these operations just as one can perceive stones, sounds, and colors. Rather, one has to *understand* to a certain degree to what operations they are due and what functions they possess. This understanding leads not away from perception, however, but to a perception that can achieve precisely this—to grasp its objects in the organization of their material as products of a particular kind of operation. Clearly, this applies already to any artifacts whatsoever, that is to say, not just to objects of art. Part of the perception of automobiles and kitchen appliances is knowledge of why they were made and what they are suitable for. Artworks are fundamentally different from such artifacts in that they are *presentations*—indeed, special *kinds* of presentations. Irrespective of what function is ascribed to them, they differ from things and utility articles in that they are made in order to be grasped as presentations of a particular kind. It is their primary function. Their materials are organized so that they present *themselves* in such a manner that we can find *something* presented by them.

What is important is this self-presentation. Artistic objects exhibit themselves in the precise organization of their material, in order in this way to bring something to presentation. Therefore, in addition to the basic operations, which allow an object to belong to one or more artifact genres, there must also be a *specific execution* of these operations so that creations of one *artistic* genre or another—or objects of an artistic species as yet unknown—can be brought into existence. It is an instance of such specific realizations of an art form—in contrast to forms of a *nonartistic* production of buildings, objects, paintings, texts, sounds, and the like—in all these cases when the objects or events produced can be grasped as presentations in the medium of the *individual constellation* of the materials used. In contradistinction to other forms of presentation and sign formation, artworks are objects that, by virtue of their individual appearing, function as presentations of human relations.

Thus aesthetic literature can be understood as a production of texts that are conspicuous as arrangements of certain words that are not exchangeable—as opposed to texts in which this is the case to a certain degree. Artistic photographs differ from many press photographs in that for the former it is precisely this perspective, precisely this brightness, precisely this depth of focus (and so on) that are important, whereas the greeting of this president by that president could have been photographed just as well in any other manner. Constructions that we classify as objects of art thereby differ from buildings that simply fulfill a purpose (without giving this purpose an informative and conspicuous interpretation) in that what is important in perceiving them are the many details in the execution, while these details may be safely ignored in the other case. Objects of art are intensive presentations in the entirely elementary sense that a person cannot get what is presented if he or she is not attentive to the *sensuous medium* of this presentation.

This medium consists in sensuously perceivable differences that have been introduced into the play of a nonarbitrary sign-constituted configuration. Where this play becomes conspicuous, objects become conspicuous in their artistic appearing. This play transpires only where a process of appearances is understood as the medium of a presentation; otherwise we would be dealing only with a simultaneity of appearances as can be observed on *every* aesthetically perceived object. Neither the objects of mere appearing nor those of atmospheric appearing have this status of artistic media; they are what they are in aesthetic perception, but they are not what they *reveal* to an understanding and interpretative aesthetic perception.

An aesthetics of the arts could be written as a theory of the relation of artistic media. Here, the materials and operations that are *primary* for a particular art form should not be the only things thematized. An art genre cannot be understood appropriately in terms of these alone. Rather, all the media *existent* in the basic constitution of an art form would have to be thematized—media through which every art form is already in communication with many others. Only thus can one do justice to the constitutive *intermediality* of the arts, which was not created by the "disorientation" [*Verfransung*] of the arts in the twentieth century, as Adorno judiciously noted, but was just brought dramatically to light by this state of the arts.[77] One inherent relation of literature to music, for instance, lies in the fact that both are concerned with sound material—music always, literature wherever it is not too closely assimilated to pictorial presentations. Literature that is presented in written form always has a pictorial quality (this having been just particularly emphasized by Concrete poetry). These possibilities can be exploited explicitly in artistic work; but they are also present where they are not used. Equally, pictures have an inherent relation not only to embossments but also to sculptures. The difference between the picture's surface and what appears presented *in* or *on* this surface contains—entirely independent of the figurative and perspective procedures of representation—a trace of the spatial that is paradoxically negated by pictorial operations but cannot be made to disappear. Frank Stella's "shaped canvases" from the early 1960s are an example of this. In addition, in the eighties Stella created in his series *Cones and Pillars* "pictures" that extend like sculptures into the spatial surroundings, much further than any relief;

he thereby inverted the picture's illusion space and placed it literally in the imagination space of its perspective. Some forms of contemporary dance theater present themselves like drama without the spoken word, here and there even without musical accompaniment (as, for instance, in Pina Bausch's creations). It is evident from this that the removal of traditionally available elements can bring inherent relations to light—here, the relations of drama to a theater of the body, to performance, to pictorial tableau. To put it succinctly, in every art form there are multiple inherent relations to other arts, even though not every art maintains these relations to all arts. These relations are not something through which the particular genre can be *expanded*; they are *fundamental* for its composition as one artistic genre among others.[78]

Constellational Presentation

But when does an object of perception belong to a determined or still undetermined artistic genre? When does it count as an object of art? Well, when it counts as such for some or for many beholders. There are no absolutely existing features through which works of art could be distinguished from other objects. There are, however, characteristics through which objects of art can be distinguished from other objects for a perception that recognizes them as a special medium of experience. This recognition is the real topic of the philosophy of art. It discusses what status objects of perception acquire in being treated as works of art, and by means of what treatment they acquire this status.

This is once again the interdependent relation of aesthetic perception and aesthetic object, which has concerned us from the outset. It exists in the field of art too. Objects of art are objects that are subject to an aesthetic treatment different from other kinds of aesthetic objects. Moreover, they are objects that deserve or do not deserve this treatment. In contrast to all objects of mere appearing and some objects of atmospheric appearing, the status of artworks is a *normative* status. They are objects that *merit* being experienced aesthetically, or being candidates for this recognition. It is only within the framework of such an evaluation that they can come to appearance as works of art. This evaluation relates to relevant objects' characteristics that can be perceived only from the perspective of their recognition as artworks. As with all states of appearing, the particular perceivable relations here are tied in their existence neither to the actual *adoption* of this perspective nor to its adoption by some *specific* person. A philosophical reflection on the constitution of art is concerned with a particular aesthetic perspective, as well as with what can be experienced from this perspective. This analysis does not attempt to clarify which objects *fulfill* the normative expectations associated with this perspective; rather, it seeks an answer to the question of *what it means* to say that objects fulfill the expectations associated with a claim to being art (one can also say, the question of what function they fulfill inasmuch as they fulfill a function as artworks).[79]

As long as they are treated as objects of *art*, they are treated neither only as objects of mere appearing nor only as objects of atmospheric appearing. They are ascribed the status of constellational presentations—the status of objects that can bring complex human conditions to light in the medium of their appearing. They are in this respect "constructs of spirit," to use Hegel's language. "The spirit of artworks," Adorno writes in his *Aesthetic Theory*, is the spirit "that appears through the appearance."[80] This spirit, Adorno elaborates, which "infiltrates" the sensuous appearance of a work, cannot be cognized independently of this appearance; but it must not be equated with it, just as it must not be equated with the intention of the artist.

Just how little the spirit of the work equals the spirit of the artist, which is at most one element of the former, is evident in the fact that spirit is evoked through the artifact, its problems, and its material. Not even the appearance of the artwork as a whole is its spirit, and least of all is it the appearance of the idea purportedly embodied or symbolized by the work; spirit cannot be fixated in immediate identity with its appearance. But neither does spirit constitute a level above or below appearance; such a supposition would be no less of a reification. The locus of [an artwork's] spirit is the *configuration* of what appears.[81]

Here, Adorno is aiming explicitly and clearly at a difference between fixatable appearance and artistic appearing. In terms of this difference he attempts to grasp the particular sensuousness of artworks. The spirit of works, he writes further, "forms appearance just as appearance forms spirit; it is the luminous source through which the phenomenon radiates and becomes a phenomenon in the most pregnant sense of the word."[82] In the second half of the sentence, however, Hegel gets the better of Adorno in an unfortunate way. That a phenomenon "becomes a phenomenon in the most pregnant sense of the word" only if it is illuminated by human spirit is not acceptable, most especially in the context of aesthetics.[83] Many objects of mere appearing are not at all infiltrated by spirit; one need only think of mountain formations or the grass at the side of the road; but even those objects that are infiltrated in one way or another because they exist thanks to human production—like our ball, or any street corner—frequently appear to aesthetic contemplation in a sensuousness that relates dismissively to all expectations of enduring meaningfulness. It is mistaken to conceive of the work of art as a kind of super thing that alone is in the state that all things really want to be in, or want to be perceived as being in. It is just as mistaken to conceive of the work of art as an aesthetic super thing that alone can be in that state in which all other aesthetic phenomena ought to actually be. We must strictly avoid assimilating all sensuous phenomena to aesthetic ones, and all aesthetic phenomena to those of art, if we want to do justice to the special position of artworks among all of these phenomena.

In general, a phenomenon becomes an aesthetic phenomenon as soon as it is perceived not in a fixed form but as "configuration[s] of what appears," to put it in Adorno's words. This cannot therefore be the sought-after feature of difference between works of art and other aesthetic objects. Nonetheless, the passage just cited contains a pregnant determination of this difference. Before Adorno allows himself to be lured to an overgeneralization, he speaks not simply of *objects* that *are* configurations of what appears but of the *spirit* of artworks that has its *locus* in such configurations. We can build upon this. The human spirit has its locus in diverse media—in the sounds and writing of language, in gestures and pictorial symbols, in sign systems of any kind; "spirit" or substantive intentionality exists in no way other than in the use of these various media of articulation. Art, Adorno argues, is *one* kind of articulation, expression, or presentation of spirit's content—the one that is executed in the medium of appearing and is tied here to "configuration[s] of what appears."

This mode of presentation differs from other forms in that it presents everything that it presents through a presentation of its sensuous medium.[84] In a trivial sense, this is of course the case with every kind of sign use. Every sentence must be visible or audible to be understood in what it says. But it does not have to be conspicuous—specifically regarded and specifically explored—as an individual constellation of words to be understood. All kinds of sign use *require* a sensuous medium, but not all of them *present* it. Not all present what they present by way of a presentation of their medium. But this is how things are with literary sentences, musical tones, artistic pictures. These present *something* by presenting *themselves*. They present something only to those who perceive them as an individual constellation of appearances (individual in the sense of not being replaceable by any other combination of elements). This perception is directed at the simultaneity of a composition or co-occurrence of appearances. Whoever wants to experience the content of artworks has to attend to this simultaneity, this interaction, this *process* (as Adorno constantly emphasizes) of artworks. Their presentation of the world transpires as self-presentation.

Here lies their capacity to bring otherwise unpresentable relations to presentation. The constellations of the work become a sign of the constellations of the world. The perception of art objects enables not just a recollection of the mere presence of things and events, nor just a making present of atmospherically articulated life situations, but an *encounter with presences* of human life. This is the relation of artistic imagination already discussed here. Its objects, it was said in the section on appearing and imagination, create a special present in which a distant or an expanded present comes to presentation. This present, with which the object of artistic appearing confronts us, is not to be disengaged from the present that the object produces through its appearing. According to the observations on the concept of presence in "Situations of Appearing," the occurrence that comes to presentation in the artwork must not be equated with external states of the world. Rather, it relates to types of human involvement in real or irreal, past, present, or future states of the world. Types of *world encounter* are thus brought to presentation, through which types of *encounter with world encounter* become possible. In one way or another, the processual sensuousness of artistic objects becomes a complex sign of the processuality of human being-in-the-world. This constitutes the objects' artistic appearing.

This artistic appearing can lead readers into unreachable, but nonetheless not entirely remote, worlds, as when reading Balzac's *Lost Illusions*; it can lead readers into a vivid making present of the interpretative situation in which they find themselves when reading an enigmatic text, such as Kafka's parable *On Equations*; it can lead beholders into an imagined and idealized Venice, as when viewing Canaletto's pictures, or to reflections on the aesthetic and cultural situation in which they are viewing Newman's *Who's Afraid of Red, Yellow and Blue IV*; it can lead listeners into the *Stellar Regions* of John Coltrane's improvisational art, which finds a musically as well as existentially extreme balance amid plunges and upswings, accelerations and decelerations, harmonies and disharmonies; or it leads into the depths of the American national anthem celebrated and lacerated by Jimi Hendrix on the electric guitar, the depths of an ambivalent apology of patriotism, which is simultaneously an apology of ambivalent patriotism.

Thus one should not think that the condition of artistic presentation described here is just a thing of painting and literature, theater or film; it is equally a matter of architecture, dance, and music—not to mention hybrids of these and other arts. Changing the music of a movie means changing the *world* of this movie. The passage of music is the unfolding of a constellation of events that is, in its own emotionality, at the same time an expression of literal and metaphorical human emotionality. It shows us its own and our motion; it moves us and shows us emotionality. By no means does the artistically imagined situation have to coincide with the real situation of its reception here, either; but it can be indeed the case, here too. More than any other art—perhaps with the exception of film—music can put us in states whose imaginative expression it is; but the character of the emotionality that it presents can be grasped and experienced just as well without adopting its moods. Arias by the mad (as in *Lucia di Lammermoor*) as well as rock music can be followed with inner tranquility. The condition of bodily and cognitive animation characteristic of music has been summarized concisely by Albrecht Wellmer:

Music's stimulation curves are always those of the body too, of a dark territory between subject and object, that is, of a body that is mimetically (in relation to the emotions) and erotically involved in the world, as Roland Barthes, for instance, illustrated by way of the example of Schumann's *Kreisleriana*; at the same time, music constitutes a "field of significance" . . . for subjects capable of language and involved existentially and interpretatively in the world.[85]

Valéry's and Chandler's Sentence

The double character of artworks cannot be emphasized strongly enough. Like all other aesthetic objects, they are events of appearing; as such they have a special presence. But the process of their appearing is a performative one through which they bring something to presentation in its presence. The special presence of art objects coincides with a special presentation of presence.

The characteristics of indeterminacy, which were discussed in connection with Valéry, are also to be found in two respects in art objects (which is why Adorno, not incorrectly, attributed an "enigmatic character" to them). The works of art are themselves indeterminate; whatever they present, they present it in observance of its indeterminacy. We have to understand how the one is tied to the other.

"Beauty," Valéry had said regarding art, "demands, perhaps, the slavish imitation of what is indeterminable in things." What is to be emphasized here above all is the second aspect: artworks make present in and on things what evades conceptually determining fixation. There is, first of all, their irreducible sensuous presence, as I explained in the section on being-so and appearing. But we have to add in recollection of the later sections that this sensuous presence can be atmospherically and imaginatively charged and equipped with elements of a supportive semblance. Furthermore, the situations presented by art are by no means always aesthetic situations; the "things" we find made present in them are certainly not just aesthetic relations. A deceptive semblance can play a role in them just as easily as all kinds of human involvement. The whole spectrum of the affective, cognitive, and practical givenness of things and events can come artistically to presentation. Whatever is presented here, it is presented in the mode of a simultaneity of characters that evade an understanding that differentiates fact by fact. One need only think of Chandler's invocation, in a half sentence, of the emptiness of the empty swimming pool thirsting for a filling, in vain.

But it is a literary sentence that presents this, and this sentence also has the feature of indeterminacy, as does of course the novel in which it appears. When Valéry says that the beauty of the work of art lies in an "imitation" of the indeterminable, then this concept should not be taken too literally. Valéry himself constantly emphasizes the constructive possibilities, the inventive character of art. What the artist invents, however, is a linguistic or other thing that not only *heralds* the indeterminacy of all things but *partakes* of it to such an extent that it itself becomes an emblem of this indeterminacy. Thus, good objects of art present for their part indeterminable objects that are destined to present the ungraspable in "things." They represent indeterminable objects, one could say in a laconic double sense. They reveal themselves in their indeterminacy, and they reveal something in indeterminacy—in the indeterminacy that is constitutive of the irreducible presence of things and events. The phenomenal repleteness in which they display something can be presented only through articulated objects on which this repleteness cannot for its part go unseen. We can therefore perceive an artwork *as* an artwork only if we take it seriously in its appearing: in its processual sensuousness, which is the medium of the contents that we can find revealed in the play of the elements of sensuousness. "Nothing ever looks emptier than an empty swimming pool"—only readers who can submerge themselves in the swinging sound, the wave motion, of this (half) sentence can imagine the metaphysical emptiness of the pool in pictorial fullness.

Good works of art (and this is Valéry's fully appropriated thought) are objects that *imagine and demonstrate* in what respect things are indeterminable in our relation to them. This double character is essential for everything that artworks can do. It is decisive for the inner tension, from which their inventions draw their inner lives. The exploration of the sensuous object and the interpretative and imaginative disclosure of the world it presents are always a fragile, often an incalculable, and not infrequently a confusing, occurrence, but it is *one* perception process in which and for which the process of artistic appearing unfolds. This process puts us in a heightened present by leading us into a (present or absent) present that is heightened for intuition.

Levels of Sensuousness

Everything has thus really been said about the special sensuousness of the objects of art. Their significant appearing distinguishes them in principle from other objects of appearing and also from all other objects of perception—even when they have the same sensuous being-so as the latter.

But let us turn once again to the painting by Barnett Newman that was presented in Chapter One. At first glance, the large-format rectangular painting is organized very simply: on the right, a big red area; on the left, a big yellow; in the middle, a somewhat narrow blue one. This can be called the *visual appearance* of the painting. It looks like this to everyone who has normal vision. The visible being-so of this object is accessible to pre-aesthetic perception. It is a different matter with the *mere* appearing (here, the mere visibility) of the multicolored surface. This play of appearances is not at all accessible to a perception serving the purposes of quick identification; it reveals itself only to an aesthetically lingering reception. Here, the different intensity and spatiality of the color zones, their balance and switching, come to the fore. In yet another manner, the object presents itself in receptiveness to its *atmospheric* appearing. It can be experienced as a strong, powerful, sublime accent in the space in which it is situated. The tricolor canvas encounters the beholder in its *artistic* appearing in yet another manner again. Only here does it become clear that in the case of this canvas we are concerned with a painting that is in intensive dialogue with other artistic pictures (not least with the other works of the *series* of paintings to which it belongs). Only here can the interaction of colors be experienced as a dramatization of basic painting and human possibilities. Only here can the painting be perceived as sublime destruction of a compositional and cultural sense of order.

This latter character of the painting is not there at all for a pre-artistic—or a pre-artistic aesthetic—perception. But it *is* there, for a perception that is able to see this object as a pictorial object, and this pictorial object as an imaginative projection of the uncontrollability of colors and forms from which pictorial works and other institutions are made. Along with this perception, the correspondences that this painting emits into its space are also transformed; now the painting colors the space with a spiritual energy that could not be sensed beforehand. The perception of the mere confrontation and intermingling of the colors now also acquires a new significance; it becomes an intensifying phase in the perception of the painting, in which the beholders' imaginative and atmospheric receptiveness is thrown back to the pure presence of the colors standing in contrast and conflict with one another.

Whether we perceive the object only in mere appearing, just in atmospheric appearing, or in artistic appearing (*including* the mere and atmospheric presence thus weighed anew), nothing changes in its sensuous appearance, its being-so, its visually discriminable facticity. It is the same red and yellow and blue surface. But it acquires a *different appearing* depending on how we allow it to affect us. How the color surface encounters us, how it "confronts" us, depends in each case on the attitude we adopt when approaching it. Works of art are objects that are grasped a particular way. What is experienced in these various kinds of perception is not a projection, however; it is not anything that our viewing would simply add; it is not anything that is not really there. Rather, each mode of encounter discovers different qualities and processes in its object. Each of the perspectives distinguished in the previous section generates different access to the *reality* of its objects.

What I have explained here about visual perception by recapitulating the Newman example could be advanced in a corresponding manner for listening (and, with some qualifications, for the close-range senses: those of touch, taste, and smell). The same general relation of sensuousness and aesthetic sensuousness would be evident. The *two* types of the sensuous givenness of something, which were distinguished in "Being-so and Appearing," led, on the side of appearing, to a distinction of three types of phenomenal repleteness on the part of perception objects. Thus, a total of *four* levels of sensuousness can be distinguished. Sensuous being-so (which for its part could be divided into subtypes) is paired with mere, atmospheric, and artistic appearing. These types of aesthetic appearing come to the fore when a sensuous object of such-and-such a kind is perceived in the simultaneity and momentariness of its appearances and therefore in an irreducible phenomenal presence.

In perceiving something as an object of art, this presence is sensed in a special way. It is not the case that here there is a thing of appearance on which artists and beholders impose interpretations, by means of which—as in a baptism—it is also metamorphosed into a substantive object of art. No, as soon as we see (or hear, or read) it as a good and substantive object of art, a different appearing, an otherwise inaccessible one, becomes evident in it. We *see* relations (or hear them, or experience them in reading) that could not be seen (or heard, or experienced in reading) beforehand. The special reality of artworks transpires in special processes of its appearing.

But they not only reveal an *appearing* different from other aesthetic objects, they also develop a different *meaning*, which separates them from the world of common expression and sign use. Their meaning, their content, is and will remain tied to their individual form and thus in turn to their specific appearing. Only in the artwork can we experience what is formed in it. Only in the presence of the work do we know what knowledge it can impart. In contrast to empirical and other theoretical knowledge, this knowledge cannot be *secured* in the form of statements. When it is said of *Who's Afraid of Red, Yellow and Blue IV* that it conveys a conflict between cultural order and its transgression, or even that it brings out how every human order arouses the forces of its transgression, then these sentences do not by any means capture the *experience* that one had with the painting and can now be formulated independently of it. At most, they formulate a knowledge that was acquired on the *occasion* of experiencing Newman's painting. As interpretative sentences, they make reference above all to the complex experience that can be had *with* this painting, an experience only hinted at by the sentence *about* the painting. This means aesthetic knowledge cannot be set down with propositional determinateness. It may lead to conceptually determined knowledge or take the latter as its starting point, but it *is* not conceptual knowledge, since it remains tied to the sensuous and signifying occurrence and thus to the specific appearing of artistic objects. All art perception proceeds from an appearing and is in search of an appearing.

Danto's Objection

It is this, however, that was continually disputed in the twentieth century. The days of artistic appearing are numbered, was a prevalent conjecture. Important currents in modern art, it seemed to many, reject any sensuous address or animation. For this reason, a departure of art philosophy from aesthetics is overdue. Above all, Arthur Danto made himself the advocate of this view. He posed the question of the status of artworks with great clarity and vividness. But the conclusion he draws fails to do justice to the state of recent art in particular.[86]

Danto's starting point is the observation that since Duchamp and Warhol objects become artworks that do not distinguish themselves externally from banal objects of everyday life. Of two phenomenally indistinguishable objects—be they bottle dryers, chairs, umbrellas, sand heaps, telephone directories, or cartons of saucepan cleaners—one can be a work of art, whereas the other one is simply what it is. Thus, Danto's conclusion runs, it cannot be objects' external appearance that is responsible for their art status. After all, both counterparts appear identical. "It meant that," Danto sums up, "as far as appearances were concerned, anything could be a work of art, and it meant that if you were going to find out what art was, you had to turn from sense experience to thought."[87] This theoretic turn away from the sensuousness of art leads to a bold diagnosis of the state of the visual arts. "Visuality drops away, as little relevant to the essence of art as beauty proved to have been. For art to exist there does not even have to be an object to look at, and if there are objects in a gallery, they can look like anything at all."[88] For Danto, it follows from the history of art since Duchamp: "The connection between art and aesthetics is a matter of historical contingency, and not part of the essence of art."[89] On contemporary art he writes: "Now there is one feature of contemporary art that distinguishes it from perhaps all art made since 1400, which is that its primary ambitions are not aesthetic."[90] Many artists of the twentieth century managed "to extrude the aesthetic from the artistic"[91]—in plain words, to chase all sensuous temptation out of the temple of art.

In Danto the term *aesthetic* stands largely for that which is sensuously perceivable. For him the dignity of recent art—and, ultimately, of all preceding art too—consists in its always having already moved beyond its sensuous appearing. Accordingly, art objects are in principle different from how they appear to the senses. They embody ideas that cannot be seen in them but are ascribed to them by artists and beholders. However art-hostile or (in the case of Danto) art-friendly this thesis is advanced, it is fundamentally wrong. What is more, it is not needed to answer Danto's insightfully raised question of the status of art in the aftermath of Duchamp.

The entire argument is subject to a grave fallacy. Objects that are phenomenally identical, Danto assumes, are aesthetically of equal value. This is not the case. The same sensuous appearance of an object, as we saw in the example of Newman's painting, can have entirely different aesthetic effects. One and the same *manifestation* of the three-part area can *appear* aesthetically in a threefold manner. As soon as one attends, while considering the simultaneity of an object's sensuous aspects, more to the mere, or to the atmospheric, or to the artistic presence of this play of appearances, there emerges a different aesthetic valency for the object. What holds true especially for art is that its gestures and contents can be experienced only in the dimension of an interpretatively and imaginatively appropriated appearing.

Confronted with this objection, Danto plays the trump card that is always used in such a situation: he refers to some of the readymades by Duchamp. Here, it seems, something becomes an object of art and therefore of interpretation, without becoming an object of the imagination tied to this object's appearing. There is a lot to think about here, but not really anything to see—beyond what can be seen anyway in a thing of this kind. Under the title *In Advance of the Broken Arm*, Marcel Duchamp affixed such a thing to the ceiling of his atelier in New York in 1915. It was a snow shovel made of metal, as was in use everywhere at the time. However one interprets this object of art, it is a clear counterexample to the view that all artworks are objects of the imagination, for this artistic object denies the sensuous transformation and imaginative transcendence that can be expected of other art objects. As Danto correctly sees, it is by virtue of this denial that the snow shovel chosen by Duchamp is distinguished from all the other snow shovels in this world, which at most just won't do the job, but they cannot deny anything. But how is this artistic denial to be understood? Where does it occur? At the level of appearing or in a sphere of reflection above it?

To accept this alternative would be tantamount to a self-disembodiment of the philosophy of art. No work of art can be understood in terms of this alternative, and certainly not the ingenious point of Duchamp's maneuver. The denial that is performed by placing a snow shovel in the space of art is possible only at the *level* of artistic appearing. Only at this level can the fulfillment of the expectations of a "different appearing" be disappointed. Without the *attempt* to see in this thing something other than an arbitrary practical or aesthetic object, it would not be possible to recognize its exhibition as an artistic operation. In its shining metal gloss, the snow shovel remains unresponsive to the expectations of an imaginative appearing; it remains dismissive of all the expectations of allurement into another state—the expectations whose fulfillment art promised before Duchamp and continues to promise after him. But it presents itself as an object of art, as an object that *entices* precisely the perception that it denies in the same move. It reveals itself solely as a banal object of use, but it *presents* itself as such in full view of those who may expect something different and can expect something different in the same exhibition space. *Its* point is also artistic appearing—one, of course, that never transpires. Like every other denial, this one also operates at the level of "accusations" directed at it.

This is why it was argued in the section "Appearing and Imagination" that not all works of art are objects of the imagination, but the status of artworks can be cognized in terms of the status of *these* objects. Even those that do not imagine a completely *different* present (like the painting by Newman) are an imaginative making present of the situation that they generate in the medium of their appearing. Even those that do not imagine anything at all (like Duchamp's object) *stage* a viewing situation whose relations they bring to light. *In Advance of the Broken Arm* establishes a paradoxical situation of art perception and thereby underscores for its part *general* expectations concerning the encounter with works of art. In the unresponsiveness of its artistic appearing, it makes jokes about the imagined worlds of art in which no one could break an arm, which is after all still possible in the midst of real art things.

Nonetheless, not all of Duchamp's readymades operate in this purely negative sense. Neither *Fountain,* proposed for an exhibition in 1917, nor *Bottle Dryer,* which had been functioning as a readymade since 1914 (to mention two other legendary examples) denies every sculptural or gestural presence, as the superbly banal snow shovel does. They both allow an imaginative presence to appear and disappear. They are objects *alternating* between art and nonart—and are for that very reason subversive objects of art. They look like banal objects and are nonetheless staged in such a way that they acquire a different appearing. So, when Danto says in one of his more cautious moments "that artworks and real things cannot be told apart by visual inspection *alone,*"[92] he is indeed right. The innocent eye cannot always distinguish art objects from other (aesthetic) objects. It does not, however, follow that the visual is without relevance in the visual arts or the sensuous without relevance in any of the other arts. What follows is only that the perception sufficient for seeing any extra-artistic object is not sufficient for the perception of an *art* object. As soon as we regard something as a work of visual art, we can discover in it visual characteristics that are completely different from those any child could ascribe to it—for who would want to say of an everyday pissoir that it *alternates* between being a useful thing and an ironic gesture?

'Art as Idea as Idea'

"Not least among the contemporary difficulties of art," we read in *Aesthetic Theory,* "is that artworks are ashamed of *apparition,* though they are unable to shed it."[93] At just about the time Adorno wrote this sentence, Joseph Kosuth set about liberating his art from this burden. "At its most strict and radical extreme," he writes in 1971, "the art I call conceptual is such because it is based on an inquiry into the nature of art. Thus, it is not just activity of constructing art propositions, but a working out, a thinking out, of all the implications of all aspects of the concept 'art.'"[94] Like the philosophical concept artist Danto later, Kosuth speaks of a "separation between aesthetics and art" already in the 1960s. The shift in emphasis initiated by Duchamp—"from 'appearance' to 'conception'—was the beginning of 'modern' art and the beginning of 'conceptual' art. All art (after Duchamp) is conceptual (in nature) because it only exists conceptually."[95]

These passages are of interest here not because they show how much Danto's theory of art is inspired by a specific direction in art. Rather, an important test for our argument so far follows from a reversal of viewpoints. It is revealing to see what happens when a theory of art such as Danto's (in its radically anti-aesthetic version) becomes an artist's working basis. Kosuth's version in the late 1960s and early 1970s is without doubt a *very* radical version. In a provocative gesture he equates artistic operations with analytical thinking.

My first use of the term "proposition" for my work was when I began my "art as idea as idea" series in 1966. The photostatic blow-ups weren't supposed to be considered paintings, or sculpture or even "works" in the usual sense—with the point being that it was art as *idea.* So I referred to the physical material of the blow-up as the work's "form of presentation," and referring to the art entity as a *proposition*—a term I borrowed from linguistic philosophy. At about the same time I began thinking of art propositions while considering the . . . *analogy* between language and art. So that in my mind I began to equate linguistic propositions with artistic propositions.[96]

In philosophy "propositions" designate the content of statements, that is, what can be expressed by different sentences with the same content. The sentences "Snow is white" and "*Schnee ist weiß*" are expressions of the same proposition, as are the two sentences (expressed at the same point in time) "The cat is on the mat" and "On the mat is the cat."[97] What is important is not the precise wording. When talking about propositions, therefore, what is precisely *not* important is that which *is* important in art according to the traditional understanding: the specific shape or "form" in which the artistic object presents itself. Correspondingly, Kosuth distinguishes the "idea" underlying his series from the "form of presentation" that it acquires in its individual realizations. The individual pieces in the series as well as the series itself are no longer to be tied to a specific form of their appearing, as with the traditional "work" of art. The idea can acquire a more or less *arbitrary* appearing. It is precisely this that the *Art as Idea as Idea* series is supposed to demonstrate.

It consists of numerous panels on which greatly enlarged photostats of dictionary entries are presented, for the most part in white lettering on a black background. The keywords are "idea," "number," "blank," "characteristic(al)," "abstraction," "letter," and so on. All of the words can be related in one way or another to discussions in art theory or can be understood self-referentially. Neither the size of the panels nor the precise graphical format of the texts is conclusively fixed by the artist. This seems to achieve what is supposed to be achieved according to the theory: the aesthetically arbitrary realization of a nonarbitrary artistic conception.

In this case too, however, the proof of the pudding is in the eating, that is, in intuition. A 1967 copy of the series is in the Sprengel Museum in Hanover, Germany. It bears the title *Titled (Art as Idea as Idea)*. The entry presented on a black panel in white letters is taken from an old English-German dictionary. "Abstraction" is the word. The explicating text is set in Gothic type. The pronunciation of the word is given first; *abßtrak'schön* is the transcription. This is then followed by standard dictionary references, among them "*Abstraktion; Absonderung; abstrakter Begriff*" and "*Abgeschiedenheit (von der Welt); Zerstreutheit; Geistesabwesenheit; Entwendung*," as well as a reference to an old usage. To the beholder who reads this in a gallery or a museum, the text is full of references to the situation of art and of the work of art, including the one before his or her very own eyes. The beholder can think about art's rejection and affirmation of the world, or wonder whether *this* object here is more a so-called abstract or more a so-called figurative exhibit. One of the points of the text is, moreover, that the little word "*schön*" (beautiful) has, for nonsemantic reasons, found its way in, which makes a temporary semanticization unavoidable. The phonetic transcription seems to be saying "*abstrakt/schön*" (abstract/beautiful). This can be read as "*abstrakt = schön*," or else as "*abstrakt ≠ schön*"; the beholder just cannot escape the question of the interplay of the abstract and the beautiful. Furthermore, the phonetic transcription brings the acoustics of this (and every other) text to consciousness and thus also the *sound* of this visual object. The signs written on its face form a musical score according to which tones can be produced that, if all the abbreviations were also read, would create more a dadaist poem than a meaningful explication. We have to *read* what is on the picturelike object. This compels us to a linear, sequential viewing movement from left to right, which is counter to a simultaneous, circling grasping of pictures—a viewing perspective that is for its part encouraged by positioning the text on the wall of a museum. This gives rise to the object's being perceived also, or again and again, as a picture—as a composition in black and in white, as the exhibition of virtually an ornament made of letters that loses all substantive meaning in this viewing. In addition, the character of the individual letters is changed distinctly by the enormous enlargement of the text. Identical letters no longer appear identical. One can see the irregularities of their application, which would be as invisible as they would be irrelevant when just reading a dictionary entry. Yet here, the letter signs acquire a pictorial quality; it seems as if they were "handmade," as if they had been applied with a paintbrush one by one to a blackened canvas. In this way, however, they lose the character of standardized tokens; they acquire a graphical individuality. The letters veer out of the text they constitute; they combine to a dance of figures that plays its bright game on the black of the background.

What we see thus *is* a picture. It is a picture on whose space a comedy of exchanges takes place: between sound and meaning, text and ornament, sequential reading and simultaneous seeing. It is a reflection on the potential of pictures—a reflection that has become a picture, a potential that can be discovered even where we are ostensibly concerned only with a text. It is moreover a reflection on the status of artistic pictures that assert their status as individual sign processes even where they seem to dispense with all distinctiveness, where they surface as if they were just arbitrary presentations of a general abstract idea indifferent to the world of the visible. As in every good picture series, individual pieces from Kosuth's series acquire their own weight. *Which* text pieces are adopted in the series, and in what format, may indeed be unimportant (within certain limits). As soon as a choice is made, however, each picture of the series acquires its own countenance. Each in its own way brings to appearance the tension between the abstract concept and the written realization of the concept words. Each individual one refuses to traverse the path from work to proposition.

To present an "idea as idea," it is necessary to have sounds or a writing system. To present *art* purely as an idea, it is necessary to have in addition the whole aesthetic arsenal of tones, lines, and other sensuous contrasts with which painting, as one of the visual arts, has always worked. With Kosuth, the *denying* use of classic painting means proves to be an emphatic *use*.

Vertical Earth Kilometer

Another possible counterexample to the assumption of an essential sensuousness of art is an installation of which almost nothing can be seen. Such a largely invisible object was created by Walter de Maria under the title *Vertical Earth Kilometer* for *documenta VI* in Kassel, Germany, in 1977. All that can be seen at the center of the wide square in front of the Fridericianum in Kassel (within sight of a laterally located statue on a high pedestal) is a sandstone plate, measuring two square meters, with an inconspicuous brass manhole cover in the middle. What is beneath remains invisible. There is none of the expository notices usually found in museums. Here, it could seem, we have a work of art that eludes sensuous experiencing, that lives solely from the conceptions that the inventor and the beholders (or should one say those already informed?) associate with it.

Among the things that one has to know is that this is a work of art. One has to know that beneath the cover a long rod extends into the earth. In the Fridericianum's exhibition halls there was a supplementary exhibition in 1977 that documented the realization of the installation, including the commentaries that the concerned citizens of Kassel made on this project. Whoever visits the installation today no longer has this illustrative material available. The visitors have to acquire their knowledge from catalogues or articles. However much information they might get about the preparatory sketches, about the genesis of the work, and about the rest of the artist's oeuvre, in the final analysis they are faced with a covering plate that, like a tombstone, enshrouds everything inside.

De Maria erected an *inverted monument*, and he did so at a place that would be ideally suited for a conventional towering sculpture. As with every work of sculpture, the location of its erection plays a decisive role here too. But there is nothing erected here, nothing set up. This art object dispenses with all displays of human power and splendor. We are standing not in front, not beneath, not at the foot of, but above a gigantic sculpture that rigorously excludes the beholder from a vision of its expanse. What we have before us is the top of the thing, which is the center of a site created by its invisible dimension. As noted, one has to know of this dimension in order to gain at this location a sensing awareness of the subterranean space that outdoes many times over all sculptural, architectural, and landscape spaces. Standing where there is almost nothing visible, bereft of the normal conditions of sculptural perception, we experience our experiential stand-point more intensively than when facing all the outstanding objects that take beholders under their direction. We sense the ground of our behold-ing, which we are at the same time in danger of losing in the absence of something to behold. In the denial of sculptural gesture, the spatial rela-tions in which sculptural gestures can at all develop become sense-catch-ing.[98] The nonvisible thus also becomes an event of appearing. To this ex-tent, the *Vertical Earth Kilometer* satisfies a classic requirement of art: to give its objects an improbable appearing.

Movements in Literature

There is nonetheless another class of art objects that can be advanced against this view: works of literature. If we assume without further discus-sion that poetry does not constitute a counterexample to an aesthetics of appearing since its language is always bound to an acoustically, rhythmi-cally, and graphically conspicuous organization, we can turn directly to the case of literary prose. Here, the objection could run, there are no relevant objects of perception at all. Many works of literary prose have emancipated themselves from the sensuousness of appearing. This is how Hegel saw it; the material of poetry is for him not the word but ideas [*Vorstellung*].[99] Many novels that dispense with the sound and rhythm of a "poetic" lan-guage use—one thinks of *Don Quixote* or Balzac's and Chandler's novels— would then be no longer objects of a specific perception. They would be objects of perception only in the trivial sense that one has to recognize the sequence of letters and words in order to be able to follow the course of a text. We would be concerned with objects of the imagination that are not objects of appearing.

In his study *Art as a Social System*, Luhmann parried this objection fittingly:

Since we began our discussion with perception, the reader might assume that all this holds exclusively for the so-called visual arts. On the contrary, it holds— much more dramatically because less evidently—for the verbal arts as well, in-cluding lyric poetry. . . . Text-art organizes itself by means of self-referential refer-ences that combine elements of sound, rhythm, and meaning. The unity of self-reference and hetero-reference lies in the sensuous perceptibility of words. . . . the artistic quality of a text lies in the choice of words, not thematic choice.[100]

The literary text is a construct that presents itself as a conspicuous constellation of words and produces through this a specific relation to the world. This conspicuousness relates by no means only to the connotations associated with the words through their recombination; it relates equally to the sound, the rhythm, the gesture of literary use. It relates to the entire movement of literary texts. Not *ideas*, we must therefore argue against Hegel, but the *word* is the primary material of literature. The primary procedure of literature is not the *presentation* of ideas but the individual *arrangement of words* according to the aspects of sound, rhythm, and a meaning that is altered (not least as a result of this). This appearing is essential to words; on the strength of *their* appearing they often open up an extensive realm of the imagination in which something—heaven or hell, thing or event—can be presented in *its* appearing.

Whoever reads a novel "just for the content," one is tempted to say, does not read it at all. But not even this is correct. Even if someone reads a novel just for the content—say, on account of the suspenseful story—he or she does not read it exclusively in this way; the reader simply does not expressly notice what is conspicuous in literary terms. "Aesthetically" attentive and "rhetorically" attentive reading always go together when novels are read, though certainly to differing degrees.[101] Anyone reading Chandler's *The Long Goodbye* might linger at suggestive sentences such as the one about the swimming pool, or might not—no matter, he or she senses the *effects* of the linguistic intensifications that generate a tense mood between the intensifications of the plot. Readers of Balzac's *Lost Illusions* allow themselves to be led by the author's long excursuses—written with sociological and economic meticulousness—into the confined world of the provincial town of Angoulême and its neighboring l'Houmeau, a world divided socially as well as spatially into an upper and a lower town; and they allow themselves to be transposed later into the unpoetic business world of the capital city, Paris. Here, readers are carried less by the rhythm of the individual sentences than by the rhythm of the continuously sweeping flow of sentences. But even here, in a prose that is sentence-by-sentence much less constructed than Flaubert's prose or even Chandler's, we can find everywhere linguistic gestures that perform, inconspicuously but perceptibly, what they speak of.

The Restoration, when it defined the status of the French nobility and awakened its hopes of something which only a general social upheaval could bring about, widened the moral gulf which, far more than the difference of locality, divided Angoulême from L'Houmeau.[102]

The space, occupied by the subordinate clause, between the noun and the verb (and that always means in literature the time that elapses between the beginning and the continuation of the main clause) measures out the gulf between the two locations of the plot in the first part of the novel.[103]

Vladimir Nabokov's novel *Pnin* commences with a distancing glance at the hero, Prof. Timofey Pnin, who is sitting in an almost empty railway carriage:

Ideally bald, sun-tanned, and clean-shaven, he began rather impressively with that great brown dome of his, tortoise-shell glasses (masking up an infantile absence of eyebrows), apish upper lip, thick neck, and strong-man torso in a tightish tweed coat, but ended, somewhat disappointingly, in a pair of spindly legs (now flanneled and crossed) and frail-looking, almost feminine feet.[104]

This artistically doddery sentence about the disproportionate appearance of the hero contains in a nutshell everything that the book is about. It tells of a Russian's situation—which is out of proportion in all respects and narrated in humorous proportion—who is living in American exile and who makes every effort (but in vain) to be at home in the new world and the new language. What's more, he is sitting in the wrong train. This is not communicated to the reader until after two pages, followed by a digression on other Pnin eccentricities, another recollection of the blunder about which the hero does not yet know anything, followed by an excursus on his two left hands, "And he still did not know that he was on the wrong train," followed by a report on Pnin's struggle with the foreign language, interrupted by a reference to the approaching train conductor, followed by a description of the efforts Pnin makes not to lose his lecture manuscript (he does lose it), and finally, followed by the arrival of the conductor, who shakes his head over Pnin's ticket. This sequence, which extends over the entire first chapter, is written in an alternation of interruptions, digressions, and perspective shifts that not only imitates and parodies the hero's seminar style but also makes present his shaken disposition—in a rhythm of dysrhythmia, as is experienced by the cardiac Pnin from time to time. The choreography of linguistic movement with which we are led into the hero's world constructs mimetically the disequilibrium with which Professor Pnin moves through the New World.

The Body of Texts

Literary texts are the resonators of the imaginative projections bundled in and ignited by them. They sound, run, and appear as such. How specifically rich in images—rich in metaphors, similes, and other means of figurative speech[105]—is not decisive here. Their primary impulse lies in the mimetic ability to produce sequences of words and sentences that themselves stand for what they speak of. This mimesis has little to do with imitation. Its artistry lies in the creation of a language that is receptive to imaginative reading because it presents itself as an instrument of our imaginative projections—an instrument that wants us, the readers, to play it according to the musical score of its letters.

Here, nonetheless, it becomes evident that there is a relation between appearing and imagination that is indeed different from the one in the visual arts or in music. In painting (but also in sculpture and music, and particularly in film), aesthetic imagination lies *in the* artistic appearing of the works: in seeing and hearing these objects, the presents they articulate are there. When I view William Turner's painting *Rain, Steam, and Speed—The Great Western Railway* (1839, National Gallery, London) I *see* a landscape dynamized to formlessness by rain, steam, and speed, even if I do not succumb to the illusion of a real presence of this landscape; when I view Barnett Newman's seemingly symmetrical painting I *see* dynamics of colors that defy any order. Each time, it is a case of imaginative seeing that in its sensitive exploration of the artistic object recognizes something that a pre-artistic perception cannot discern. In many forms of literary prose, on the other hand, the imaginative reading of the artistic appearance of a text is merely upheld. It possesses a different sensuousness—a different "different appearing"—from the arts that are primarily visual or sound arts. The sensuousness of its texts evolves with and consists of a (frequently expanded and transformed) meaningfulness of its words that is itself not accessible to sensuous intuition. The empathic reading of a piece of prose executes its imaginative projections on the basis of a receptivity to the prose's rhythm, acoustics, and gestures, but not in toto *as* a sensuous perceiving, however steered and intensified by knowledge and reflection. In this sense, we are concerned here with the *scores* of aesthetic perception—scores or notational systems that call for a perception specifically directed to acoustics, gestures, and graphics.[106]

All art perception, it was said,[107] proceeds from an appearing and is in search of an appearing. This holds also for the reading of literary prose, but with an important qualification. Perception here is in search of, *among other things*, the appearing of the body of texts; at the same time it unfolds as an *imaginative* making present of the world imagined by the text. A second qualification seems necessary with regard to the presence of literary texts. All art, it was argued,[108] produces a special presence and in this way presents something in its presence. But what kind of a presence could it be that is produced and underlined by the novels of Balzac, Chandler, or Nabokov? What kind of a presence could it be that is not just presented but made present by poetic productions?

It cannot be a presence in a spatial sense. Nonetheless, the text of a literary reading possesses its own presence. It too is an object that comes to perception in an individual phenomenality—in interplay with precisely these words and signs. What is intuited here is an otherwise inconspicuous presence of *language*. The latter reveals itself in its play; it shows the readers how they are players of this play. Literary texts do not reveal this—as the philosophical theories of Humboldt, Frege, or Davidson do—by way of a presentation *on* language. They reveal it through the loud or quiet presentation of their *language*. They reveal it by constructing before the readers' eyes and ears *versions* of a linguistic access to the world. In these versions, it becomes perceptible to what *extent and how*—different each time—our conscious life is a linguistic life. In the literary text, language becomes evident as a part of the presence of our life. Whatever presence it might imagine within its space, the literary text lets its language become present in the formation of this space.

The individuality of literary texts has its own character. As with panel pictures, for whose beholding there must be optimum lighting conditions, and with movies, for whose presentation there must be optimum technical conditions, it seems obvious to say that the coupling of simultaneity and *momentariness*, which is so important for objects of mere appearing, does not play a role here. Unlike that of sculptures, buildings, or scenes of nature, the processuality of a text or a picture is not linked to a constant variety in their appearing—a variety determined by wind and weather, varying light, and changes of perspective. But this would be only half of the truth, because here we are not concerned with unchangeable objects, though they may not be subject to the slightest change materially speaking (in the precise sequence of letters).

The constitutive changeability of literature refers neither to its typology nor to the possibility of literary readings in which texts are presented in close analogy to the performative interpretation of music. Rather, it refers to the changes of the involved languages themselves—both the languages in which the texts originated and those into which they can be translated. With changes in historical languages, the physiognomy of the texts composed in them changes too. What changes is the way in which a literary text is situated in its source language (or its translation-determined target language). The body of texts moves not in a static, but in an ever-dynamic linguistic space, though the steps of this change may first be as unnoticeable as the movements of the minute hand of an analog watch. In this sense we are also concerned in literature with elements of the momentariness of its appearing. The language of poetry, too, has a here and now that is subject to historical time. It changes in that the language of its readers changes. It changes with us. After all, every change in language is much more than just that, a change in language; it is a change in the cultural world in which we move in using our language.[109] The presence that comes to appearance in the texts of literature is not the here and now of a body-centered space; it is the here and now of a historical time. It becomes discernible in the vibrations that its language produces in ours.

The Father of the Thought

This echo of language in the expansive spaces of historical time occurs even in the smallest of literary forms. "The clock strikes. Everyone" goes one of Stanislaw Jerzy Lec's deadly short aphorisms.[110] The pendulum of an old clock swings in these words; the death bell tolls in them; even the owners of digital chronometers do not escape the timeless logic of this sentence. This too is a linguistic *gesture* that must be perceived in its appearing to be able to be read as literature. Brevity and sparsity become here the stylistic device of laconic speech—in contrast to the entirely unadorned language of a washing machine's operating manual, which is scarcely worth a lingering read. Linguistic asceticism is also a form of literary animation.

One of Bertolt Brecht's Mr. Keuner stories bears the title "The Father of the Thought":

The following reproach was made of Mr. K.: all too often in his case the wish was father to the thought. Mr. K. replied: "There never has been a thought whose father was not a wish. But what one can argue about is: which wish? One does not have to suspect that a child might have no father at all in order to suspect: determining fatherhood is a difficult matter."[111]

This unassuming text lives from a clear rhythm, a complex dramaturgy, and a conceptual irony carried by these two elements. It begins with a critique of Keuner's thought, a critique sparked by a common saying. To the thesis expressed in it, which is itself an antithesis, Keuner responds for his part with an antithesis. This thesis is then in turn transposed so that there is finally a surprising synthesis. The construction of the text follows the scheme of a dialectical movement. The thesis (Thoughts are not an expression of interest) is followed by the antithesis (Yes, they are); this is then followed by the synthesis (They are an expression of interests, but it is *uncertain which ones*). The change of positions is marked by colons, which furnish the anecdote with firm divisions. Nothing is left here to the flux of natural and obvious assumptions. The apparency, supported by an idealized lore, that it is fatal for a thought to be born of wishes is just as shaken as the opposite materialist assurance that all thinking is an expression of interests. The concluding point takes seriously in a melancholy manner the common saying mentioned at the beginning. To be sure, all thinking gets its motivation from the motives of human practice, but from which ones it does cannot always be said, and it does not have to be said if a thought is welcome in the light of the world. What Brecht sketches here with gentle mockery about the basis-superstructure model is a pragmatic understanding of the autonomy of thinking that neither banishes thinking to a pure sphere of the mind nor condemns it to be in slavish service of the passions.

All this (and more) is achieved by the text in the space of 70 words, while my interpretation has thus far availed itself of about four times that. The little text organizes a play of movement and countermovement through which it itself becomes a reflection of the latitude that it ascribes to thinking. Even in this self-confidently unadorned shortest of stories, therefore, we find again the relation that is decisive for literary speech. Its language develops *in itself* a characteristic of the matter about which it speaks in the constellation of its words. Here too language becomes present—in turning back and forth the alluring set phrase, which is carefully led astray, about the illegitimate intellectual fatherhood of wishes. As with the painting by

Newman or the installation by de Maria, a presence is not imagined here that goes beyond the presence of the artistic object. Here, too, interpretive perception is moved to an intuitive involvement in an exemplary situation generated purposely by the text. Readers are prompted to retrace what happens when they think that they are thinking.

7. A Play for Presence

But art is not everything. Its objects expand the human world by worlds of an improbable experience; its processes load human perception with unimagined energy, but they are not the highest authorities of aesthetic consciousness, since there is no highest authority here. Works of art are not the sole model of an arousing aesthetic situation. Anyone stepping out of the movie theater, the theater, the opera house, the art gallery, or a reading and into the night of a city not only sees and hears once again cinema, theater, opera, paintings, and rousing speech but also breathes an air filled with the sounds and voices, movements and images, smells and gestures whose never-to-return aroma is not the outcome of a staging. Anyone departing the office, the production plant, or lecture theater for the openness of any day and pausing perceptively at a thing or a scene never just projects art onto life but enters into the appearing of the real, an appearing that cannot be substituted anywhere. Anyone entering a state of aesthetic watchfulness in a landscape (be it natural or urban scenery or in a more intimate scene—be it the bed or another podium) not only applies an education acquired in art but gives oneself over to a unique state that is as unrepeatable as an unrepeatable performance can be. Without doubt, art is a culmination point of the aesthetic, whose degeneration would leave a huge gap in humans' consciousness of themselves, but it shares its sophistication and coarseness with the encounter with unbridled aesthetic sensations. Passion for what appears holds not only for art; it holds also for a lingering in the ever-vanishing time of life, wherever this lingering might occur.

This passion for the play of appearances has a lot to do with the passion for playing. But there is an important difference. Every game is played for *presence*, but every aesthetic game is played for an *intuition* of presence.

We play because we—we play when we—want to be moved for the sake of being moved. This being moved can be bodily or emotional, or both. The point of playing is bodily or mental agitation. In the situation of playing we want to become present to ourselves in a special way. We want to be at the center of the play, in the middle of the game. We want to be in a situation that does not point beyond itself but nonetheless generates unforeseen conditions. We want to be in the possibilities of an extraordinary presence.

This applies to children's games as much as it does to adults', to regulated no less than to unregulated. Play is performance-oriented action; its primary ends lie in performing the particular action itself, however many purposive undertakings within this frame may be necessary and however many ends going beyond this frame may be connected to the performance. It is not an enduringly fixed action; it lives off the uncertainty of its course. It is an involving action; it consists in giving oneself over to the situation of the action. It is, finally, a temporally limited action; it stands in contrast to a normality of the rest of life, no matter how this normality is grasped. Even the person who plays a game of patience out of boredom moves for a brief period into a time that is subdivided differently.[112]

The process of aesthetic perception possesses many or all of these characteristics of play. In concentrating on concrete and momentary presences, the process is out to experience being moved sensuously and emotionally for its own sake. It unfolds as a lingering at, or in processes that are cognitively as well as practically indeterminable and intractable. The arbitrary or nonarbitrary (but in principle voluntary) step into this game is also tied to the expectation of becoming involved in a temporally limited occurrence that is only partially controllable by one's own action and reflection, and that, precisely on this account, causes a strain on bodily and intellectual powers.

But the game of aesthetic perception not only follows a special course that is closely related to other games; it also has an objective counterpart that is accessible in its subjective processes: a play of appearances. This makes the difference. Aesthetic perception is play, and it is attentiveness to a game. It is a playful going along with a game that is not solely *its* game. As argued earlier,[113] the two "games" involved do not have the same meaning. On the one side, it is a particular intuiting activity and thus a subjective play; on the other, a particular sensuous givenness and thus an objective play: of the simultaneity and momentariness of the appearances perceivable on an occasion.

Unlike other games where the game does not begin until the players start it, the objective aesthetic game that can be experienced by any player is in general not *started* by an act of play; but it is always *accessible* in the activity of perceptive play. This is an activity of perception *par excellence.* Its performance includes not only diverse and diversely complex perceptions, like a lot of play; *here we play for perception,* for the perception of a simultaneous and momentary occurrence that is presence at this moment. The highly immaterial dividend that can be earned here concerns not only a heightened intensity of being present in mind and body but also a heightened intensity of the *consciousness* of presence; not so much bodily *exertion* but primarily an intuiting *musing* in presence. When we play, we engage fully in the present. When we play aesthetically, we engage fully in the intuition of a presence.

Works of art play a *double* game here in that artworks play both *their* presence and *a* presence—the one they create and the one they present (which can in turn be the one they have created). They establish for the recipients a presence that is *split*, ranging from drastically to unnoticeably so. One cannot lose oneself in this presence in the way one can on a football pitch or in a game of billiards. But one can immerse oneself in the intuition of this presence. Every exertion in the *presence* of art requires a commitment to the presence of *art*—to the play of appearances of artistic objects. From this there often follows not only an intuitive and imaginative consciousness of but also an intuitive reflection on present and/or absent presences.

Nonetheless, the aesthetic consciousness of presence is not by nature reflective. Neither consideration of mere appearing nor consideration of atmospheric appearing is tied internally to reflective consciousness, which even so does not lessen the intensity or radicalism of this kind of recourse to the present. It is therefore not reflection and not imagination that distinguishes in principle aesthetic play from other games. The decisive difference, which in respect to imagination and reflection can be sharpened at any time, is the one between a sense of presence gained through dynamic exertion and a sense of presence gained through intuitive lingering. Because the step from one to the other—fraught with consequences as it can be—is often just a small step (and sometimes almost not one at all), aesthetic play often attracts nonaesthetic play, and the latter often aesthetic play.

From the perspective of actors, the play in a theater is not merely the presentation of a situative, imaginative, and illuminative play of appearances; it is also giving oneself over to a reality that is transformed in comparison to everyday reality. Conversely, the game of a fulfilling sexual exchange is not only a reciprocal bodily exertion, which lets one forget everything else for the time being, but also a conscious sensing of one's own bodily disposition mirrored and heightened in the other's perceivable sensing. The actions of professional athletes in the arenas of modern mass sport aim not only at winning money and honor, which after all could be achieved in other ways; they are practices of a public exertion that is limited by rules and takes place in situations that are in principle imponderable and in which all success and failure is rewarded with the enjoyment of the irreproducible presence of what is occurring. From the perspective of the spectators, it is a matter here, as Hans Ulrich Gumbrecht correctly says, of "performances that are directed exclusively at the production of presence."[114] The public spectacle of modern sport is an aesthetic event that allows spectators to take a collective time-out from the continuities of their lives—a time-out that does not, like the time-out of art, lead them to imaginative projections and reflections about the game of their lives. This is not art and should not be art; it does not have any meaning and should not have any; it is an aesthetic spectacle of its own kind that finds fulfillment in the visible genesis and passing of spectacular events. The exerting and intuiting realization of presence are extraordinarily close to each other here, so close that they determine each other; but they do not coincide here, because they are divided between the positions of the athletes and spectators. Both parties do, though, come together in a celebration of the uncertainty of their situation.

The aesthetics of sport is also just one example among many. But it is a good example for the affirmation of the imponderable, an affirmation that accompanies all aesthetic success—good aesthetic production no less than excited aesthetic reception. So far I have not said anything about aesthetic pleasure. On the one hand, that was not necessary since we were entirely concerned with processes and objects of a perception executed for its own sake (too). On the other hand, the reservation was justified in the fact that only now, after a long passage through various forms of the aesthetic, can we plainly say what a pleasure it is to perceive something in its appearing and for the sake of its appearing. It is a pleasure in being intuitively aware in various ways of temporary presences of life.

Aesthetic pleasure is a pleasure of finite existence in finite existence. But in this finiteness aesthetic intuition discovers the opportunity to make present infinite possibilities that cannot be experienced from the theoretical and practical perspective. The aesthetic object is an object experienced in its indeterminacy; the aesthetic situation is a situation open to the indeterminacy of both its world and the world as a whole. Much as consciousness of the fact of an extensive cognitive and practical indeterminateness and of an indeterminacy of the world can be crippling in many contexts, it can also be liberating. It is liberating when it emerges as consciousness of unexplored, undetermined, open possibilities that exist here and now. This consciousness emerges when something is perceived in its sensuous particularity and for the sake of its particularity. This consciousness becomes aware that it is not the future but the present that is radically indeterminable. In a certain sense, of course, the future is much less determinable than anything that occurs in the present or occurred in the past. But the future is *too* indeterminable to be *experienced* in the repleteness of its indeterminacy, which is the privilege of the ephemeral present.

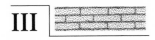

Flickering and Resonating

BORDERLINE EXPERIENCES OUTSIDE AND INSIDE ART

Aesthetic objects have always been famous, and infamous, for being in essence appearances. Not what they are, nor what they seem to be, but rather how they appear to us—that is what is above all important in their perception. The aesthetic object is what is appearing—that which interests us in how it encounters our senses. It does not have to interest us exclusively in this respect (no work of art interests solely our senses), but the possibility is ruled out that it does not interest us in this respect. Its entire being is based on its appearing.

Kant

When Kant calls the aesthetic object at one point a "play of shapes," then he means little else.[1] He speaks of a givenness that should be neither conceptually fixed nor practically used but can be appealing in free beholding. Kant calls this beholding disinterested. In it, all those interests are secondary that go beyond the presence of what is appearing. Disinterested beholding is a beholding that is eager for what is appearing, how it comes to intuition in the process of its appearing. It is not examined in respect to being and semblance, but perceived in its particular appearing. Whatever we treat aesthetically, Kant believes, we take seriously in its particular appearing and thus in a presence that can (and not infrequently must) appear frivolous from a theoretical or practical perspective.

In this Kant saw an important moment of freedom, virtually a proof of freedom. In the aesthetic state, we experience the world as being determinable by us precisely by forgoing the theoretical and practical treatment of the world. The processing play of shapes on the side of the aesthetic object correlates with a free play of the perception and distinction faculty on the side of the aesthetic subject. The diversity of what is appearing correlates with a diversity of being able to perceive, a diversity of which we can fully avail ourselves in the presence of what is appearing without subjecting ourselves to the internal limitations of theoretical knowledge or instrumental action. In the aesthetic state, Kant argues, we experience our determinacy as being determined by us, without having to carry this determinacy to the point of determining a restrictive position.

Nietzsche

As Nietzsche saw in *The Birth of Tragedy*, there is also a threat to human autonomy lurking in this confirmation. In the aesthetic experience of the type described by Kant, Nietzsche says, another experience can become evident: that of the disappearance of shapes and thus the experience of a "dread" that arises in the loss of the determinacy of reality. This shock cannot and does not have to be transformed into a pleasurable experience by reflective *effort*, as Kant envisions this for the sublime; it can, Nietzsche thinks, be affirmed as such—as a liberation from the prescripts of autonomy, as a shattering of the semblance of fundamental cultural orientations. The "Apollonian" construction contains an invitation to "Dionysian" destruction.

Nietzsche says at the beginning of the book on tragedy:

Schopenhauer has described the tremendous *dread* that grips man when he suddenly loses his way [*irre werden*] amidst the cognitive forms of appearance, because the principle of sufficient reason, in one of its forms, seems suspended. If we add to this dread the blissful ecstasy which, prompted by the same fragmentation of the *principium individuationis*, rises up from man's innermost core, indeed from nature, we are vouchsafed a glimpse into the nature of the *Dionysiac*, most immediately understandable to us in the analogy of *intoxication*.[2]

In this state, human beings lose their way not on account of *appearances* but, as Nietzsche puts it, because of "the *cognitive forms* of appearance." The *principium individuationis*, which is no longer in force here, is the principle of the spatiotemporal and shapelike distinguishability of the given. Thanks to this identification possibility, the given can be ascribed this or that *appearance* as well as this or that *cause* for its appearing. Nietzsche's wording at this point leaves open the possibility of an encounter with what is appearing, for which there is no cognitive form available because it cannot be identified as a spatiotemporal shape—or as a play of such shapes. We would be concerned here with something that is appearing but that cannot be grasped as a relation of appearances, or followed as a play of appearances. We would be concerned with an acoustic or visual *resonating* [*Rauschen*].

Transcendence and Immanence

Admittedly, Nietzsche does not use the concept of resonating. He just says that what happens in breaking the *principium individuationis* is "most immediately understandable to us in the analogy of *intoxication* [*Rausch*]." Contrary to my hypothetical reading, which goes beyond the wording of the text, Nietzsche assumes that there are no appearances at all outside the *principium individuationis*; that is, Dionysian intoxication is to be understood not as a dedication to what is appearing but as a transcending of it. I consider this to be the wrong track, one that leads to the artist metaphysics that Nietzsche later criticized in his "Attempt at a Self-Criticism" as being "arbitrary" and "fantastic."[3] His efforts were not "idle," though, as the author also says there. They were the beginning of the theoretical recognition of a phenomenon without which contemporary aesthetic practice would be unthinkable.

In a manner highly fraught with consequences, Nietzsche points out that inherent in every aesthetic organization—in every formation of an "Apolline semblance," to use his terminology—there is the tendency to overstep or underrate its sense-catching order. Where this happens, *what is appearing* aesthetically is transformed into a radical *process of appearing*. Its perception pushes abstention with regard to determination, which Kant established, way beyond the limits he set; its perception becomes an experiencing of the limits of the determinacy of ourselves and our world.

Along with other theorists today, I am of the opinion that the transcendence of shape projected here is among the fundamental possibilities of aesthetic perception.[4] More resolutely than the young Nietzsche, however, I believe that this transcending is to be understood not as going beyond the world of appearance but rather as losing oneself in this world. Resonating is a phenomenon not of the transcendence but of the radical immanence of appearing. It is the extreme form of aesthetic appearing and is therefore a potential though improbable state of aesthetic objects of all kinds.

Rauschen *and* Rausch

The resonating I speak of should not be equated with intoxication.[5] Resonating is a process on the part of the object, something that is the object of our perception. Intoxication, on the other hand, is a subjective state. Just as every intoxication does not result in the perception of a resonating, every resonating does not produce intoxication in those who perceive it. Even when this effect occurs, resonating is not comparable with a drug that induces intoxication. It is not the *cause* but simply the *occasion*. Moreover, it is the occasion for a perception that, as Nietzsche correctly underscores, has in some features a character similar to intoxication, without however being intoxicating in the physiological sense.[6]

Thus, even though there are no sequential relations between the objective state of resonating and the subjective state of intoxication, the phenomenon of resonating cannot be analyzed without reference to the state of its perception. Like every other aesthetic phenomenon, resonating must be understood in terms of its perceptibility. The analysis of the constitution of resonating and the analysis of the constitution of its perception as a resonating are one. Even if a resonating can be given independently of its *current* perception, its constitution cannot be understood independently of the *possibility* of this perception. To perceive an optical or acoustic occurrence as resonating—and not simply as noise or silence, fullness or emptiness—presupposes a perception that turns to the phenomena in question for their own sake, precisely because there is not really anything to perceive in them.[7] Aesthetic resonating, of which we speak in an apparently subject-independent sense as if it were first given and then perceived, is an appearance occurrence that is or would be a worthwhile occasion for a special aesthetic intuition. Its description must therefore also be a description of *interest* in its presence.

Mere Versus Artistic Resonating

Whereas Nietzsche has solely art in mind, I speak of resonating "outside and inside" art. For this reason, I have spoken thus far of aesthetic objects, and not just of artworks. The great significance that the appearance mode of resonating has inside modern art can best be recognized in comparison to the value resonating can have in aesthetic practice outside art. I would like to call extra-artistic resonating *mere* resonating; it is a resonating and nothing more. From this I distinguish *artistic* resonating; it is an enduringly foreign element in the process of artistic articulation.[8]

An Occurrence Without Something Occurring

Examples of mere resonating are the rustling of the trees in a wood, the roaring of a mountain stream, the rumbling of a big city, static in the airwaves, the foaming or flickering of a sea, the shimmering of a desert, the flickering of a monitor, or the flurry of a heavy snowfall.[9] The resonating that Nietzsche bequeathed to aesthetic theory as a problem is a literal or a metaphorical resonating. It is an acoustic or visual phenomenon. It is a flickering and/or a resonating. It is an occurrence perceivable through the sense of hearing or seeing without something occurring that has form (or can be followed and determined unequivocally); in short, it is *an occurrence without something occurring.*

The rustling of the trees in a wood is a sound, or actually a multitude of sounds, whose source cannot be detected by listeners. They are surrounded by sounds that to them do not follow from individual tones or tone sequences that through listening could be traced back to a specific sequence of events. It is no different with the sounds of a city. Here it may well indeed be possible to distinguish individual noises or sounds (machine noise, voices, sirens), but the tone of the city follows from a multitude of such sounds that cannot be individuated in their resounding and fading. Knowledge of the source of the particular resonating (the movement of leaves and twigs in the wind; the machine-generated and human energy of city life) can in no way compensate for this powerlessness of apprehension, because this is the powerlessness of the simultaneous sensuous reception of a highly complex occurrence. It cannot be remedied in hearing—and it is not supposed to be remedied at all.

Nor in vision.[10] To look onto a sunlit sea surface in largely calm conditions is also a perception of resonating (in the terminological sense now explicated); we perceive a stirring of light and water that cannot be followed as an orderly movement.[11] The example of the calm sea (like that of a shimmering desert) shows that the phenomenon of resonating arises not only where we are confronted by an extraordinary fullness of events; it can also crop up precisely where circumstances are pretty empty in comparison to other lifeworldly surroundings. Here too, however, resonating appears by virtue of the fact that in this emptiness—or acoustically speaking, in this silence—an extraordinary event fullness is perceivable, a fullness that does not reach perception outside of aesthetic attitudes. Even in what is the purportedly empty, therefore, resonating proves to be the presence of a fullness—more precisely, of an overabundance of shapes ensuring that a "play of shapes" (not to mention individual shapes, transformations of shapes, or shape sequences) can no longer be discerned.[12]

Only where we are able to discern such things can we speak not just of an *occurrence* but of *something occurring*; only here can we state and follow *what* is occurring. Everything *occurring* in this sense is a given that is subject to a perceptible change in visual or acoustic shapes. Even in an occurrence such as resonating, where nothing occurring can be discerned anymore, *there is* of course still something occurring; here, too, there are states that are subject to change, and this is what gives rise to an occurrence in the first place (as could be easily established with the aid of recording or measuring devices). However, that which triggers this occurrence is no longer discriminable to sensuous perception. Thus, even though one can in principle say that there is no such thing as an occurrence without something occurring, it is precisely this that remains a real possibility for perception, and especially for aesthetic perception: to be confronted by something occurring in which nothing particular occurs. Even though the beholder knows that a lot occurs, it seems nonetheless as if nothing occurs—as if only an occurrence occurs. This is the paradoxical case of resonating.

Yet it is seldom the case that *nothing whatsoever* is distinguishable in resonating; it often appears as a clouding of the distinguishable, as a ceaseless loss or change of shapes that makes it impossible to follow assuredly the transformations taking place. To this extent, resonating is always a matter of degree; "absolute" resonating—occurrence without any trace whatsoever of what is occurring—represents a limit concept. Furthermore, particular nuances can always be distinguished in resonating; the resonating is loud or quiet, roaring or banging, rasping or puffing, whimpering or flickering, shimmering or flowing, swirling or streaming, whizzing or fizzing, and so on. But all these are characteristics of the occurrence that can be felt or stated without being able to say something definite about what is thereby occurring. They are determinations of resonating *as* a resonating —as acoustic or visual movement without which our determination faculty is helpless.[13] Resonating is always an occurrence without a phenomenally determinable something that occurs.

Formless Reality

Much as this can be frightening, it can also be fascinating. Resonating can fascinate instead of frighten us only so long as we can also turn away from resonating, so long as it is up to us whether we want to perceive an event chiefly as resonating or otherwise. It can fascinate only where it is not resonating that overpowers us (against our will) but where we are the ones who give ourselves over to resonating and occasionally allow ourselves to be overpowered by it.

In attentiveness to mere resonating, an *encounter with formless reality* takes place. The real, which is otherwise perceived in this or that form and is ascribed this or that meaning in this or that form, appears here without these forms and without the meaning usually associated with them. What was previously located in a social or cultural order, what previously had an existence that could be anticipated and fixed, now reveals itself in a submeaningful appearing. In this way, there occurs for perceivers an encounter with the limits set on the shaping, understanding, and availability of the world—one can also say, an encounter with the limits of one's own, uniquely historical, uniquely cultural world. Reality reaches appearance in a nongraspable version. As we continue to know and master, it can indeed continue to be grasped and mastered as this or that reality; yet it reveals itself here as a reality that, for all the grasping, can never be fully grasped or mastered.

An Enduring Passing Away

At this point, we have to guard against a serious fallacy. The experience of formless reality, which allows attentiveness to resonating, is an encounter neither with the thing-in-itself (as Schopenhauer conceives of it) nor with the primordial source of all being (as stated in Nietzsche's text on tragedy),[14] nor with a higher being or meaning, as one could assume with Heidegger or George Steiner, nor with "raw being" in the sense of the later

Merleau-Ponty, nor with an otherwise interpretation-free reality. The perception of resonating is also an "as" relation to the world; the acoustic and/or optical occurrence that we grasp *as* resonating could also be heard or seen differently, for example, as noise or interference with the picture. The perception of resonating presupposes an aesthetic act. The possibility of resonating does not exist without the ability to act toward it *as* a resonating; it does not exist without the ability to experience a disengagement of reality from the possibilities of grasping reality.[15]

To this disengagement of the perceived there corresponds a disengagement of perception. Mere resonating can be sensed only where perception has liberated itself from all teleological orientations; it is then, like the course it takes, no longer organized in terms of something, ordered according to something, aimed at something. Here lies a lingering at what is appearing that is radicalized in comparison to all other aesthetic perception. The lingering relates not just to the presence of something appearing; it relates to an unfolding, to losing oneself in something present that no longer appears as an object of knowledge or action. In the discernment of resonating we surrender our determination faculty; we determine ourselves toward nondetermination. We no longer experience, as in Kant, our determinacy through us; we encounter reality in a temporary relinquishing of this determinacy of ourselves and the world. We give up determining the *phenomenon*; we give up determining ourselves *relative to* the phenomenon. We give up *ourselves* to the extent that we are determined in terms of our acting toward the world in an asserting and determining and mastering manner. All interest in resonating stems from pleasure in self-surrender.[16]

In giving oneself over to resonating lies our ability to leave the strenuousness of self-maintenance behind us—as Adorno said in recollecting Eichendorff and in the spirit of Schopenhauer.[17] Here, nonetheless, there is not really a departure from self-maintenance; rather, there is an aesthetic being oneself (a mimetic being oneself, Adorno would have said) in view of the surrender of that self-maintenance that is executed in the modes of self-assertion and self-determination. This philosophical interpretation of resonating is plausible only if we can say what the subject gains in this receptive relinquishment. By virtue of its perceiving at the boundaries of perception, its listening at the boundaries of hearing, its seeing at the boundaries of vision, the subject reaches the exceptional state of a differenceless presence—a presence with which it can be one. The experience of resonating is thus (like Dionysian "intoxication" in Nietzsche) a mystical experience, but it is so in a purely formal sense. It is not experience of participation in unspeakable meaning or inconceivable being (at any rate not necessarily so).[18] It is experience of the presence of an irretrievable temporal appearing, an experience that can be welcomed as the experience of a unique duration, as the condition of an *enduring passing away.*

Formed Formlessness

That is all, but it is not enough. Up to now I have spoken only of mere resonating, not yet of artistic resonating. The general concept of resonating, as I drafted it in terms of extra-artistic examples, is not sufficient for determining resonating inside art. If Nietzsche is right, without a concept of *this* resonating we have understood nothing about art.

When I stated earlier that the perception of resonating is an encounter with *formless* reality, then this should not be equated with an *unformed* reality, because in the resonating of art we are concerned exactly with a form of formless appearing. In contrast to the resonating of nature or of the city, the resonating of art is an arranged resonating and its perception an arranged encounter with a resonating. This resonating, though it sometimes continues to follow from contingent operations, is no longer a contingent process. Artistic resonating *reveals itself* as resonating, and it transpires *within* a play of shapes.

Some Genres

The connection between occurrence and what is occurring with which I have been dealing—no occurrence without something occurring, but some occurrences without something perceivable occurring—is, for all intents and purposes, presented by Bruce Nauman's installation *Anthro-Socio*, which was to be seen at *documenta IX* in Kassel, Germany, in 1992. On approaching the Fridericianum one could hear only a loud noise or howling—one could not tell—that on getting closer proved to be the scream or song—one could not tell—of a voice played continuously on tape; on entering the installation, the voice's sounds could then be deciphered with some difficulty as various lines of a text that were presented in infinite repetition. The resonating proved to be speech that, in concentrating on the medial arrangement's stream of images, was lost again in resonating. Related effects are found in Steve Reich's early compositions, for instance in the piece *Piano Phase*, in which a short phrase is played by two pianos at first in unison, then unnoticeably more and more desynchronized, until finally doubled and quadrupled, whereby an acoustic space and rhythm of a particular kind emerge, ones that cannot be traced back in listening to the ever-identical starting element. The clear and simple acoustic figure with which the piece opens loses itself in a musical occurrence that does not allow any individual occurrences to come to the fore.

To come out of and to enter into resonating is a frequently employed procedure in modern musical composition. (Nietzsche declares it, exaggeratedly, to be its fundamental pattern.) Wagner used it already, especially in his overtures; the prelude to the first act of *Lohengrin* arises out of a sound field formed by a few stretched tones echoing through the orchestra in order, in the end, to scatter in the same tones. A piece such as *Continuum* for harpsichord (1968) by György Ligeti abides by a limited variation of minimal intervals that are presented in a prestissimo that exceeds every conventional notion of the instrument's playability. In his *2 Études* for organ (1967/1969), there occur perpetual sound modulations of such a minimal level that the individual steps remain largely inaudible, as a result of which the acoustic sound space enters the appearing of a standstill whose spectrum ranges from flowing to speeding.[19] In *Atmosphères* (1961), an orchestral resonating forms the acoustic backdrop against which sound forms crystallize and dissolve again, are sketched and erased again, to end in the silence of a simultaneously composed resonating that is empty, as it were. John Cage has made this resonating silence audible in not a few of his works—for instance, in the piece for piano entitled *4:33*, in which the pianist goes on stage, sits at the piano, and does *not* play for four minutes and thirty-three seconds and thereby gives a sound to the silence that in musical practice is otherwise regarded as a supposedly toneless presupposition of musical sound. Following a suggestion of Sabine Sanio's, this can be understood actually as a musical definition of resonating: what otherwise forms the vague background of perception comes to the fore, without however being released out of its vagueness. The background of listening is pushed to the foreground *as background*.[20]

In the 1960s, jazz also developed its own language of resonating, as in Coltrane's playing since *Ascension*, in which the improvisations let themselves be propelled beyond every melody line into ecstatic phrases from

which the playing returns to a melodious ductus. Similarly, the saxophonist David Murray executes today a self-surpassing improvisation on traditional or traditionally commencing themes. With Cecil Taylor such a cal-
culated exhaustion is the basic principle of a treatment of the piano not as
an instrument of melody but as an orgiastic resonator. This triumph of the
occurrence over what is musically occurring is not at all confined to free
jazz. In his later years, the tenor saxophonist Ben Webster made it part of
his style to allow every melody phrase to ebb in a vibratory resonating—an
indication of the toneless breath from which all tones stem, an indication
of the limited bodily energy that manages to transform its pulse into
rhythm and playing and song.

Nor is artistic resonating by any means solely a matter of noise and
sound. In Pina Bausch's or Johann Kresnik's dance theater there are situations of an unsurveyable stage occurrence, or states of sparseness and un-
eventfulness that dramatically undertax structure-forming perception where
it was previously dramatically overtaxed.[21] In painting, Pollock, who not
coincidentally took his orientation from music and operated with dance
modes when painting, created resonating paintings, in the strict sense;
while others, such as Gerhard Richter or Sigmar Polke, have infused their
pictorial inventions with a subcutaneous resonating that does not allow a
definite shape to form in the picture—a refusal to form definitive shapes,
a refusal that became obligatory, one would almost like to say, through Picasso in figurative and portrait painting.

Finally, literature too is at home in resonating. Aside from evident
examples such as Schwitters's language-tone compositions, the tonal pieces
of Concrete poetry, or sound-underscored poems from Morgenstern to
Brinkmann, aside from the *topic* of resonating, which is central to all literature since Eichendorff, Tieck, and others, modern literature has developed languages of resonating that affect the specific *text as a whole*. One
need only think of Virginia Woolf's *The Waves*, Joyce's *Finnegans Wake*, or
Bernhard's *Correction*, in which resonating and (in the case of Bernhard)
the roaring [*Tosen*] of water are indeed introduced as a substantive motif,
but done so within the text of a language movement that can itself assume
all the characteristics of an aesthetic resonating when read in a brisk, non-
analytic manner. The language flow swamps the semantic and syntactic
structure of the sentences and sentence sequences, which then no longer
provide any specific opening or narrative, utterance or allusion, but are

now just elements of an independent linguistic life that captivates the reader for stretches as resonating speech.[22]

Christoph Marthaler's Faust

These states are not simply there; the aesthetic opportunities that they represent have to be sought and grasped both outside and inside art so that they can grasp the perceivers. In Christoph Marthaler's theatrical production *Wurzel aus Faust 1+2* in the Hamburg Schauspielhaus in 1994, there is a scene in which Faust, played by a darkly musing Josef Bierbichler, speaks his famous monologue, which in Goethe begins with the words:

> Habe nun, ach! Philosophie,
> Juristerei und Medizin,
> Und leider auch Theologie
> Durchaus studiert, mit heißem Bemühn.
>
> [I have, alas! Philosophy, / Medicine, Jurisprudence too, / And
> to my cost Theology, / With ardent labour, studied through.][23]

This text is not, however, spoken. What the actor, after a long struggle, squeezes out of himself haltingly and dolefully are just the vowels of the text ("aaaa, uuuuu, aaaaaaaa, ii-oo-o-iiiie," and so on). Only an extremely disfigured text is presented, accompanied by some snatches of dialogue that allow the theatergoer to recognize which passage from *Faust* (together with its famous presentations and interpretations) is being given over to resonating here.

This example gives us reason to verify in respect to artistic resonating the very relativity that has already been ascertained for simple resonating. Just as the resonating of the forest can be perceived other than as resonating (as a sign of the health or ill health of the forest), the resonating of the distorted monologue can be perceived other than as resonating. To the extent that we know Goethe's work, we can subject the stammering to a reconstructive listening that silently supplies the authoritative text to the distorted sounds. Then we would have decided against perceiving a resonating; we reconstruct from memory the language forms that the presentation shattered. However, we can also give ourselves over, in listening and viewing, to the antideclamatorily performed sound sequence and regard it for the moment as an original. We then practice a forgetful listening that decides against the presentation of thoughts and for the creatural groaning that suffocates all thinking here. We hear the body's doubt about the mind's achievement; we see the mind's desperation about the body's dissonance.

Being and Revealing

Artistic resonating is a borderline phenomenon in art, no matter how great or small a place it may occupy in individual artworks. No work of art can be simply the upshot of a resonating; it would be indistinguishable from occurrences of mere resonating. Every work of art is a construction and presentation of a special kind. As construction and presentation, it is an articulated creation that displays its supporting parts in such a way that the interaction between them becomes the center of its perception. Art objects articulate themselves in the interaction of their supporting parts, and usually they also articulate in this manner something, a content, that can in no way be disengaged from the how of its appearing, and can therefore never be expressed independently of the work; but it can be addressed interpretatively in various ways.

The work of art is, in other words, an appearing of a special kind. It does not simply appear; it *reveals* itself in its appearing. It presents its appearing. It directs its beholder to explore and discover, understand and interpret, marvel at and follow the construction of its appearance. The beholder who wants to *have* something from the artwork has to *take* it in one previously unspecified way or another.

This applies also to resonating. When Adorno writes in his essay on Eichendorff, "*Rauschen* is not a sound but a noise,"[24] then this is true indeed of simple (but not of all artistic) resonating. The resonating in Steve Reich's *Piano Phase* is not just noise; it is sound through and through, formed from the phrase that is played in unison at the beginning but then varied beyond recognition through relentless repetition, shifting, and multiplication, to resound once again in unison in its own form at the final moment. This resonating is a rhythmic sounding that on account of arranged overdetermination cannot be heard by the listeners as an organization of sounds or sound sequences, though they can recognize that it is an organized sound. Even where artistic resonating originates in chance techniques, it is always a matter of an arranged or staged or scenically permitted chance occurrence—as the term chance *techniques* already says. Resonating in art is often not a contingent occurrence; where it is one, it is always a matter of an invited process—indeed, one could say, of a summoned process.

However it is set up, resonating transpires in the work of art as a dissolution or nonoccurrence of acoustic, linguistic, figurative, choreographic forms; expressed in terms of the theory of production, it transpires as forming beyond the formation of forms. The work reveals itself as the formation of a formationlessness from which the work's forms stem, in which they disappear, against which they must assert themselves. It makes itself the pointer of a process of formation finding and formation loss. Yet, it makes itself the pointer by being this process and by revealing it as a process. Artworks, insofar as and so long as they unleash the energy of resonating, are what they reveal and reveal what they are.

Energies of the Artwork

What the work of art reveals in this way is above all *its* process, not a general, extra-, or transartistic process of becoming and passing away. The latter—that an artwork reveals becoming and passing away per se—might be said of individual works, but certainly not of all works in which resonating has a place. (Reich's *Piano Phase* shows the acoustic and rhythmic overflowing of a piano phase, and nothing more.) For this reason again, an interpretation of resonating must be rejected that, in respect to art, intimates that there occurs in resonating the revelation of a meaning or being that is otherwise inaccessible.[25] Gilles Deleuze probably makes a mistake of this kind when he says in his study on Francis Bacon, which is devoted to the antifigurative and thus potentially resonating energies of his work, that painting and music are to be defined as the attempt to make forces that are invisible and/or inaudible visible and/or audible.[26] This would mean that these forces already exist somewhere and just have to be brought to light in the medium of the artwork. But the work of art brings nothing to light; it brings to appearing, and it brings first of all itself to appearing, in such a way that we the beholders can frequently find *something* brought to appearing. The forces operating on or in the work of art are *its* forces—produced by the construction of the work, operative in the dynamics of its appearing.

Deleuze's reference to "forces," "energies," and "sensations" is nonetheless important. After all, one could say, it is precisely in states of resonating that the energetic moment of the work gains the upper hand over the forms forged by these energies. The work presents itself as something forming, not as something formed. It presents what is forming in its forms and beyond them. It would be incorrect, though, to play what is forming off against the forms it exhibits and conceals, for instance, by saying that the processuality of the work disavows the work's own forms. Rather, the work intensifies the interaction of forms in the phases of its resonating; it heightens the sensation of these forms by allowing them to evolve from resonating and to pass away in resonating. In this way, resonating participates in the play of the work's shapes. Artistic resonating is indeed an overflowing of the work's energies beyond the play of its parts and shapes, but it is an overflowing of the energies of a *work* that created that play and its figures and, on the strength of the dynamics of its appearing, brings them again to light from out of every disappearance. This is why I stated earlier that artistic resonating transpires differently from mere resonating, namely, as a resistant, irregular, agitated movement within a play of shapes.[27]

Artistic resonating too creates a possibility for mystical experience. It consists not so much in becoming one with the presence of a work as in being part of its kinetic energy. (Only with certain art forms, especially music, can this come close to the mystical experience of simple resonating, since music envelops the listener in his or her total situation and thus of all art forms—including architecture—overcomes most completely the difference between object and beholder.) In this experience too, nothing but the sensuous appearing of the work is opened; no extra-artistic meaning for which the work could serve as confirmation is revealed. The work is the source of *its own* energy of appearing; only in this way can it also bear witness to other energies, if the case may be. Perceiving resonating provides the possibility for losing oneself in the movement of a work—of letting oneself be carried by the work's movement out of what otherwise matters in real and irreal worlds.[28] We are then in the movement of Bernhardesque sentences, in the rhythm of Reichian tone and sound repetitions; we store the power of the screams of manifolded Naumanian protagonists; we pause for a moment in the enduring passing away of Ligeti modulations; we move with the form metamorphoses of paintings by Picasso or Polke. We are one not with the work but with the movement of the work. All perception of resonating in art has the form of a dance, however motionlessly we perform it.

Cinematic Resonating

Nor is this formal mysticism of resonating inside art something elitist or exclusive. The movie *Broken Arrow* by John Woo (USA 1997) leads constantly into sequences in which the movie theater's sound-image space is filled with a visual and acoustic occurrence where individual specifics can no longer be discerned. This resonating gains the upper hand especially when weapons and explosives of the most diverse kinds (from hand grenades to nuclear weapons) do their work. But it is also present in the background in other action sequences when we encounter an overabundance of actions and reactions that cannot be assimilated or sequentially ordered anymore. The disappearance of unequivocally identifiable shapes and forms is the normal state of affairs in this kind of cinema, which is as much a resonating cinema as it is a narrative one. A pure U.S. action movie almost always steers toward states of obscurity out of which the rogue (played this time by John Travolta) and his adversary in the service of the good (played this time by Christian Slater) resurface as expected in order to work on a new crisis of the senses. The "getting into trouble and getting out again" that narratively dominates these movies also dominates their perception, in the form of "getting disoriented and getting oriented again." These movies are made for that reason: they want to put us in the intoxication of perception that can be satisfied solely in the perception of resonating. Resonating and intoxication are more closely connected here than anywhere else. Cinematic resonating allows us audibly and visually to let hearing and seeing pass away.[29]

A lot of popular music follows a similar pattern—or, to be more precise, a lot of that popular music that has not yet been worn down to a listening agreeable to everyone. In comparison to the numbers and video clips that dominate markets, the popular music produced and distributed in comparatively underground conditions is frequently a music of resonating that produces effects, uses tones, and mixes sounds and styles that are successful later (or were successful earlier) only in milder and purged versions. In recent decades, artistic resonating has drawn a lot of its most productive energy from the fringes of pop music. One could describe the history of popular music since rock 'n' roll, if not before, as the repeated attempt to revitalize ever anew the waning energy of resonating. Even the techno sound must be understood as the attempt to create a music that can be listened to without a detour through sense, meaning, and individual expression; it is to be listened to *somatically*, as a direct transference, so to speak, of the work's energy onto the bodily disposition of its listeners. However, since schematization, automatism, and habit quickly took root here too, the next attempts to create short, strong numbers inaccessible to the intellect have already been in progress for some time now.

It is not by chance that we are again speaking of music here; after all, because it touches the most passive of sense organs, music is an art that overwhelms more so than other arts; because it runs its course in time, music is an art that passes away more so than other arts. In agreement with Nietzsche, music can thus be called the instructress of aesthetic resonating, even if in our day cinema has stepped up beside it with equal entitlements. These arts are pioneers of a persisting sensuous and imaginative perception precisely at that point where, in their time frame, listening to something and seeing something are processes that pass away on us.

The Children of the Dead

In the Austrian mountains an automobile accident occurs. On a stretch of road damaged by a burst water pipe, a Dutch touring bus propels an oncoming, speeding minibus with daytrippers from the roadway. The latter's occupants are now lying in the most horrible of poses in the most beautiful of vacation areas:

Like a playful dog, woolly and pert, nature jumps around its guests, circles them, whirls them through the air, does not catch them because a different flying stick is more attractive; moodily, nature places its paws on this or that one, lets loose again without considering that it has completely squashed, lacerated its playmate. It sniffs at the pieces, cries its sorrows into the daylight until night comes, and then it cries a different song, from the depths of the throat. Nature! Expansive are its clumsy jumps, expansive too are the rescue vehicles, which are already approaching. Endlessly fascinating are such human-sized dolls as are lying around here, limbs spread-eagled, the mouths are not talking anymore. Branches have broken off, the leaves are already flaccid on them. Tall in the noonday warmth are the heaps of human beings. Decoration for the countryside off which the country lives, they stretch all the way up the embankment, as far as the roadside restaurant, and they even stretch inside, where those still alive rummage about and rescue their belongings from the heap of rubbish; they have been spared and can now exert themselves on the fitness trail.[30]

Elfriede Jelinek's Language

The passage comes from Elfriede Jelinek's 1995 novel *The Children of the Dead.* It is an excerpt from the book's beginning, which is a prelude to the natural disaster that occurs at the end, when the narrow-mindedness, blindness, and dullness of the native inhabitants and tourists in an Austrian valley are punished by a gigantic landslide. People who formerly led the lives of the undead are brought by nature into the realm of the dead, against which they had previously insulated their lifeworld with unflagging energy.

In the critical reception of the novel, it was appreciated mainly for its narrative pattern, as a novel critical of the times, one that employs the constructions of the Gothic novel and zombie cinema in order to expose the heaps of what has been repressed, heaps on which clean, tourist-appealing, and politically harmless Austria is constructed. This is certainly not incorrect, but it skips over the linguistic process that unfolds through this narrative construction. The book maintains a pitch-black and deadly comical humor that is serviced not by the plot but by the talk about the place and time and occurrence of the events. A lot does indeed occur, and a lot of specific things, but this is just the exterior of what transpires in the literary text. What actually occurs are the incompatible languages of which the text is composed. There is no style here that could be characterized as such. The language that Jelinek writes often switches a number of times to a different idiom in the same sentence without favoring a particular one or without aiming primarily at satirical or parodical effects.

Strictly speaking, what is presented in the novel *The Children of the Dead* is not the text of a novel, but rather a hypertext in novel form, a wild language mix that knows no source or base language. Among the idioms knavishly tangled up here, without being woven together, are the language of the geography textbook as well as that of advertising for consumer goods and political parties, the language of art criticism no less than that of magazines for beauty and fitness, the language of news programs and sport broadcasts no less than that of the later Heidegger, the edifying speech of religious texts no less than that of the *Heimat* novel, the set phrases of TV entertainment no less than the stereotypes of pornography, penny dreadfuls, and romantic poetry. The terror that Jelinek spreads is a linguistic terror. She has invented an un-German language that relates to correct German usage as the undead, of which it speaks, relate to the legal status of either the living or the dead. This is not a language that one could humanly take pleasure in; above all it is not a language that one could examine as to whether its descriptions are appropriate. It is a language that, whatever it speaks of, speaks of the inappropriateness of all speech. By means of its ceaseless change of style, it denies not only the authority of its own speech but that of all the types of speech with which its thoroughly tactless speech comes into contact. It touches all of them.

That is why this text, though it says something definite word for word in each sentence, repeatedly morphs into a resonating—into a language buzz formed by thousands of set phrases, a language that reads like a roaring, never-ending, incomprehensible curse on the dangerous power of a speech that buries every conceivable object beneath it with naturelike insensitivity. Readers are pulled into a torrent of dismay about the stream of public and private speech, but in such a way that they cannot be sure at any time whether they are swimming with or against the current of false language.

A Limit Case of Consciousness

Both the aesthetic perception of arbitrary objects or situations and the perception of art reach a limit in resonating. Although mere resonating is just the upshot of a physical process (the audible or visible becomes equivocal), artistic resonating is the upshot of an articulation process; the forms in which a work presents itself become equivocal. But because this equivocality is part of the strategy of the artistic operation, the perception of artistic resonating cannot be understood, like that of mere resonating, as a departure from all teleological orientation; in this respect it is less radical. Nonetheless, this perception is consciousness of a resonating within human articulation attempts; it is consciousness of a waning resonating [*Verrauschen*] on the part of their constructions and distinctions—and is therefore as subversive as ever. All resonating produces a loss of coordinates, to which a loss of coordinates on the side of perception corresponds. Nietzsche, who has only artistic resonating in mind, believes that it gives rise to a sensuous mental tumbling. He speaks mutatis mutandis of the "rolling and tumbling" of musical experience, of a resonating music that is perceived in the mode of a literal or metaphorical tumbling. Mere resonating, by contrast, does not trigger such a tumbling; it is more like lingering in "stationary time," more precisely, in an enduring passing away. Its predominant form of reception is not so much tumbling as being absorbed. Nonetheless, it is once more characteristic of the aesthetic power of art (and again primarily that of music and film) that it can combine these two states or allow them to morph into each other. It then creates states in which we lose ourselves through processes that can make us lose our way.

Yet both types of resonating and its perception have something important in common. The audible or visual perception of resonating represents not only the beginning and the end of aesthetic perception; in a certain sense it represents the beginning and the end of *all* perception. Not in a genetic sense, however, only in a cognitive one. Resonating leads us to the edge of our developed capacity to perceive—to where we can no longer recognize anything but can nonetheless perceive with the greatest intensity. Resonating, that extreme of appearing, thus acquaints us with a limit of conscious being.

Thirteen Statements on the Picture

For some time now both inside and outside philosophy, there has been vigorous discussion about the picture and related phenomena (the relation of which to the picture itself is still largely unclarified): film, video clips, "interactive" picture use, computer design, and cyberspace. One reason for the interest in this topic is the rapid change in the pictorial worlds within which we live. This change has enormous influence on the realities of our lives, even if this does not give us reason to cast the concept of reality overboard, as has happened in some overreactions. A plausible concept of the picture is entirely dependent upon a comprehension of extrapictorial reality.

In recent decades, there has appeared a series of subtle, epistemologically, aesthetically, and art-historically arguing reflections on the status of pictures; I refer directly and indirectly to these reflections in the following theses. I will, however, confine myself entirely to remarks about "material pictures." These are perception objects among other objects of perception. I will not touch at all upon the topic of "mental images." Encouraged by the unwariness of other authors—or simply the unwariness of a philosophy that could not be restrained by the quietism of the later Wittgenstein—I will attempt in what follows to draft a general concept of the (material) picture.

It would of course be more precise to say that I will attempt to expound a plausible concept of what has counted and still counts as the central phenomenon of the picture within the tradition of picture use, up to

and including the present-day cultural practice that is much instrumental-
ized by new technical media. What a picture is is not laid down once and
for all. Pictures are objects that are subject to a certain comprehension and
treatment within which they alone acquire the status of pictures. Consequently, we have to speak of this treatment, that is, of what we do with objects of a certain kind when the question is raised as to "what a picture is."
(That much Wittgenstein must be permissible.) Nonetheless, pictures are
objects that in their use as pictures acquire a dynamic of their own that is
not subject to the direction of those who view them as pictures. A theory of
the picture has to keep both things in mind: the pragmatic and the processual constitution of pictures.

When I say that what is essential is to understand what *counted* in the
past and *counts* in the present as a picture, then this implies by no means
that responsibility is to be shifted to a history of the picture that could in-
vestigate what was regarded at various times as a picture and examine what
power devolved upon diverse pictorial media at various times. Rather, what
is important is to comprehend the *understanding* from whose perspective
we encounter pictures, whatever kind they may be and whatever power may
fall to them. This might seem entirely hopeless since there are so many different objects that we grasp as pictures: advertising boards, press and vacation photos, video and film footage, and figurative and nonfigurative paintings, just to mention a few examples. Is there *one* understanding at all that
can support the perception of such diverse pictorial forms?

I believe so. The differing forms of the picture are indeed based on
diverging understandings in each case, but there is an understanding—
and, on the side of the object, a relation—that is present in all of these
comprehension modes. This becomes evident when we turn to the constitution of "nonfigurative" artistic pictures, which are in some respects completely different from most other pictures (especially from most culturally
and politically powerful pictures). According to an interpretation propa-
gated by Clement Greenberg and radicalized by the philosopher Arthur
Danto, the meaning of these pictures is to say with artistic means what a
picture actually is.[1] However one-sided—and, with regard to American
painting of the 1950s and 1960s, unjust—this interpretation may be, it
does provide the theory of the picture with a decisive pointer. In the context of the question of the constitution of the picture and its perception,

the so-called abstract picture proves to be the most concrete and therefore the paradigmatic case of the picture.

In spite of this somewhat eccentric view, far be it from me to add yet another theory to recent theories of the picture. Occasioned by current discussions and relying on such disparate witnesses as Nelson Goodman and Gottfried Boehm, I would like to make some observations as to what a unified understanding of the picture and related (or just ostensibly related) phenomena *could* look like. This is why the text in this chapter retains the character of notes and commentaries endeavoring to sketch step by step how the appearance of pictures differs from the other appearances of the visible world.

I start with some statements that attempt to delimit the phenomena central to a theory of the picture (statements one, two, and three). There follows the thesis on the methodological primacy, first of artistic pictures over nonartistic ones and second of nonfigurative pictures over figurative ones (statements four, five, and six). On the basis of this, a useful concept of similarity can be formulated with which figurative pictures operate (statement seven). Statements eight, nine, and ten endeavor to further elaborate the special sign character of pictures with the help of phenomenological characterizations. Statements eleven and twelve compare the constitution of pictures with the simulated space of cyberspace and the virtual space of traditional cinema. The final statement employs the compiled observations on the reality of the picture for a moderate Platonic conclusion.

Statement One: Pictures are presentations that present
something visible within the space of a surveyable surface.

There are pictures only where the pictorial object can be distinguished from what is presented in or on the pictorial object.

Pictures are not just more or less complex visual patterns, like many ornaments. Pictures are not just what they are. They *refer* to something that they are and are not. (Pictures of unicorns are not unicorns; blue pictures that refer to their own blue color are not *simply just* blue.) Pictures, in other words, are a special kind of sign. They present something; they refer to something that is visible on their surface.

This *visibility* does not have to be evident at a glance. There are pictures that are not in this restrictive sense "surveyable." Barnett Newman wanted his huge painting *Who's Afraid of Red, Yellow and Blue III* (1967, Stedelijk Museum, Amsterdam) to be placed so close to beholders that they could not survey it at a distance. But this picture too can be surveyed in vision; what is required is just a small movement in front of it (as is also the case for instance under many sacred ceiling frescoes).

The *surface* of a picture does not have to be a *flat* surface. But a curved surface appears as a picture only as long as it is perceived in vision as a curved *surface* and can be demarcated from its surroundings. Otherwise the picture becomes an element in an architectural arrangement or a theatrical performance, in a sculpture or an installation; it becomes an element of an object that is itself not a pictorial object, however much it makes use of pictorial procedures.

Unlike pictures, sculptures gain their identity primarily from a difference between the sculptured object and the spatial situation, from their position *within* the space in which they are viewed. The picture, by contrast, has a specific position *toward* the space in which it is viewed; it is always positioned over against its beholders even if they do not view it frontally; it reveals itself, inasmuch as it reveals itself, from the front.[2] Unlike a sculpture's space, the space of a picture is not part of the real space of its appearance; it emerges solely from the difference between pictorial object and pictorial presentation.

The appearance of a sculpture is the appearance of an entity in space. The appearance of a picture is an occurrence on the surface of the pictorial object.

This difference between picture and sculpture can of course be glossed over and transgressed in many cases from both directions; but what happens in this glossing over and transgressing can be understood solely in terms of the *difference.* For instance, the slashed canvases by Lucio Fontana that are usually classified as "paintings" are objects *between* picture, embossment, and sculpture. By "damaging" the canvas—for example, of the 1963 work *Concetto spaziale* (Sprengel Museum, Hanover)—the picture is opened to the real space behind the surface on which the metaphorical space of a pictorial representation traditionally extends. The picture is opened to the space behind the canvas, which nonetheless remains closed insofar as it is a framed object hanging on a wall, an object that also prevents a view through a *passe-partout* behind the canvas. Moreover, this pictorial and sculptural object provides a continuously changing view to any-one moving in front of it. If one moves from a frontal to a lateral view, the thin cavity of the gash becomes narrower and narrower until it acquires the character of a black line, which then finally becomes invisible too; the em-bossment consisting of a canvas open to real space is transformed into the picture consisting of a painting surface that appears still untouched.

The relation of pictures to other objects as well as to language is ex-posed in Joseph Kosuth's laconic triptych *One and Three Umbrellas* from 1965 (Galerie der Gegenwart, Hamburg). In front of a white wall, on the left, there is a black-and-white photograph of a black umbrella hanging from a nail in front of a white wall; in the middle there is a black umbrella of the same make, position, and size hanging from a nail; and on the right there is a picture panel (of the same size as the photograph on the left) on which the text of the entry "Umbrella" from an English-German dictio-nary can be seen. We see only one real umbrella, but reference is made three times to umbrellas: first, in a photograph of one; second, through a specimen of one; third, in a linguistic definition (in translation) of one. Picture, specimen, concept (of the same thing): if we recognized what dis-tinguishes and connects these three, we would recognize how pictorial ob-jects are in the space of a linguistically disclosed world.

Every theory of the picture has to explain on the one hand how the pictorial *object* relates to the pictorial *presentation* and on the other how *pictorial* presentation relates to other (for instance, linguistic) representa-tions. In addition to these aspects, there is a further one as soon as we are concerned with figurative pictures, that is, with objects that are presented *in the picture*. The complex differences involved here are brought into play by Kosuth, into the play of an artistic performance. The picture of an um-brella is an object completely different from the umbrella. It is a flat object on which something is presented. On the other hand, this representation differs radically from the conceptual *designation* of an object, as we find it on the enlarged reproduction of a dictionary entry. The object *represented* in the picture on the left has therefore a character different from the real object in the middle, but also different from the object on the right that is designated with the words *umbrella* and *Regenschirm*. On the left, in the photograph, we *see* an umbrella, though only in the middle is there an um-brella *present*. All of these differences can be clarified only if the interrelationships involved are also clarified—between thing and picture, between picture and language, between things outside and inside the pictures.

Statement Two: Pictorial signs are not (just) symptoms.

Pictures present something that is visible on them, and its meaning is not exhausted in pointing to the *cause* of pictorial appearance. The meaning of pictures cannot be adequately characterized through the causal path of their genesis.

The tracks of a horse—the imprint of its hooves—on sand are not a picture of the horse or its hooves. Nor is a fingerprint a picture of the finger whose calluses can be read from this imprint; something can be recognized but nothing can be seen in it (unless someone declares the imprint to be a picture).

Mirror images are pictures in a limited sense. They are presentations that remain bound to the presence of the objects presented and are to that extent their symptoms, not signs that can designate independently of their designata. (Mirror images are *like* pictures of external objects. In the rearview mirror of our automobile we see not pictures of automobiles but other automobiles from a particular *view* generated by the mirror.)

A photographic picture, by contrast, does not become a picture by virtue of the fact that it was produced by the light rays emanating from its objects. In this regard, it—the negative or the print—would be nothing but a visual pattern. It becomes a picture by having the *function* of referring to one situation from out of another.[3]

Statement Three: Pictures are more or less compact signs; signs are "compact" when it is essential that they be realized with comparative precision.

That some pictures can be faked is due to their not being "notational" signs (in the sense of Nelson Goodman's terminology),[4] that is, they do not belong to a notational system with differentiated syntactical parameters (such as conventional music notation or the letters of the alphabet). Pictures are syntactically (in their internal articulation) and semantically (in their substantive references) "dense." Signs are syntactically dense when their meaning-constituting elements cannot be demarcated unequivocally from one another (as they can be in the case of the letters that together form a word). Signs are semantically closed when they do not refer unequivocally to an object or a thing (as they do in designating numbers by figures). According to Goodman, a pictorial presentation also has the syntactical property of relative "repleteness": comparatively many *aspects* of the sign medium are constitutive of its function as a sign (whereas for a letter it is not usually important how it is specifically executed). Essential for the constitution of a picture—*every* picture, not just artistic ones!—are always a multitude of properties and form differences on the part of the pictorial object.

Along with these syntactical features there is also the semantic feature of relative succinctness that distinguishes the picture from the (once again relative) diffuseness of language.[5] A picture is worth a thousand words, as the saying goes, and not by chance. The picture of the umbrella viewable at a glance in Kosuth's installation reveals much more about the folds of the umbrella hanging (half open) beside it than even an elaborate description could. Pictorial representations are succinct also insofar as many of their constitutive features can refer *individually* to something; by no means do these features represent something as something only when taken *all together*. Many of the individual parts of a figurative picture serve the characterization of pictorial content; one need only think of a portrait, or the photo of an automobile accident. An arbitrary *segment* of many pictures also gives a rich characterization of the objects visible in it. A pictorial sign can provide a much more detailed representation of something than a sentence can.

This succinctness, though, holds also for the characterization form of pictures that Goodman calls "expression," the pictorial explication of properties attributed metaphorically to the picture.[6] In a picture that is an expression of "sorrow" (and in this sense "has" sorrowfulness), this mood is frequently characterized not only by the picture as a whole but by a multitude of details that in themselves also disclose the world in light of a despondent state. The picture series *18. Oktober 1977* by Gerhard Richter (1988, Museum für Moderne Kunst, Frankfurt am Main, Germany), which goes back to police photos and is kept entirely in gray and black tones, refers to the death of the members of the Red Army Faction incarcerated in Stammheim high-security prison. In each picture, and in each picture segment that points out details, there is an atmosphere of crippling disorientation, of which the entire series reminds us under strict avoidance of ideological commentary.

Nonetheless, objects that are grasped as pictures can possess the properties of syntactical density and repleteness as well as semantic density and succinctness in more or less large amounts. The invariably *compact* pictorial signs are not necessarily *individual* signs that are calibrated for a *single* realization.

I call signs "compact" if they acquire their meaning from the specific execution of their particular (kind of) realization. In contrast, say, to letters, which are executed individually in every handwriting and yet retain the same value as letters (insofar as they remain legible, that is to say, *somehow* satisfy the letter scheme), the meaning of a picture changes as soon as we distinctly change its execution. The word *distinctly*, though, points to the relativity of this difference, a relativity underscored by Goodman too. Not every marginal change of a pictorial sign changes the meaning of the picture in question. This is why there can be equivalent copies and photographic prints of one and the same picture.[7] But in contrast to the letter *a* written in this or that way within the framework of a text, what is important for an *a* picture—a picture whose motif is (among other things) the letter *a*—is precisely this *particular* execution. But even in this case variations are possible. At the launching of a new computer font, the journalists in attendance could be each presented with the *same* photographic print of a page in this typeface (which is possibly not to be distinguished from the nonpictorial *paper printing* of the same specimen). On the other hand, in the case of Magritte's *La trahison des images* (1928–29, County Museum of Art, Los Angeles)—the ostensibly conventionally painted picture of a pipe and the sentence "*Ceci n'est pas une pipe*" below it in the painting—what is important is *precisely this* painterly execution of the letters, presented as a parody of the neat handwriting practiced in school.

The *particular* execution of the signs constitutive of pictures—an execution less arbitrary in comparison to other signs, for example, alphabetic characters—is therefore not necessarily an *individual* execution. It is possible "that there are a number of instances of the same sign."[8] Various photographic prints of the dictionary entry that Kosuth uses in the installation can be instances of the same picture. Since the invariably *compact* pictorial signs are by no means grasped invariably as *individual* signs, we have to distinguish between pictures in which the particular execution of the pictorial sign is *more or less* important and pictures in which it is *strictly* so.

Artistic pictures, it seems, are always individual pictures. This would be too simple, however. There can be two phenomenally identical photographic prints of the one artistic negative, prints in which the *same* picture can be seen. An artistic computer picture too can be repeatedly "started up"; or it can be calibrated to appear differently on different monitors (the "same" picture would mean in this case the same picture-generating *program*). Traditional paintings, by contrast, are usually grasped as individual signs that are bound to precisely this material realization. The reproduction does not give us the full picture. Here too, exceptions are at least conceivable. A gifted copyist could in fact create the *same* picture again—at least in respect to the relevant *phenomenal* properties of the pictorial sign (but not in respect to its properties as an art-historic and culture-historic *document*; these remain tied to the original). Not all artistic pictures that we treat as strictly individual pictures are bound in principle to exactly this material realization. Nonetheless, the individual picture is still today the paradigmatic case of an artistic picture. The pictures of art are grasped as unique creations that are to be regarded and preserved in exactly the form in which the artist created them.[9]

In contrast to individual pictures, there are instances of the picture where the particular form of the pictorial sign is of much *less* importance.

Pictograms are pictorial information bearers of little syntactical repleteness and without semantic succinctness.[10] In the case of the lady depicted on the restroom door, for instance, what is important is not the detailed execution of the sign but solely the circumstance that one can recognize it as the sign for a person of the female sex.

Furthermore, "singular" pictures can be distinguished from "general" ones. The photo of a lion in an encyclopedia, for example, is used to illustrate *general* properties of this biological species, not to present *this* lion. General pictures are much less succinct than singular pictures.[11]

All of these are differences in the *use modes* of pictures; the same picture can be used as a pictogram (male lion on a restroom door), or as a general picture (lion in an encyclopedia), or as a singular picture (this excellent specimen of a lion!). It also depends on these use modes if and when the *reproduction* of a picture represents a loss of its pictorial quality, a fake, creation of a new picture, or simply duplication of one and the same picture. Here it becomes clear that different types of pictures have different identities as pictures, which also means that different types of treatment of pictures create different types of pictures. Nor do artistic pictures exist simply on the strength of an inner magic; rather, they exist because their creators and beholders *treat* them as artistic pictures—frequently on account of the so-called magic forces that can be attributed to them in this comprehension.

> *Statement Four: In comparison to the basic form*
> *of the individual artistic picture, nonindividual*
> *but compact instances and nonsingular but*
> *general instances represent subsidiary forms.*

This is a purely methodological thesis. "Subsidiary form" does not imply "weaker," or "less important," or "less powerful" (it frequently[12] implies merely "artistically weaker"). In pictograms and general pictures, for instance, aspects of the pictorial sign can be disregarded that cannot be ignored in other cases. Singular nonartistic pictures are—in a syntactical sense regarding the composition and the relations of the sign's elements— poorer than artistic ones, which for this very reason makes them more informative and effective. We can glean a lot of information from any newspaper photo at a glance; from Piet Mondrian's *Broadway Boogie Woogie* (1942–43, Museum of Modern Art, New York), by contrast, nothing at all is to be gleaned. Understood in this way, pictorial density and repleteness can often mean less (unequivocalness and information), even if they represent more in other respects.

These are practical differences, which are not important here. In what follows I am interested in a theoretical distinction that allows the status of pictures, in contrast to other visible objects and other types of signs, to become as clear as possible. Accordingly, the term *subsidiary form* is a purely theoretical concept. In these picture types, the general constitution of the objects treated in human cultures as pictures cannot be grasped as well. In artistic pictures, by contrast, the basic constitution of pictorial objects—and thus the difference to visible things and linguistic signs, which Kosuth presented exemplarily—stands out more clearly. Along with Gottfried Boehm, I am of the opinion that singular art pictures consisting of individual realizations constitute the paradigmatic case for a theory of the picture, and furthermore that reflection on the status of these pictures has to include from the outset so-called abstract pictures.[13]

Statement Five: Art pictures are (mostly individual)
signs that allow the self-referentiality of all pictures
to become conspicuous.

Art pictures (and there should be no doubt about this) are a special case of picture. One could say that they *work* with the difference upon which the other pictures tacitly *rely*—if one does not want to say that they *play* with this difference.

The difference in question is that which is between the surface of the picture and what can be seen on or in the surface. Boehm, whose trailblazing suggestion I shall discuss below (ninth statement), termed it the *iconic difference*. Accordingly, I said in the first statement that pictures are presentations that present something on a surveyable surface. The relations of the presentation are decisive. Pictures are visible surfaces that are treated by picture users in such a way that they display certain relations visible on them. One can also say that pictures refer to these relations. The photograph Kosuth uses reveals an umbrella; the photocopy he uses reveals an entry in a dictionary. It is not just bright and dark parts that can be seen on the two suspended panels; the distribution of these parts *reveals* to the competent beholder on the one hand an umbrella and on the other a text from a dictionary. *That* is what these pictures present, and they *present* it. In the dictionary, by contrast, from which the enlarged copy of the entry is taken, the text is not by any means presented as text; this does not occur until Kosuth changes the context. What was previously an informative entry printed on paper is now presented in its graphic (legibility and) *visibility* as a component of a picture-reflective triptych. What is otherwise simply a legible arrangement of signs now becomes inspirited as an *arrangement* of colors and forms.[14]

We are thereby in the midst of the constitution of *artistic* pictures, for in them the relation between visible (on the pictorial surface) and presented (by the pictorial surface) appearance becomes *conspicuous*. It becomes a central occurrence of the picture. The self-referentiality latent in all pictorial phenomena becomes more or less dramatically apparent in the art picture. It becomes apparent wherever a picture is perceived as an artistic picture.

In artistic pictures, the self-referentiality of the sign is much less inconspicuous than in other cases; here the self-presentation of the picture is not simply a function of its presentation of a world. What is important is not just—or not at all—swift recognition of what is presented on the pictorial surface. It is not settled conclusively how the elements and nuances on the pictorial surface are to be grasped. Rather, the appearing of the pictorial surface here is a *counterpart* of what is revealed in and through the picture. What an art picture reveals follows here solely from deliberate attentiveness to how the picture reveals itself, that is, attentiveness to its constitution as an individual sign medium. The artistic picture reveals how it reveals what it reveals. In everything that an art picture reveals, the *process* of differentiating between pictorial object and pictorial presentation is felt (or thematized, or it even becomes the primary motif).[15]

We can therefore distinguish between (nonartistic) pictorial surfaces that present something in their domain and (artistic) ones that present *an occurrence of the presentation* in their domain. This is why the relation, which is decisive for all forms of picture, can be studied so well in artistic pictures. In its demonstrative pictoriality, as one could say, the peripheral phenomenon artistic picture is the paradigmatic case for the theory of the picture. The hardest of these cases is for its part a peripheral phenomenon within the quantitatively marginal domain of artistic pictures.

Statement Six: All pictures present; most pictures represent.

Although the vast majority of pictures (including artistic ones) are representational—"figurative"—pictures, a unified theory of the picture should take its orientation from the case of simply presentational pictures, yet do so in such a way that pictorial representation is recognized from the outset as the natural case of a picture. (Not as *the* natural case, however, since nonfigurative pictures by children are pictures in just as fundamental a sense as figuratively representational pictures are.)

Here there is a strong movement against almost the entire tradition of picture theory, which always took its orientation from pictorial representation, in order then (in the twentieth century) to look for additional explanations for the nonfigurative picture.[16] In my view it is not constitutive of pictures that they bring to appearance something that is not there. It is not generally the case that pictures bring to intuition something that they themselves are not (as has been argued again recently by Lambert Wiesing and Reinhard Brandt).[17] All illusionism in picture theory has the ground cut from under its feet by abstract art, especially by monochrome painting, concept art, or the early works of Jasper Johns and Frank Stella. A plausible theory of the picture has to match the complexity of the representational picture as well as Concrete painting.

Gerhard Richter's 1992 *Abstraktes Bild* (Sprengel Museum, Hanover) is part of a series, started in 1976, of often large-format color compositions that mark a distinct shift in his work.[18] The painting, which measures 200 by 180 centimeters, presents a thick and inhomogeneous colored surface dominated by green and above all brown tones, which the artist imbued with continuous horizontal and vertical structures by using long wooden beams. While still wet, the paint was spread smoothly, employing these big trowels, into narrow segments of irregular width, varying between 5 and 20 centimeters. The traces of this design are apparent everywhere. One can see how the somber, polychromatic paint sphere got its visible form under deliberate bodily effort. One can also see that the rhythmic organization of the painting's body in the vertical came after its arrangement in the horizontal, since the upright color beams clearly dominate the flat ones. In this way, the painting generates a tension between the subterranean surge of color and the processing of this color in forms. Moreover, the painting manifests traces of the moment of its composition, which is reflected in the dynamics of viewing the picture; when doing so, the vertical traces of the painting process call for greater attentiveness than the horizontal ones. In this tension, the nominally "abstract" painting proves to be a highly concrete creation. With its structure of thick layers of oil color, making it almost like an embossment, the painting brings to light a bodily labor of/in paint in which the forces of the reticently shining undercoating and its rhythmic organization balance each other.

At the same time, however, it is still possible to grasp this painting not just as a presentation of its forces, but over and above this as a representation of energies outside the picture. The verticals, for instance, can be seen as a close-up of tree forms, through which the painting can then also be grasped as the unfolding of a natural process (just as Richter's best landscapes *alternate* between abstraction and landscape). Nonetheless, this view is anything but mandatory here; this or any other painting from the series of multicolored *Abstrakte Bilder* coming from Richter's workshop and numbering in the hundreds can be appreciated in intuition without being seen as a presentation of states outside the picture. It then appears as a picture that moves in the rhythm of the to and fro of its colors.

Seen in this way, the picture does not represent anything, even though it does indeed present something. It reveals features and references that are left to the beholder for visual and interpretative exploration. As is the case with Barnett Newman's *Who's Afraid of Red, Yellow and Blue IV* (1969/70, Nationalgalerie, Berlin), which was discussed in Chapter One and the sections of Chapter Two "Appearing and Imagination," "Situations of Appearing," and "Constellations of Art," one can speak here of a reintensified self-presentation of the artistic picture. What it presents can be recognized *solely* in how it is presented since the reference to object forms known elsewhere does not exist. Nevertheless, a picture that does without a reference to recognizable forms of the external world is just as much a picture as its representational siblings. Thus, if (according to the fifth statement) it is correct to say that art pictures are the venue for the open or latent self-referentiality of all pictures, then it must be possible to study this self-referentiality in abstract pictures too. This means that here those fundamental factors are already gathered that are *generally* characteristic of the givenness of pictures.

If we bear these possibilities of nonfigurative picture production in mind, then the process of figurative picture production proves to be an *additional* achievement. It is not the case that abstract pictures somehow foreshorten the status of the picture. Rather, it is the case that figurative pictures expand this status; they present *their* appearing in order to refer to *other* appearances. *By virtue of* the phenomenal features they possess, figurative pictures refer to objects or imaginative projections *outside* the picture—to real objects such as pop stars, duchesses, or trees, or to fantasy creations (often first engendered by the picture) such as unicorns or imaginary cities. This is the prevailing case of pictorial *representation*, which has dominated picture production at all times.

I use the term *representation* here in the uncontroversial sense of a reference to states that are not at the same time (literal or metaphorical)[19] states of the sign in question, in the sense of referring in contrast to mere showing, of representation in contrast to mere presentation. In all pictorial representation, the elementary pictorial presentation is always included.

This is the case because all pictures present something on their surface—be it "just" the surface character of the picture, its color, its boundaries, and the like. The fact that limited surfaces with boundaries become pictorial signs does not imply a reference to forms of a real or fabricated extrapictorial reality, as the example of abstract painting shows. Rather, what is essential for the existence of pictorial signs is that they show something that is on or present with their surface. Without this (attentiveness to an) indicating function, which refers presentationally to *particular* properties of the pictorial object, we would have just a visual object but not a picture in front of us. A canvas by Fontana can refer to the vulnerability of this canvas, as well as to its space-dividing qualities—all properties that the material pictorial object possesses. In being grasped as a picture, the pictorial object *refers* to aspects of its appearance, irrespective of whether it also refers to things or events in the world. This *highlighting of aspects of its own appearing* is the decisive pictorial operation, a highlighting that is constitutive of abstract and figurative pictorial surfaces alike.

Even so, few pictures remain at the level of this elementary self-referentiality. By no means all pictures—and certainly not all abstract pictures—are largely *signs* of the properties they actually possess. Only some abstract pictures are restricted to this. Pictures, it can thus be affirmed, refer to states that reveal themselves in the pictures, or else to things, events, or imaginative projections outside the picture. It is probably an appropriate interpretation of Gerhard Richter's laconically and ironically named work *Abstraktes Bild* to say that it raises to consciousness the often chameleonlike nature of art pictures. It presents its own relations of color and form and at the same time opens up the possibility of seeing relations of nature or the human condition present there. Similarly, Fontana's canvas is a pictorial object that presents its own vivid properties (and, over and above this, arouses erotic associations). Newman's huge canvas *Who's Afraid of Red, Yellow and Blue IV* dramatizes the relations of color and form as well as color and surface, with the effect of underscoring the autonomy of color vis-à-vis the form and surface of its presentation. Here too, it is a matter of world presentation *by virtue of* a highly opaque self-presentation of the artistic object. With his painting, Newman stages a dispute between the forces of the ("beautiful") order and the forces of a ("sublime") transcendence of the most beautiful (symmetrical, balanced) order. His series of paintings lets us experience the fact that human beings can tolerate their systems of order only if they are able to transcend these systems—a project that is scarcely less ambitious than *The Ring of the Nibelung*.

*Statement Seven: Pictorial representation operates with
forms that are similar to the objects represented.*

According to Nelson Goodman's much discussed view, the feature of
similarity is irrelevant in the analysis of pictorial representation. This is,
however, implausible. The assumption that the concept of similarity is not
needed results from an erroneous assimilation of picture and language,
which is part of Goodman's program.[20] The difference between verbal and
pictorial representation lies not solely in a lesser syntactical repleteness and
semantic succinctness but also in the similarity of representation and the
represented, which is constitutive in the case of the representational picture.

Everything depends, of course, on how this similarity is conceived. It
should not be understood as a similarity of the *picture* to it objects; rather,
it exists between objects that we can identify *in* the picture and those we
can identify *outside* the picture. Accordingly, my proposal is this: an object
identifiable in the picture is similar to an extrapictorial object if it is *sortally
analyzable* using the same predicates.

In general, independently of the picture problem, it should be said
that one visual appearance is *similar* to another if both can be analyzed sortally in the same way in their description. This already shows that a relation of similarity cannot be a *sufficient* feature of pictures. For something
to be regarded as a pictorial representation, it has to be grasped—Goodman is right in this respect—as a *sign* that *refers* (in one way or another) to
the objects that we can distinguish in it. Contrary to Goodman's view,
however, pictorial representation presupposes similarity of the kind mentioned as a necessary condition.

"Sortally analyzable" means that we can distinguish (or, in the case
of cubistically painted guitars and the like, reconstruct) a *relation* of parts
in this object, just as we can in the corresponding real object. The relationship of similarity that is sought consists in a more or less far-reaching
sameness of form relations. (In the case of a cow in a picture, the horns
and hooves are distributed in approximately the same relation to the ears
and the back as on a cow seen from the corresponding perspective in the
meadow.) In that sense, it is understandable to speak also of degrees of
similarity, such as those that come into play when we ask *how realistic* a
picture is. Accordingly, realism would be not—at least not simply—a
"matter of habit" but a matter of the *ease* (or of the very possibility) of distinguishing and sortally analyzing objects on the surface of the picture.

Moreover, the thesis of a *pure* conventionality of perspective can be doubted from this viewpoint. Rather, perspective is comprehensible as a procedure for the most faithful pictorial representation of the visibility of spatial object *relations*.

> *Statement Eight: Pictures are sign events—objects*
> *about the world that are also perceived as independent*
> *objects in the world.*

To be objects of the world and objects about the world: in a trivial sense this holds for all objects or events that we treat as signs. They are all occurrences in the world that have the function of a *reference* to something (or in the service of a *contribution* to such a reference). In the case of the picture, though, this triviality is the departure point of a substantive observation. The surface of a picture is not of secondary importance in comparison to its sign function; rather, in a special way it emerges as a source of references. Art pictures, but also many other conspicuous images (be it in advertising or in personal recollection) are not just a ground on which something appears presented; they *appear* as a ground on which something appears presented.

The element of truth in picture-theoretic illusionism—as is defended today by Reinhard Brandt, for example—probably consists in underscoring the special presence of the picture in comparison to all other types of representation. The picture *refers* not just to something; it is in a special way *present*. Still, illusionism necessarily misses this specialness because only in very rare cases are the objects or circumstances that are presented in the picture perceived *at the expense of* a perception of the pictorial medium (of the pictorial surface). When this happens, a picture is perceived not *as* a picture but as a (real, extrapictorial) presence of what is *represented* in the picture.

The disappearance of the pictorial surface is not constitutive of the perception of pictures—not even in the form of an undisguised semblance (in Newman, Fontana, or Richter there is not such a semblance). The special presence of the picture consists not in a seeming presence of the particular pictorial content but in the thereness of the picture itself as an *appearing ground* for (re)presented appearances. The presence of the picture is not an illusion; it does not imply an "as if" (as if the represented object or the represented scene were there). It is the presence of a presenting appearance that enriches reality with specific phenomena by appearing concurrently as *appearance* and as *presentation.*

Kosuth's triptych highlights with subtlety this intermediate position of the picture between real thing and mere word or text. The picture of an umbrella is closer to the umbrella thing and its perception than the concept (or the explication of the concept) "umbrella" is to the matter it designates; nonetheless, it belongs, like concept and text, to the domain of signs that refer to something that does not have to be present in the act of verbal or pictorial reference. Like the word, the picture is not a substitute for the thing. Nonetheless, it is part of the process of perceiving a picture that we attend to its particular (and sometimes individual) appearance, whereas we can simply read words without paying specific heed to their graphical execution. Words too, especially when they confront us enlarged and isolated on an exposed surface (this being the third point of this threefold metaobject), can acquire a pictorial status. Then they refer not so much to what they designate as to their own arrangement and form; or, to be more precise, then *words* do indeed continue to refer to what is normally intended by them, but the pictorial surface on which they now reside refers to a choreography of lines, strings of words, and sounds—to which no one looking up something in the dictionary would pay attention.

The picture *is* (the abundance of appearances visible on its surface) and it *reveals* (something on, in, or through this medial appearing). Because of the features of repleteness and succinctness (and often also similarity), and depending on the *degree* of these features, pictures are signs whose sensuousness one cannot often overlook when using them as signs—in contrast to the use of plain words (outside literature). They are frequently less transparent than other signs. The pictorial sign is not of secondary importance in comparison to what it refers to. *In its appearing, it brings something to appearance.*

> *Statement Nine: There is no real conflict between the phenomenological and the semiotic theory of the picture. Pictures are surveyable surfaces that make something visible; both sides could agree on this basic formula.*

As soon as one lays emphasis on the specialness of the pictorial sign, on its special sensuous conspicuousness, the sign-theoretic analysis touches phenomenological theories of the picture, as were developed for example by Jean-Paul Sartre and Maurice Merleau-Ponty, Michael Polanyi and Richard Wollheim (almost exclusively in connection with the paradigm of the artistic picture).[21] Boehm has recently reconstructed this tradition under the guiding concept of "iconic difference." "What encounters us as a picture," Boehm says, "rests upon a single basic contrast, that between a surveyable total surface and everything that it includes in terms of inner events."[22]

What, in all historical variety, pictures "are" as pictures, what they "reveal," what they "say," is therefore due to a fundamental visual contrast, which can also be called the cradle of all pictorial sense. Whatever a pictorial artist wanted to represent—in the twilight darkness of prehistoric caves, in the sacred context of icon paintings, in the inspired space of the modern atelier—its existence, its comprehensibility and effectiveness are due to the particular optimization of what we call the "iconic difference."[23]

The picture-theoretic discussion is currently distinguished by a considerably far-reaching opposition between a (more) sign-theoretic and a (more) phenomenologically proceeding position. The phenomenological viewpoint grants that pictures can be signs, but it disputes that they are necessarily signs, as its opponents claim. On closer examination, however, this opposition proves to be artificial. Only if the concept of the sign is arbitrarily constricted is it possible to dispute that pictures are always signs too. If, on the other hand, the iconic difference established by Boehm is explicated as a relation of visual *presentation*, then a sign relation is always already implied in the reference to what is particularly presented on the pictorial surface, and indeed long before this presentation—as a fulfilled or an unfulfilled reference—points to something outside the picture.

Pictures, Boehm says, "*unfold* the relation between their visible totality and the wealth of their *represented* multifariousness."[24] Pictures, this means, present (something of) what appears on their ground. To grasp the meaning of this presentation, it is necessary to pay attention to the difference between the arena of the pictorial medium and what is displayed or made visible here. It is not simply the pictorial surface that is exhibited (just as in DIY stores we find painted surfaces exhibited on which we can see what the obtainable paints look like).[25] In exhibiting a picture, what occurs on the expanse of its surface is always exhibited at the same time. The picture not only *contains* certain appearances (of color and form), it *refers to* its own internal references. It is through this reference to its appearing that it first becomes a picture.

For this reason it is correct to say that a visual object becomes a picture precisely when it becomes a sign of what occurs on its surface. A visual object becomes a picture precisely when its surface is *grasped* by its beholders as a sign of what appears on it.

That it is in fact a sign relation can be recognized in a series of simple comparisons. Let x be a visible surface (in the sense of the comments on the first statement) on which something can be seen. A number of relations are possible:

> "y is visible on x." Here there is not yet a pictorial relation. The spot on a table or pants does not make the table or pants into a picture of something.
>
> "y appears on x (without x being y)." The shadow of a flower appears on the table; that something appears on something does not in itself produce a picture, either.
>
> "x makes y visible." Only where *this* relation exists, only where it is a matter of visual *presentations*, can we speak of pictures.

Pictures are presentations in the medium of appearing—in the medium of the appearing of a surface on which something appears as presented. A picture of apples is something different from an apple pattern on a pajamas. This sign status of the picture can be illustrated by another comparison. The reference of a figurative picture is of a type different from the reference of a linguistic term and the direction of figurative vision. There is *no ball at all* to be seen in the sentence "I see the ball." If on the other hand I say "I see the ball," then I am usually referring to an object that is located somewhere in my spatial surroundings. Yet, we do say "I see the ball" even when it is a matter of a picture in which a ball can be seen— we see the ball *in the picture.* The ball in the picture, however, is neither a ball nor the illusion of a ball, nor simply the pattern or figure of one, but the sign of a ball: presented, formulated in the medium of the difference between the visible surface and the figure presented (and not just visible) on it. What distinguishes pictures from ornaments is the presentation, the highlighting of aspects and references of what is appearing.

Only a sign-theoretic *and* a phenomenological comprehension of the picture, I would like to conclude, does justice to the phenomenon of the picture; only an integral access provides the basis for an appropriate explication of those related phenomena, mentioned at the outset, with respect to which we are not even sure whether and to what extent they are *pictorial* phenomena.[26]

> *Statement Ten: To see something, to see something as something, and to see something in something are three basic instances of seeing; they come together in seeing pictures.*

Surveyable surfaces that in their appearance bring something to appearance call for complex seeing. Richard Wollheim has described it as the capacity for "seeing-in."[27] I see something in something that I do not see as that which I see in it. I see a cow on the surface of a picture without therefore seeing the picture as a cow. I see in the dark parts of the photographic print an umbrella without thinking this print is an umbrella (or viewing it as an umbrella). This special seeing presupposes, however, *other* skills in visual perception.

The general concept of seeing is that of seeing something; all living beings capable of seeing can see in this way. They are in a position to distinguish objects and movements by virtue of visual perception.

To see something *as something*, on the other hand, is a much more specialized ability; the ability of conceptual distinction is included in it. The mere seeing *of* something becomes seeing *that* such and such is the case, for example, that there is an umbrella hanging there. In contrast to a seeing that simply perceives, here it is a matter of epistemic seeing.[28]

To see a picture, we have to be able to perceive an object among other objects—and we have to be able to perceive it *as a picture*. Identifying and reidentifying forms in pictures (as many animals master) is not enough here.[29] Identifying something as well as the more elaborate identifying of something *as* something are indeed necessary presuppositions of seeing pictures, since to recognize a pictorial presentation it is necessary to have the ability to discriminate visually what is specifically presented. What is decisive for the perception of pictures over and above this is to recognize what is presented by the picture not simply as something given but as *something presented*. If a person standing in front of Kosuth's installation were to see simply two umbrellas, and not see that only one of them can be opened, he or she would indeed see to the left an object that *others* would classify with good reason as a picture, but the person himself or herself would not perceive any pictorial object. He or she would see only the *object* of the picture, without seeing that it is the object of a picture.

Only the person who masters *seeing-in* has this competence. I see in these colors and forms an umbrella, a cow, the Duchess of Kent, a reflection on painting, or a parody of abstract expressionism. Seeing-in enables us to see in an appearance—that of the pictorial surface—another appearance (or to see something else appear): an umbrella, a cow, a duchess, a developmental stage in painting, and so on. When we speak of pictures, an additional element must however join the appearing *of* something *in* something else: the fact that one appearance (say, that of an umbrella) is *brought* to appearance in the medium of the other appearance (that of the pictorial surface). A cloud in which we see Churchill's face is not a picture of Churchill.

This means that not seeing-in per se but just a particular *use* of this ability is constitutive of seeing pictures. When I see in the cloud a ship or in this smudge a face, I still do not see a picture of a ship or a face. Picture-specific seeing-in enters a *sign relation* (constitutes it or reconstructs it). It grasps the visual object as the presentation of something.[30]

Like seeing-as, seeing-in is a form of epistemic seeing. Even so, seeing art pictures in particular is not exhausted by such an epistemic orientation. It is in unceasing exchange with a "seeing seeing"[31] that sees everything seen in the picture emerging from and passing into the process of its colors and forms.

The fact that picture-specific seeing-in presupposes a seeing-of as well as the more specialized seeing-that means that it is founded on abilities that can be realized independently of picture perception. Pictorial seeing-in is possible only where a successful seeing-of and a successful seeing-that are available, which means there are pictures only where there is a visible world in advance of pictures.

Statement Eleven: Cyberspace is not pictorial space
but simulated space.

With reference to Henri Pirenne and Michael Polanyi, and using the example of figurative painting, Richard Wollheim has developed a "two-foldness thesis" about the picture, on which Boehm bases his more general thesis of an underlying "iconic difference" and I base my observations on the (open or latent) self-referentiality of the picture. The thesis states that pictures can be perceived as pictures only if attention is an attention "divided" between the pictorial medium and the pictorial presentation, no matter how dominant each attention may be in the particular case. I have to pay attention to what is visible on the pictorial ground in order to know what is presented on this ground (or, in the case of monochrome pictures, presented through this ground).[32] But precisely this twofoldness, of which Boehm and Wollheim plausibly speak, is no longer given upon entry into the cyberspace of simulated spaces.[33] Cyberspace is indeed an exciting visual phenomenon but not a pictorial phenomenon; "pictorial spaces," as Benjamin fantasizes them in his essay on surrealism,[34] are either not spaces or not pictures. The picture is a surface phenomenon that cannot be transferred into (real or imaginary) spatial relations. Where the space becomes a picture or the picture a space, we are concerned no longer with pictoriality but with a visual phenomenon that is sui generis.

For this reason, Lambert Wiesing's linear progressive history—from the figurative panel painting via the video clip and CAD up to cyberspace—seems to me not just too stylized but also wrong in terms of consistency.[35] In the appearance space of cyberspace (which is in principle a space not just of visual but also haptic and acoustic appearances), the difference between pictorial medium and pictorial content loses all foundation. Only here does the medium become invisible. Here the medium is a program and an apparatus that together produce independent sensuous appearances. The iconic difference disappears.

Yet here too there is a twofoldness, though it is of a nature completely different from that in the case of the picture. The difference constitutive of cyberspace exists between the real space of the body's presence and the virtual space of bodily unreachable, but nonetheless visible, objects. But this is a twofold position of the bodily *subject* of perception (vis-à-vis objects that are in principle reachable and unreachable), whereas in the case of the picture it is a matter of a twofold givenness of the *object* of perception. The one twofoldness has to disappear so that the other one can appear. Seen phenomenologically, therefore, there is no continuum between pictorial space and virtual space. In terms of the theory of signs, it is a different matter; all pictures are signs, whereas there is no sign relation at all constitutive of cyberspace. It is an appearing space alone.

To make the difference in question clear, one can imagine a cyber-space that is equipped with pictures: in a computed visual space, objects appear that, as a ground for presented appearances, differ from their equally virtual environment, which is only appearance but not the presen-tation of appearances.

> *Statement Twelve: Film's virtual movement space*
> *is located between the simultaneous appearance*
> *of pictures and simulated space of cyberspace.*

Just as pictorial worlds and simulated worlds are sometimes equated with one another today, the world of film was confused with the world of pictures for a long time. The central question for a theory of film is what dif-ference it makes to project a film strip, which—like the film of traditional movies (before the advent of video film and digital film production)—con-sists of a multitude of individual pictures, as continuously moving pictures. The movement alone does not constitute the decisive difference. Otherwise the glance from a moving automobile at a construction-site fence with pic-tures would amount to the perception of a film. Rather, everything depends on *how one is moved* by the cinematic occurrence.

Like many others, Siegfried Kracauer held the view that film is just an "extension" of photography and therefore is itself a form of picture. "Moving pictures," Kracauer believed, share the essential properties of the photographic picture.[36] Theorists such as Roland Barthes and Gilles De-leuze have with good reason opposed this superficial impression.[37] Films, Deleuze says, are not moving pictures but "movement" pictures. Even Er-win Panofsky, to whom Kracauer refers to support his aesthetic realism, described film in a way that allows a fundamental difference between film and picture perception to become clear.[38] Under the rubrics "dynamiza-tion of space" and "spatialization of time," Panofsky describes cinematic perception as the experience of a virtual space that, detached from the po-sition of the viewer, is in permanent movement.[39]

Without going into the difference between photography and film in detail here,[40] the peculiarity of film can be characterized with reference to the primary material and to the primary operation of cinematic presenta-tions. The material of film is by no means individual pictures, but rather technically fixated and reproducible *movement traces*—photographically produced (or computer-generated) sequences of patterns that (can) change independently of the viewers' perspective. The fundamental operation of film can (following Panofsky) be seen to be the creation of a virtual movement space. Here there emerges a difference between events in bodily space and events in pictorial space. This is again a genuine relation that should not be assimilated to the iconic difference of the picture or to the situative difference of cyberspace. Film has in common with the picture the fact that it is a presentation that is executed on a surface in space; it has in common with cyberspace the fact that the opening up of a dynamic space is what constitutes its presentation.

Viewing a film differs both from the situation in front of a simultaneously presented picture and from the situation of an entirely simulated space. The pictorial occurrence, of which we spoke, transpires within a state of simultaneity; the cinematic occurrence, of which we now speak, unfolds as a process of succession. The difference between perceivable and presented appearing in the picture becomes here a difference between a static bodily space and a dynamic, solely visually accessible space. It generates the experience of a twofold space; the space of the film opens within the space of the movie theater. In contradistinction to cyberspace, the difference between the two spaces remains apparent: with a glance to the side we exit the virtual space of the film. Cinema up to now has kept us *in front of* its space, however much the accompanying sound installations may draw us into what is occurring on the screen. Future cyberspace funfairs, laboratories, libraries, and artworks, by contrast, will *take us into* a virtual space that reacts to each movement of our bodies with a change in its perspectives.

The picturelike phenomena I have glanced at in conclusion differ most clearly in respect to their position on the space (and time) of their beholding. The unmoved *picture* is seen in a space; it is given to us simultaneously; in many forms (of pictorial representation), it lets us see a virtual, bodily inaccessible space. In *film* we see a virtual movement space that lets us participate in the movements that are performed independently of the position of our bodies. In *cyberspace* we see *within* a virtual space that changes independently of the position (but not of the movements) of our bodies.[41]

*Statement Thirteen: Pictures cannot take the
place of the real.*

This is so because there are pictures only where a (real) pictorial ground can be distinguished from a (real or irreal) occurrence in the picture. Without the reality of the material pictorial object, there is no picture (just as there could be no films or cyberspaces without projection rooms and processors).

Because pictures are sign events (see the eighth statement), they easily awaken the impression among theorists and cultural critics that they could undercut the difference between world and sign; there is, the claim goes, a possibility or a danger that the world will be replaced by pictures. If the picture analysis so far is correct, this danger does not exist, for reasons of principle. All pictures operate with the difference between material pictorial object and material or immaterial pictorial appearance. They therefore cannot occupy the place of the world since, as pictorial objects, they always have to be anchored in the world.

If we were in fact to drown in a "flood of pictures," as many critics of our times believe, we would not drown in a flood of *pictures*. That the world has become a picture can mean at most that more and more things of the world are assuming the twofold character of the picture, a thing in the world and a thing about the world—that is, that more and more things are *also* acquiring sign character. It is only because the picture reaches into the world that it can reach far beyond it.

The perception of the difference between picture and nonpicture is a presupposition of the perception of pictures. We should note that it is not merely the *difference* between pictorial and nonpictorial objects that is a presupposition of the existence of pictures, but the ability to *perceive* this difference. Anyone not able to perceive this difference is not able to see pictures.

From this perspective, Plato's cave simile is phenomenologically correct. The cave's occupants are incapable of knowing reality precisely because they are incapable of knowing the presented shadows as pictures. The existence of pictures is thereby a proof of the existence of a world beyond pictures. Whoever can see pictures, runs the conclusion from Plato's imagery, is in principle immune to world blindness—though only in principle.

We could not understand one sentence, not to mention translate it, if there were not things there that did not comply with our sentences in all respects. We could not perceive a picture if paper and canvas were not distinguishable from everything that is presented to us on them. Not the slightest would we understand of movies if the inertia of our perceiving bodies did not carry us into the occurrences of acoustic space—and out again. Only the person who knows the way out of the movie theater's cave knows the way into the world of playing shadows. Without the difference between external occurrences and their imaginative comprehension, there would be no pictorial occurrence there. We are "in the picture" only if we believe we are not in the picture.

V

Variations on Art and Violence

I

A woman sits knitting in her living room. It is in the morning; her husband is at work, her child is at school. The television is on. There is a cooking program on, which the woman is watching with obvious pleasure. All of a sudden she glances to the large window looking onto the veranda. There, in broad daylight, she sees someone wearing a black mask, who, with the help of a poker, is trying to enter. The viewers know that it is one of the two kidnappers recruited by her husband, who has gotten himself into financial difficulties; they do not yet know that the abductors will tie up their victim, take her away in the trunk of their car, and later murder her. The woman is still staring in disbelief at what's happening behind the window. She follows it as if it were transpiring on an extended TV screen showing a highly astonishing scene. Spellbound by this appearance, she reacts by fleeing and screaming only when one of the kidnappers immediately scrambles in through one of the broken panes. An episode from late-night programming suddenly materializes in the serene world of morning programming. The performance of the two crooks may be histrionic, but it bursts the window of fiction that the woman had secured prior to their attack.

In this grotesque scene from the movie *Fargo* by Ethan and Joel Cohen (USA 1995), the basic components of a violent occurrence are all gathered together. Two culprits attack a victim, and they do so in full sight of viewers who follow the incident from a distance. Here, however, there occurs a multiple exchange of roles. The victim is first presented in the role of a viewer until she notices that *she* is in fact the one in danger. As soon as the figure realizes this, the part of the distanced observer is then left to the viewer. Subsequently, there is another exchange of roles when the woman being hunted through the house bites one of the abductors in the hand. As a result he breaks off the pursuit and quietly goes looking for ointment in the bathroom. While he is treating himself there, his fixed stare comes upon a mirror in which a movement of the shower curtain is visible; this puts him instantly back into the role of the culprit who chases his victim— who had hidden behind the curtain—until she lies unconscious at the bottom of the stairs, which she fell down in panic.

2

In many circumstances, violence is a threefold relation today. Violence is committed, violence is suffered, violence is observed. In this triangle, violence is realized conjointly with perpetrators, victims, and spectators—though in very different meanings of "realized": inflicted, painfully felt, followed from a distance. It is not infrequent that these realizations imply one another, for instance, when violent acts occur only because the actors know that there are spectators who can perceive and witness their role as actors. Such a violent triad evolves, for example, when youth gangs or warring parties perform violent acts in front of or for TV cameras in order to demonstrate their own presence, strength, or vitality to those absent (and to themselves).

Angela Keppler opens her study "*Über einige Formen der medialen Wahrnehmung von Gewalt*" (On Some Forms of the Medial Perception of Violence) with these far-reaching theses.[1] However, the triadic relation in which violent acts frequently occur is by no means tied to a medial occupation of the spectator position. Through medial presentation there emerges simply a doubling of the observer standpoint: perception through the medium (television, for instance) is subject in turn to the perception of those to whom it is addressed. The scene of violence is also determined here by the triangle of perpetrator–victim–spectator. Nonetheless, the process of violence, as Keppler makes clear, is not tied to a triadic situation. "Two are enough for violence. Violence should not therefore be *defined* through the presence of spectators, much as the social distribution and character of violence can be investigated only in consideration of the observing third party."[2] Nonetheless, even if individual violent occurrences can be limited to the model of the encounter of perpetrators and victims, the reality of violence—expressed sociologically, the *meaning* of violence— cannot be understood independently of the additional position of (shocked or enthusiastic) spectators. Even a violent act perpetrated secretly is often committed—today as well as in the past—in cognizance of the perspective of absent others.

If this is the case, artworks that thematize violence, or are themselves in a certain sense violent, are in remarkable proximity to what they make present from a safe distance. They too make a violent occurrence available for viewing to an audience. Violence in art is always an event in front of and for addressees (who are not of course beholders in every case; the position of the "spectator" of violent events can be adopted by listeners and readers too). Violence presented by artworks or done through artworks opens up for its part a triadic situation of the kind just sketched—and thereby represents a *variation* (though an incisive one) of the relation of the actual exercise of violence.

Irrespective of which of these situations we are thinking, the positions of those involved in a violent occurrence—involved actively or passively, in close proximity or from a distance—can change multiply. As every fistfight in a Western shows, the supposed victim can become the culprit and the alleged culprit the victim. Or the two positions can fade into each other to such a degree that they are occupied by both parties at the same time. Similarly, culprits can become spectators or, *as* culprits, be spectators (as is the case in many situations of torture). Conversely, spectators can become culprits or, *as* spectators, be culprits (commencing with the applause with which a violent act is greeted). Finally, spectators can also become victims of a violent act or, *as* spectators, be victims of a violent presentation. The scene sketched from *Fargo* plays through some but by no means all of these position changes. In the extreme case, arrangements are conceivable in which a person involved adopts all of the basic positions simultaneously: those of the culprit, the victim, and the spectator. The best known example for this is probably the situation depicted in Kafka's short story "In the Penal Colony." In front of the traveler, who is visiting the penal colony, the officer, who is supposed to supervise the torture of a person using a machine he constructed, metamorphoses into a delinquent who carries out his own execution with the help of this device.

It is also characteristic of violent acts that in their course execution and presentation frequently intermingle—be it where violence is actually *committed* and at the same time presented to a public; be it where it is artistically *imagined* with more or less shocking effects for the unaffected affected observers; finally, be it where an artistic presentation, which is itself not a presentation of violent occurrences, appears violent. Without doubt, these are very different cases: we have to see what they have in common to be able to see clearly what keeps them apart.

3

In the scene from *Fargo* described at the outset, the beginning of a violent act unfolds as the intrusion of the real into a world of semblance. What first seems to the woman character sitting in front of the television like an episode from a TV program proves suddenly to be a very real occurrence impinging directly upon her. The desperate and equally futile attempts of her husband, a dishonest car dealer, to get out of his misery describe murderous circles into which the involved and uninvolved are drawn. Violence surfaces as an indicator of a hard reality that cruelly asserts itself. "Now it's getting serious"—the emergence of violence signals a breach with the usual course of life.

A relationship between violence and reality is in the nature of things. Violence and sexuality are the two serious cases of bodily human encounter. Interaction occurs here not as a gestural or verbal drawing close that is occasionally *accompanied* by contacts; it occurs *as* contact. It happens as a massive or tender, one-sided or reciprocal grasp of the other's body. Those involved do something to one another in a good or a bad sense. Inherent in even voluntary sexual exchange there is always the element of avoiding a violent interchange. Violence does not occur when the other person does not suffer something that he or she could experience as a violation of his or her body or personal integrity. Violence occurs when one person inflicts bodily injuries on another, be it to subject him or her to one's will or to take pleasure in his or her pain, or both.

This violence unfolds as the infliction of bodily injuries with the purpose of tormenting or subjugating the victim. Violence understood thus is physical violence. Unlike the standard surgical operation or the regulated sport of boxing, the aim of violent inflictions is to make the victim of this treatment *suffer* against his or her will, be it as a means to an end or to take pleasure in one's superiority.

Those who commit violence are concerned with breaking the resistance of the world on the body of the other. Violence is a form of human interaction in which there is no more room left for negotiating common conduct, for coming to mutual agreement. Those who suffer violence experience it as an irrevocable occurrence. The reality that is held simply at a distance in normal conduct impinges upon the body of the victim. There is no escape. The scope of reality contracts to the point of one's own tormented body. This can be called the particular facticity of the violent occurrence. The victim is caught by a powerful movement that shows no consideration for the limits of the body.

Beholders of artistic works are safe from such ordeals. They might be surprised or shocked, but nothing happens to them. Real violence does not befall them. However, it is not without reason that what art is getting at in its works is frequently described as a touching. Being touched or stirred or overwhelmed, being captivated or carried away is a justified expectation concerning the perception of works of art. But these are all metaphors from the domain of bodily distress, which is not really supposed to happen if aesthetic perception is to remain possible. The viewer or the listener is caught by a powerful movement that shows *a* consideration for the vulnerability of his or her body.

In this particular nonviolence of the artwork lies its affinity to violence. It wants to touch without physical violence, but at the same time unfold a reality that is as distinct from the normality of existence as other borderline cases of life. *One* of the forms in which artworks attempt this is the representation of violence. Another is the representation of sexuality, and yet another is the exposure of the materiality of the artistic object; art knows aphrodisiacs other than the presentation of violence. It does not have to turn to the representation of violence in order to let the public feel the power of its constructions. The representation of violence is just one *among various* means with which art touches people. The work of art wants to touch the beholder not with real violence, nor with the apparency of such violence, but with *its* reality, the reality of the artwork. It lures the perceivers into a play of appearances that seizes and touches them without their being literally struck.

4

From the beginning I was trying to see if I could make art that did that. Art that was just there all at once. Like getting hit in the face with a baseball bat. Or better, like getting hit in the back of the neck. You never see it coming; it just knocks you down.[3]

This statement of Bruce Nauman's is probably the most brutally formulated metaphor for the violence of art. However, it cannot and does not want to obscure the fact that the violence of art differs categorically from all real violence aimed at physical and mental injury. Art might reach the "pain threshold" of its addressees with its pictures, sounds, or movements, but it always gives them the possibility of avoiding this excessive prospect. It offers them scope for being able to react autonomously, whereas real violence aims to restrict or destroy precisely this freedom.

Art *guarantees* this freedom—for all the excessive demands and seduction, agitation and captivation, irritation and disruption that it generates on the side of its addressees. Measured in terms of a strict and literal concept, it is always a *metaphorical* violence with which art attempts to overwhelm its recipient. With just slight exaggeration it can be said that, in this meaning, a moment of violence is inherent in all art.[4] Its works aim at an animation that takes beholders for a short time out of the certainties and self-evident truths of bodily and mental orientation and thereby brings about a welcome disturbance of their perception and understanding. In this sense, but only in this sense, every aesthetics of art is an aesthetics of violence: an interpretation of the power with which its works create a reality on which its addressees' life reality breaks.

This performative force of artworks can unfold independently of any representation of violent events. The metaphorical violence of artworks has, however, a special meaning precisely when it makes violent occurrences the *content* of its presentations. The presentation of violence lives here off the violence of the artistic presentation. It is only in terms of this relation that the potential of artistically treating the phenomenon of violence can be understood. Only because art possesses a special *power of presentation* can it reveal *what is violent about violence* as no other medium can.

The internal connection between execution and presentation, which is generally characteristic of relations of violence, finds a particular realization in art. Today and in the past, but today to a far greater degree, art that thematizes violence is confronted on the one hand with real violent incidents as they occur in full view of the public, and on the other with the representation of these incidents in contexts of information and infotainment. In one case, the representation of violence is tied directly to the violent act; in the other, it refers to (supposedly or actually) real violent acts at another location. Making violence artistically present, by contrast, entangles beholders in an *imagination* of violence at *their* location. At a location where real violence is absent, making violence artistically present gives expression to a reality of violence by binding perceivers to the process of its *presentation.*

5

In the scene from *Fargo* this comes about in such a way that the difference between the medial and the real scene is placed once again into the film. The violence represented occurs as an incursion of reality upon a seeming world of domestic and familial peace, from the perspective of which the prelude of the real violent act appears like a purely fictional presentation. As an indication of *reality*, however, this violence can come to appearance only because the director has allocated it the status of a *formal* indicator. There occurs a sudden acceleration of events, which is accompanied by a crescendo of sounds: the conversational tone of the TV program shifts into the noise of breaking glass and the screaming of the victim. Things are getting serious for the figures represented, but things are also getting serious for the representation of these figures.

Here lies a basic law of all artistic treatment of violence. The evocation of a human borderline case represents at the same time an aesthetic borderline case. If art wants to make of *violence* an event, it has to make of *itself* an event. If it wants to show an outburst of violence, it has to permit a climaxing of its means. To show (literal) violence, art has to trust its (metaphorical) violence.

This interconnection exists entirely independently of the type and execution of the particular violence motif. Whether it be the narrative of the violent return of Ulysses to Ithaca in Homer's epic; or Giotto's representation of those condemned in *The Last Judgment* in the Scrovegni Chapel; be it the terrifying *Martyrdom of Becket*, which Master Francke painted circa 1425 as part of *The Altarpiece of St. Thomas a Becket* for the

English Trading Company (Kunsthalle, Hamburg, Germany); or Caravaggio's painting of *Judith Beheading Holofernes* (Galleria Nazionale d'Arte Antica, Rome); or the obsessive sketching and painting of dead, decapitated, and dismembered bodies by Géricault; whether we think of the consequences of violence in Shakespeare's royal plays or of the soberly brutal battle painting in Flaubert's novel *Salammbô*; whether it is stories of the victorious, just violence in the classic Western or those of the defeated, unjust violence in Mafia and police movies—scenic escalation is always accompanied by aesthetic escalation. Precisely in the comic treatment of violence in movies such as *Pulp Fiction* by Quentin Tarantino (USA 1994) or also *Fargo*, incredible contrasts are made that signal in their own way the incursion of violence. The fissure constituted by physical violence appears as a fissure of artistic form. The power of represented violence lives off the power of the representation of this violence. Whether it wants to or not, art plays its game with the violence it shows.

6

This game can be played in quite different ways. Let us stay with film for the moment. In connection with Keppler's study, we can distinguish entirely different functions played by the representation of violence in movies of recent times. Ornamental or *choreographic* violence, which serves largely as a suspense element in action movies without the violent event itself being given its own significance, differs from the staging of *contingent* violent incidents in which fistfights and shootings are presented as much as possible as *real* occurrences. In the James Bond movies and related ones (such as *True Lies* by James Cameron [USA 1994]), but also in an elegiac late Western such as *Last Man Standing* by Walter Hill (USA 1996), violent occurrences remain to a certain extent irreal; they are an important stimulus for the continuity of the plot, in shaping the rhythm and, it could be said, in performing the visual music of these movies. By contrast, in films that show violence as an expression of social or individual pathologies—for instance, *Falling Down* by Joel Schumacher (USA 1993), *Natural Born Killers* by Oliver Stone (USA 1991), or also *The Silence of the Lambs* by Jonathan Demme (USA 1991)—the process of violence and the threat of violence are presented in their real horror; they are presented to the viewer *in their seriousness*.

Here, the element of an *hallucinatory* representation of violence is frequently added—as in Stone and Demme, and especially in *Lost High-way* by David Lynch (USA 1996). In this case, violence appears irreal in the other direction, as it were: not by screening out its horror but in forming visions of violence that, beyond the imagination of real horror, can terrify even hardboiled viewers. What is represented here is not really violence but a violent *phantasm* that holds individuals or societies spellbound.

Older cinema also knew *heroic* violence in which an idealized individual or a group persists against all possible perils; the violent act and its effects are embedded here in the myth of the virtually omnipotent hero. The violence committed does indeed appear as real, but it remains ultimately an episode within a narrative about the reestablishment of nonviolent social conditions. As a dramaturgical model, this treatment of violence still survives in action movies today, though in a highly disillusioned form, as it is represented by the *Die Hard* films, for instance (*Die Hard,* John McTiernan [USA 1988]; *Die Hard 2: Die Harder,* Renny Harlin [USA 1990]; *Die Hard: With a Vengeance,* John McTiernan [USA 1995]). Bruce Willis, the leading actor in these movies, is the exemplary disheveled hero of our times.

Cinema's fictions of violence can therefore be presented predominantly as *irreal* events, mainly as *real* incidents, or largely as the *transgression* of all real horror. The dividing lines often remain blurred, though. They do so particularly where a movie does not operate within the ambit of a given schema but makes an art of making experienceable the irregular reality of a violent occurrence. This art consists above all in thwarting habitual, prevalent, hackneyed, and thus harmless representations of violence. Only where the schematized pictures of violence have been roughened up, where their gloss has been scratched, where artists have broken with their recognizability, where the unequivocalness of their treatment has been abandoned can the incursion of violence be represented.

7

This equivocalness in the representation of violence is a sign not only of a notable cinematic treatment. For instance, driven not least by competition from film, modern visual art has desisted more decisively than other arts from the heroic representation of violence, up to the point of largely forgoing the presentation of scenes and acts of violence. Instead, the nameless horror of the twentieth century has been frequently made the object of the pictorial visualization of a violence incomprehensible in its causes and effects. An extreme example are those *Black Paintings* by Frank Stella, executed between 1958 and 1960, which refer in the title to the horrors of the Third Reich without in any way being a rendering of what happened.[5] Gerhard Richter's picture series *18. Oktober 1977* (1988, Museum für Moderne Kunst, Frankfurt am Main, Germany), which is gray and black, shows the dead founders of the Red Army Faction in an atmosphere of distress and disorientation, desperation and sorrow, without any attempt at further commentary. The series draws the distinctness of the police photos, according to which the pictures were made, back into the indistinctness of an historical event that has neither been understood nor coped with. Bruce Nauman's *Concrete Tape Recorder Piece* (1968, Neue Galerie, Kassel, Germany) consists of a tape recorder encased in a concrete block; it contains a continuous recording of human screams, which would necessarily remain inaudible at any imaginable volume of playback. His installation *Musical Chair* from 1983 (Froehlich Collection, Galerie der Gegenwart, Hamburg, Germany) is a sharp-edged, cross-shaped steel mobile mounted at the beholder's eye level; set in motion it collides with a steel chair also suspended from the ceiling and generates a hard, penetrating tone. The creation awakens recollections of torture scenes, evinces traces and vibrations of a lurking violence, is a reminder of power instruments that can be thrust through the body of victims, is the hallucination of an ever-present threat—and yet remains a free-floating ensemble that steers the horrors it makes public into the peacefulness of its restrained movement.

8

Constellations of this kind prevail also in the literature of the twentieth century. Since Dashiell Hammett's novel *The Glass Key* (published in 1931), the American crime novel's lonely heroes, shorn of a heroic mission, have to survive beatings that can be called simply ornamental in their compositional function. Since the war novels that succeeded the First World War, heroic violence is still possible in literature in a refracted form at the most. What prevails is the representation of violent incidents that, even when they are the result of intentional terror, are presented as an ultimately contingent, meaningless occurrence—as in such novels as *The Quiet*

American, by Graham Greene; *Die Ästhetik des Widerstands* (The Aesthetics of Resistance), by Peter Weiss; or *Death in the Andes*, by Mario Vargas Llosa. The representation of violence in modern literature too often fades into hallucinatory writing. A glaring example of this is the novel *Blood Meridian, or, The Evening Redness in the West*, by Cormac McCarthy, first published in 1985. The novel is about the campaigns of marauding gangs of headhunters in the American West in the middle of the nineteenth century. In alternation with detailed and intensive images of the countryside, there are recurrent descriptions of cruel fighting. In their first appearance in the novel, the "savages" attack a party of bandits:

Now driving a wild frieze of headlong horses with eyes walled and teeth cropped and naked riders with clusters of arrows clenched in their jaws and their shields winking in the dust and up the far side of the ruined ranks in a piping of bone-flutes and dropping down off the sides of their mounts with one heel hung in the withers strap and their short bows flexing beneath the outstretched necks of the ponies until they had circled the company and cut their ranks in two and then rising up again like funhouse figures, some with nightmare faces painted on their breasts, riding down the unhorsed Saxons and spearing and clubbing them and leaping from their mounts with knives and running about on the ground with a peculiar bandylegged trot like creatures driven to alien forms of locomotion and stripping the clothes from the dead and seizing them up by the hair and passing their blades about the skulls of the living and the dead alike and snatching aloft the bloody wigs and hacking and chopping at the naked bodies, ripping off limbs, heads, gutting the strange white torsos and holding up great handfuls of viscera, genitals, some of the savages so slathered up with gore they might have rolled in it like dogs and some who fell upon the dying and sodomized them with loud cries to their fellows. And now the horses of the dead came pounding out of the smoke and dust and circled with flapping leather and wild manes and eyes whited with fear like the eyes of the blind and some were feathered with arrows and some lanced through and stumbling and vomiting blood as they wheeled across the killing ground and clattered from sight again.[6]

This is not heroic violence that is taking place here, nor is it terrorist violence following some strategic plan, nor is it satanic violence observing a hedonistic strategy. It is the outbreak of blind violence that stops at nothing, that takes hold of everything, people and animals, victims and culprits. McCarthy imagines a naked violence that knows no civilizatory restrictions. He describes the bloodiest seriousness. Where, however, an unbridled violence is to be described in its terrifying course, it has to be sketched with great meticulousness. A word-by-word precision is set in motion, one that goes way beyond the presentation of the mere factual. Thus, McCarthy's description intensifies into the acoustic picture of the horses thundering in panic across a blood-soaked battlefield with the whited eyes of the blind.

Dust stanched the wet and naked heads of the scalped who with the fringe of hair below their wounds and tonsured to the bone now lay like maimed and naked monks in the bloodslaked dust and everywhere the dying groaned and gibbered and horses lay screaming.

This is how the description of the massacre ends. The extreme violence has to become extreme language so that it can be presented as extreme violence.

The representation of violence here is not only a means for building suspense, but it is that too; it is not only the testimony of a possible real event, but it is that too; it is not only the imaginative projection of a drama of cruelty that surpasses everything, but it is that too; it is not only the representation of an excessive reality but is also the excessive representation of a reality. Violence functions in this passage not only as an elixir of reality, but also as a drug of appearance; the incident described is imagined with all the writer's power *as real*, but it is at the same time *imagined* with all his power.

9

The two severed heads lay on a crumpled, gray-white, bloodied cloth. Cushions placed under the sheets supported the heads. If the raw cuts on the throats, if the watery congealed blood had not been visible, one could have gotten the impression of a couple surprised by death lying beside each other in bed. . . . The woman's face was turned to the man. Her mouth was slightly open, a speckle of the white of the eye glistened between the shadowy eyelids. Strangely naked, the ear protruded from the hair that had been cut short for the guillotine. The man's face, having the beginnings of a beard around the hollow cheeks, was still imprinted with horror. The deeply sunken eyes were open, the mouth was also wide-open, the gaping lips, the teeth, the tongue seemed to be still bearing the final scream. They must have had to drag him to the guillotine, the woman had already given up beforehand. It would have been inappropriate to equate the expired expression on her face with peace, for how could it have been possible to connect the idea of peace with her existence, even after the advent of the ultimate peace. And yet her features, palely lit on temples, cheekbone, nose, and chin, contained something soft; her head lay there like an overripe piece of fruit fallen from a tree. The man had been torn out of his existence. The chin muscle, the sharply protruding nose, and the dented contours of his bald head still expressed a charge of energy. While the woman was completely disempowered, he defended himself violently as long as there was a breath in him.[7]

On first reading this passage, it appears almost obscene to employ such attention to detail and interpretive pleasure in describing the heads of two decapitated human beings. It is therefore a relief for the reader to discover that this passage is the description of a painting. In the second part of *Die Ästhetik des Widerstands*, Peter Weiss describes Théodore Géricault's painting *Têtes des Suppliciés* (Heads Severed, 1818, Nationalmuseum, Stockholm, Sweden)—or rather he describes the impression that the painting in a side room of Stockholm's Nationalmuseum makes on the novel's young protagonist. This scene with a painting description makes preparations, in terms of motif, for the detailed depiction of the execution of a group of resistance fighters in the third part of the novel. The description of the painting commences without preparation at the start of a new paragraph. "The picture was painted in black and white and a small supplement of brownish and reddish tones," runs the text already after the third sentence, so that readers know relatively early where they stand. But as soon as they have reassured themselves that "it is just a picture" that is being subjected here to an extremely intensive viewing, the precarious relation this *picture* has to its object immediately forces itself upon the readers. For here we are in fact concerned with the highly poignant visualization of a cruel incident. The picture uses its whole artistic ambition to make visible and sensible a state that is the outcome of a very real occurrence, the guillotining of two people. It is precisely this art to which the description of the writer, Peter Weiss, bears eloquent witness. "A speckle of the white of the eye glistened between the shadowy eyelids"—this is how things are when an artist makes violence between people his subject matter. Between the horrors he lets flare up, there shines the paint with which he banishes them.

10

Observations of this kind have led Karl Heinz Bohrer to speak of violence and aesthetics as being in a "relation of mutual determination."[8]

While referring to works such as Delacroix's *Death of Sardanapalus*, Flaubert's *Salammbô*, and Francis Bacon's paintings, Bohrer defends the thesis that in order to track down the meaning of artistic representations of violence it is necessary to evade the question of a substantive meaning in these representations. He cites a sentence of Bacon's from an interview with David Sylvester: " . . . I want very, very much to do the thing that Valéry said—to give the sensation without the boredom of its conveyance."[9] There it is again: the longing for the most direct artistic contact possible. The artist makes violence into an appearance because he or she wants to make appearances forcefully.

The correct observation that there is a genuine artistic interest in (the representation of) violent occurrences should not lead to the conclusion that what is important here is solely an intensification of the metaphorical violence of artistic representation. Artists such as Nauman and Bacon, Delacroix and Flaubert, McCarthy and Weiss are also interested in the phenomenon of violence itself. Otherwise violence would be able to acquire merely an ornamental status in their works. Whatever the effect of the representation of violence is in each case—be it as sheer animation, as an indictment of predominant conditions and powers, as a revelation of human abyss, or as a disinterested visualization of physical and mental processes—the fascination of the violence shown always emanates from a fascination in showing it; in this respect Bohrer is right. But this fascination often applies also to imaging a *reality* of what is shown. Art brings violence to perception in a manner in which it cannot or must not be perceived in other contexts. Precisely because it transfers real violence into the play of its appearances, art—unlike any discourse, report, or statistics—can articulate the infliction that lies in the suffering or also the perpetration of violent acts. Art's intuition can linger in the eye of violence as no involved or uninvolved person can.

The artistic necessity of treating the human case of committing violence as an artistic case does not justify the generalization "that art and the *theme* of violence determine each other,"[10] since the metaphorical violence of art can after all be executed without any representation of violence. The general affinity of art and violence is a matter of its artistic *execution*, which shakes in various ways the certainties of the bodily or bodily based disposition. In this formal affinity lies the reason also for the special *substantive* reference of art to violence. The metaphorical violence of artistic presentation, which is as such not tied to the theme of violence, opens up at the same time the possibility of a heightened *presentation* of violence—a presentation, however, that does not have any affinity to the literal *committing* of violence. By virtue of its distance, art comes close to the occurrence of violence in a way in which it would be neither possible nor bearable to do in the real perpetration of violence.

II

Part of the basic relation of violence is not only perpetrating and suffering violence but also viewing it. This relation is present in every representation of violence. The occurrence or the outcome of an act is presented, which allows a distinction between victims and perpetrators, no matter how much these positions change, interchange, and even blur. Like many incidents of staged or documented real violence, art's imagination also releases a violent incident for viewing by an audience. How art does this, how it lets violence be perceived—*in contrast to* all the other kinds of direct and indirect appearance of violence—is what decides the relationship between art and violence. What is special about the artistic treatment of violence can be understood only in reference to the phenomenon of violence itself. What makes the treatment of violence artistically so incisive cannot be separated from the fact that it is anthropologically so incisive.

After all, real violence can move and touch, repel or attract its observers. Quite a few forms of violence have always been committed in front of and for the pleasure of spectators—be it in front of prisoners to force them to confess, in front of opponents to demonstrate one's own strength, in front of the medial public to give it a message, or in front of an audience that wants to take delight in acts of violence. Many spectators of violent *acts*, which are as such also *presentations* of violent acts, are not sufficiently impressed or moved by the mere presentation of violence; it has to be real violence, real pain, real infliction with which they want to be served for this or that reason.

This interest on the part of spectators is by no means perverse from the outset. Watching a war report on television, the viewer would like to be put in the picture not about posed but about real acts of war. The interest of the viewer is in a representation of real violence. However, it is not as such tied to an interest *in violence*; it can apply solely to its *represen-*

tation. We just want to be informed about what is going on in the world. The perception of the viewers is guided by an interest in violence *itself* as soon as it includes the *affirmation* of certain forms of *perpetrating* violence. Then, to a certain extent, the observer of violent acts adopts the attitude of those who inflict violence on others. They become accomplices of a (single or collective) culprit who shows off his or her acts by carrying them out. The perpetrators of such violence and their affirmative spectators have a common goal: the resistance of the *world* is to be broken in one way or another, not just the resistance of a received *representation* of the world.

12

Here lies a categorical difference of the representation of violence in the context of art. From terrorist attack to violent pornography—but also in some "official" military campaigns—violence is *perpetrated* so as to be shown. In art, by contrast, violence is *shown* not in order to be perpetrated but to be able *to be shown.*

This showing differs fundamentally from presentation in news footage, which frames the violent event in text and film editing and pushes it one way or another into the background. It also differs fundamentally from the presentations of reality TV, which presents or re-creates violent incidents in an intentionally artless picture language intimating "realness," thereby transporting them into the surveyable order of standardized narratives that tell of risky police raids or heroic rescuers.[11] When artworks integrate this schema of medial reporting into their operation, as happens not infrequently today, then there is always a break with these conventions; they are needed to show the showing of violence in society. Thus, in *Natural Born Killers* Oliver Stone has tried (albeit with dubious success) to enact the "violence in the heads" of his violent heroes using the stylistic means of an overstrung TV picture language. In procedures such as this one, it is a matter of getting a new view of the horrors of the perpetration and results of violence—new in comparison to the established pictures of violence that have become routine for filmmakers and audiences. Here too it is a question of transferring literal violence over to a merely metaphorically violent imagination.

Even so, the artistic primacy of presentation does not apply absolutely. It would be incorrect to say that in general violence is shown in art *just* for the sake of showing it. There are works of art that want to prompt *resistance* to violence (*Die Ästhetik des Widerstands* is certainly one of them); they show violence so that it will *not* be committed. However, not all representations of violence in art have this moral motive. Cormac McCarthy does not appeal to nonviolence; he shows a violence disconnected from civilizatory restraint; that's all. By contrast, older art knew very well the more or less unrefracted representation of heroic violence—a violence in alliance with the powers of truth and religious belief. Yet, it probably holds for art since the First World War that an affirmative representation of violence no longer plays a part. This is the case not so much for moral or political reasons but above all for aesthetic ones. A modern representation that is free of traditional stylization takes from the represented violence the gusto and aura that enable an affirmative image of its perpetration. Modern art reveals the monstrosity of the manifestation of violence. The object of its creations is not a glorified, eroticized, and in this sense fictitious violence, but real violence.

It is precisely real violence that is frequently committed in order to be shown—and this violence is realer than all the violence presented *as* real in art! Realer it certainly is; in demonstrative acts of violence, nonetheless, real violence is by no means presented *in* its reality for all those involved. The self-presentation of literal acts of violence relates not only to the *results* but above all to the *potential* of this violence. What it has done and what it can still do are what is demonstrated. For this demonstration to be successful, however, the *occurrence* of violence, which is physically and mentally risky for all involved, must not be presented openly. Where violence is supposed to horrify, the horror of committing violence must be excluded. In particular, war propaganda that wishes to have some prospect of effect must not look into the center of a violent situation. It must not show, and it will not show, what it means to be exposed to violence as a victim or as a culprit. It might present the insignia of power and means of violence; it might dress their acts in the mythology of a sports competition, but it will pass over the process of violence itself. The promotion of violence can work with *indirect* means at the most, for instance, by presenting the supposed or actual cruelty of the *opponent* to be fought. It is also frequently the case that to support acts of war a social condition is projected that is to be constructed or reconstructed by acts of violence. The promotion of violence is then presented as the promotion of the cessation of violence. The naked presentation of violence remains a taboo wherever the willingness to commit it is to be demonstrated, roused, or strengthened.

Presentation in various arts operates against this instrumentalization by showing violence in a way peculiar to the arts. Unlike actually perpetrated violence, unlike violence in the news, and unlike the mere play with violence without any intention to represent (as in many computer games and some action movies), all representation of violence in art is set on this showing. It emanates from it and always returns to it. It frequently includes a reflective thematization of inner-artistic and extra-artistic *presentations* of violence. It always claims distance to the relations whose presence it imagines. Art wants to touch not with violence but through the *appearance* of violence; it wants to make violence experienceable without experiencing violence; it does not want to commit violence; it wants to remind us of the violence that, though not operative, is nonetheless lurking in all human relations.

There is indeed an element of coercion here. Art forces the beholder, the reader, and the listener to encounter possibilities of violent human encounter. Even so, the source of this coercion is a particular pleasure—pleasure in the fact that what is otherwise a cycle of violence becomes a play of appearances. Art, whether it wants to or not, plays its game with the violence it shows; it creates latitude for perception where violence robs its victims of all latitude.

13

A violent relation can exist even in creating such latitude. Up to now we have been observing largely the beholder and what he or she is burdened with in terms of metaphorical, real, and imagined violence. But the artist is also part of the game in which metaphorical violence is generated and occasionally literal violence is presented. He or she is also subjected to a particular violence, the one present in becoming involved in artistic processes. Thus, not a few artworks are signs of an exhaustion, and even destruction, of energies to which they owe their own genesis.

A video sculpture by Bruce Nauman from 1996 bears the laconic title *Work* (Froehlich Collection, Galerie der Gegenwart, Hamburg, Germany). The artist's face can be seen in vertical movement on two monitors, one placed on top of the other. The head, which faces the viewer, jumps into the picture, only then to drop out of it immediately. The top monitor shows it in an upright pose; the bottom one, on the other hand, shows it in an inverted, upside-down position. The expression on the face, which is without makeup, is marked by the effort of constantly jumping into the installed camera's field of view (or of letting itself fall to that point, as the inverted picture suggests). The video recordings could have been shot in a fitness studio or during a military or paramilitary training program; in any case, the face is marked by a bodily activity that is unrelenting, tiring, and perhaps even coerced. By virtue of the mirror-image montage of the video pictures, the head continually disappears for a moment, only to immediately pop up or down once again. The moment the face appears on one of the screens, the lips form the word "work," always with the same intonation; its staccato repetition constitutes the acoustic dimension of this work and gives it the character of an acoustic sculpture.

This word is spoken in a loud, hard, commanding tone. But it is only for an instant that it can be actually understood; the two picture sequences and their two soundtracks are arranged in a marginally desynchronized rhythm. Within a time frame of about one minute, the two heads appear just once in symmetrical motion. Correspondingly, the ceaselessly uttered word acoustics can be heard in unison—and thus clearly—only for a fraction of a second. Immediately, the visual and acoustic harmony shifts again in favor of an increasingly—and soon again decreasingly—asynchronous appearing. This produces the effect of a tense, cascading, well-nigh-chaotic act that reaches a relaxed state for only fleeting moments.

One could be tempted to see here the allegory of a work society that forces, without interruption or end, the bodies of the people organized in it to be unconditionally available for labor. But this is not entirely plausible for the simple reason that Taylorized labor is in dramatic decline. It would perhaps be more credible to see in Nauman's little video shrine another self-declarative art object that enacts effectively the paradoxes of its status as art. It could be said that, following this line of argument, footage seeming to come from a surveillance camera is arranged here into the choreography of a minimalist ballet; a conflict unfolds between the weightlessness of the video pictures and the weight of the movement they show; an object announces its artwork status with a crackling voice in the halls of a museum, thereby undermining all the certainties of its position.

But this too is off the mark because the figure visible on the monitors addresses and satisfies the ceaseless demand directed primarily at itself. It utters the unchanging commands, and it follows them in uninterrupted practice. It is the artist himself who, in this situation, lays himself open in full view of his viewers. The sculpture exhibits the vulnerability of an artist who devotes himself body and soul to the creation of works that, for their part, aim at a direct somatic reaction on the part of the addressees. Yet through the artwork the artist remains at the same time shielded from the beholders, to whom he lays himself open in word and picture. The video image produces an incorporeal picture of corporeal exertion, on the one hand through the picture detail that shows only the face, and on the other through the artificially arranged reproduction on a continuous videotape, which is evidently neither the presentation of a currently occurring action nor the recording of an excessively long one. The sound-and-picture constellation of this sculpture thus proves to be the *staging* of unconditional artistic labor, but in the concrete *instance* of art, which Nauman stands up for with his own face.

Unlike the sweeping installation *Anthro-Socio*, which is indeed baroque in comparison to *Work* and which also operates with contrasts between harassed corporeality and technical artificiality but without bringing the person of the artist into play, *Work* has an almost intimate character. It has such a nature despite its formal stringency, obsessive rhythm, and aggressive rhetoric. As in Kafka's short story or with the dictators horrified by themselves whom Francis Bacon painted, one figure here occupies all the positions visualized in the triangle of violence. The body that the face marked by effort represents in the monitors is at the same time subject and object of the torture inflicted on it; the face that we see, however, is the mask of the artist himself. The beholder looks into the eye of a passionate *beholder* who was the first addressee also of *this* object created for seeing and hearing. In this constellation, *Work* is a study on the position of the artist who, in full view of an avid audience, consumes himself in an effort to create something lasting that goes beyond his own effort.

Much as he is whittled down by this effort, it nonetheless leads occasionally to moments in which something fits together, in which something succeeds, in which the tension eases. At the same time, however, these moments are the poison that drives the artist to further exertions of energy, just to arrive yet again at a state of lucky artistic coincidence. This pulse of losing and finding oneself determines all of his reactions; the search for the work becomes the imperative of a life that is under the compulsion of a vivid objectification of its own reactions. *Work* is a hallmark of the dissonance of art and life in which one inflicts violence on the other without one being able to yield to the other. The two monitors on top of each other lay a loud trail of quiet violence that all those inflict on themselves who care in their lives about the life of their works.

REFERENCE MATTER

Notes

CHAPTER ONE

1. Alexander Gottlieb Baumgarten, *Theoretische Ästhetik*, trans. and ed. Hans Rudolf Schweizer (Hamburg: Meiner, 1983).

2. The idea of this complementarity in Baumgarten is analyzed by Brigitte Scheer, *Einführung in die philosophische Ästhetik* (Darmstadt: Wissenschaftliche Buchgesellschaft, 1997); the spirit of her argument is shared by Gottfried Gariel, *Zwischen Logik und Literatur. Erkenntnisformen von Dichtung, Philosophie und Wissenschaft* (Stuttgart: Metzler, 1991).

3. Immanuel Kant, *Critique of Judgment*, trans. Werner S. Pluhar (Indianapolis: Hackett, 1987), § 12, p. 68.

4. Ibid., §§ 9, 14, pp. 62, 71–72.

5. Kant's frequently misunderstood insistence on the "purity" of aesthetic judgment at the start of his theory has precisely this methodological point: to secure first the basic phenomenon of aesthetic intuition in order then to be able to analyze the special phenomena of the aesthetic. There is no purist aesthetic norm whatsoever associated with this.

6. Georg Wilhelm Friedrich Hegel, *Hegel's Introduction to Aesthetics*, trans. T. M. Knox, intro. Charles Karelis (Oxford: Oxford University Press, 1979), p. 19.

7. Philosophers from Schelling to Adorno have tried repeatedly to reverse this order of precedence. Such reversals, however, merely reproduce the compulsion to establish an order of *precedence* where only a *constellation* of forms of world interpretation can prevail.

8. From the revelation of the absolute to the self-contemplation of cultural worlds, this is the course taken by the history of art (and of our dealings with art) in Hegel. The best interpretation of Hegel's diagnosis of the times is still Dieter Henrich, "Kunst und Kunstphilosophie der Gegenwart," in *Immanente Ästhetik und ästhetische Reflexion*, ed. Wolfgang Iser (Munich: Fink, 1966), pp. 11–32.

9. Arthur Schopenhauer, *The World as Will and Representation*, vol. 1, trans. E.F.J. Payne (New York: Dover, 1969), p. 179 (italics in original).

10. Ibid., p. 195.

11. Ibid., p. 197.

12. I have formulated a more detailed critique of Schopenhauer in Martin Seel, *Eine Ästhetik der Natur* (Frankfurt am Main: Suhrkamp, 1991).

13. Friedrich Nietzsche, *The Birth of Tragedy out of the Spirit of Music*, trans. Shaun Whiteside, ed. Michael Tanner (Harmondsworth: Penguin, 1993, p. 16.

14. On this interpretation, see Karl Heinz Bohrer, "Aesthetics and Historicism: Nietzsche's Concept of 'Appearance,'" in *Suddenness: On the Moment of Aesthetic Appearance*, trans. Ruth Crowley (New York: Columbia University Press, 1994), pp. 113–47; and Seel, "Die Macht des Erscheinens: Nietzsches ästhetische Marginalisierung des Seins," *du*, 1998, *6*, 26–28.

15. Chapter Three of this study is concerned with this topic.

16. By contrast, the discovery of appearing in early Nietzsche remains ambiguous insofar as it tends—under Schopenhauer's influence—to interpret the recourse to appearing as a participation in the chaotic essence of things.

17. Paul Valéry, *Eupalinos, or The Architect*, in *Dialogues: The Collected Works of Paul Valéry*, vol. 4, trans. William McCausland Stewart (Princeton: Princeton University Press, 1977), pp. 65–150, at p. 80. (Quotations from the original are taken from Valéry, *Eupalinos; ou l'architecte, précédé de l'âme et la danse* [Paris: Gallimard, 1924], here p. 101.)

18. Ibid., p. 76.

19. Ibid., p. 92.

20. "Why did you never experience this when present at some religious festival, or when taking part in some banquet, while the instruments filled the hall with sounds and phantoms [*et que l'orchestre emplissait la salle de sons et de fantômes*]?" p. 94 (French edition, p. 125).

21. Ibid., p. 95. ("*Cet édifice d'apparitions, de transitions, de conflits et d'événements indéfinissables,*" French edition, p. 126.)

22. Ibid., p. 147.

23. Ibid., p. 97.

24. This is also Hans Blumenberg's position in his classic interpretation of "Eupalinos," "Sokrates und das 'objet ambigu': Paul Valérys Auseinandersetzung mit der Tradition der Ontologie des ästhetischen Gegenstandes," in *Epimeleia: Die Sorge der Philosophie um den Menschen*, ed. Franz Wiedmann (Munich: Pustet, 1964), pp. 285–323.

25. Valéry, *Eupalinos, or The Architect*, p. 96.

26. Martin Heidegger, "The Origin of the Work of Art," in *Poetry, Language, Thought*, trans. Albert Hofstadter (New York: Harper & Row, 1971), pp. 15–87, at p. 45.

27. "When truth sets itself into the work, it appears. Appearing [*Erscheinen*]—as this being of truth in the work and as work—is beauty. Thus the beautiful belongs to the advent of truth, truth's taking of its place" (ibid., p. 81; translator's note: translation altered slightly).

28. Ibid., pp. 45–46.

29. Ibid., pp. 46–47.

30. Theodor W. Adorno, *Aesthetic Theory*, ed. G. Adorno and Rolf Tiedemann, trans. Robert Hullot-Kentor (Minneapolis: University of Minnesota Press, 1997), pp. 93–94.

31. Adorno, *Negative Dialectics*, trans. E. B. Ashton (London: Routledge and Kegan Paul, 1973), p. 10; translator's note: translation altered slightly).

32. Adorno, *Aesthetic Theory*, p. 86.

33. Ibid., p. 79.

34. "Artworks are neutralized and thus qualitatively transformed epiphanies. If the deities of antiquity were said to appear fleetingly at their cult sites, or at least were to have appeared there in the primeval age, this act of appearing became the law of the permanence of artworks, but at the price of the living incarnation of what appears. The artwork as appearance is most closely resembled by the *apparition*, the heavenly vision" (ibid., p. 80).

35. Ibid., p. 82.

36. The forms of aesthetic reaction alluded to here are systematically distinguished in Chapter Two, the section "A Play for Presence."

37. Adorno, *Aesthetic Theory*, p. 87.

38. Ibid., p. 80.

39. Ibid., p. 72, and Adorno, "Valéry's Deviations," in *Notes to Literature*, vol. 1, trans. Shierry Weber Nicholsen (New York: Columbia University Press, 1991), pp. 137–73, at p. 172. "*Le beau exige peut-être l'imitation servile de ce qui est indéfinissable dans les choses*"; Valéry, "Autres Rhumbs," in *Tel Quel II* (Paris: Gallimard, 1943), pp. 103–97, at p. 161. (Translator's note: in Adorno's second text, Valéry's sentence is translated as "The beautiful demands perhaps the slavish imitation of what is indefinable in things.")

40. Adorno, *Negative Dialectics*, p. 28.

41. Bohrer, *Suddenness*; Rüdiger Bubner, *Ästhetische Erfahrung* (Frankfurt am Main: Suhrkamp, 1989); Albrecht Wellmer, *The Persistence of Modernity: Aesthetics, Ethics and Postmodernism*, trans. David Midgley (Cambridge, Mass.: MIT Press, 1991); Christoph Menke, *Die Souveränität der Kunst: Erfahrung nach Adorno und Derrida* (Frankfurt am Main: Suhrkamp, 1988).

42. On the relation between knowability and unknowability, see Seel, "Bestimmen und Bestimmenlassen: Anfänge einer medialen Erkenntnistheorie," *Zeitschrift für Philosophie*, 1998, *46*, 351–65.

43. See Seel, "Ästhetik als Teil einer differenzierten Ethik," in *Ethisch-ästhetische Studien* (Frankfurt am Main: Suhrkamp, 1996), pp. 11–35.

44. "The world is unique"; Theodor W. Adorno and Max Horkheimer, *Dialectic of Enlightenment*, trans. John Cumming (London: Verso, 1979), p. 220.

CHAPTER TWO

1. In place of the concept "perception" I sometimes use, for reasons of style, the concept of "intuition" as a designation for the *entire* sensuous receptivity of human beings, not just the sense of *visual* intuition.

2. In contrast to this, Hans Rudolf Schweizer and Armin Wildermuth suggest proceeding, in epistemology and aesthetics, "from a reality that facilitates access by means of rationality"; *Die Entdeckung der Phänomene* (Basel: Schwabe, 1981), p. 9. This, however, is possible only in the strongly "foundationalist" fiction of "a comportment toward phenomenal reality that is unrefracted" by any conceptual categorization (see p. 37). Contrary to this, I am seeking the aesthetic relation *in the midst of* the culture of human possibilities.

3. Adorno, "In Memory of Eichendorff," in *Notes to Literature*, vol. 1, ed. Rolf Tiedemann, trans. Shierry Weber Nicholsen (New York: Columbia University Press, 1991), pp. 55–79, at p. 65.

4. Martin Heidegger, *The Basic Problems of Phenomenology*, trans. Albert Hofstadter (Bloomington: Indiana University Press, 1982), p. 249.

5. Important observations on the temporal structure of aesthetic perception are made by Bohrer, *Suddenness*, and Michael Theunissen, "Freiheit von der Zeit: Ästhetisches Anschauen als Verweilen," in *Negative Theologie der Zeit* (Frankfurt am Main: Suhrkamp, 1991), pp. 285–98.

6. What is even more complex is the interwovenness of purposive and end-in-itself action in the case of artistic production; on this, see my "Über die Arbeit des Schriftstellers (und die Sprache der Philosophie)," in *Ethisch-ästhetische Studien* (Frankfurt am Main: Suhrkamp, 1996), pp. 145–87.

7. A phenomenology of sensing in connection with art is developed by Ulrich Pothast, "Bereitschaft zum Anderssein: Über Spürenswirklichkeit und Kunst," in *Im Rausch der Sinne: Kunst zwischen Animation und Askese*, ed. Konrad Paul Liessmann (Vienna: Zsolnay, 1999), pp. 258–82.

8. Kant, *Critique of Judgment*, p. 44.

9. "Presence in the existential sense is not the same as being there or being available"; Heidegger, *The Basic Problems of Phenomenology*, p. 266. (Translator's note: translation altered. Heidegger's German sentence is "*Gegenwart im existentialen Sinne ist nicht gleich Anwesenheit bzw. Vorhandenheit*" [*Die Grundprobleme der Phänomenologie*, p. 376], and Hofstadter renders it in English as "The present in the existential sense is not the same as presence or as extantness"; but the Heidegger-specific nomenclature he employs does not suit the present context.)

10. Bohrer, *Suddenness*, and *Das absolute Präsens: Die Semantik ästhetischer Zeit* (Frankfurt am Main: Suhrkamp, 1994).

11. What these places actually are varies, of course, to a great extent historically, culturally, and individually. My arbitrarily chosen examples do not include any claims about what are good or bad places, opportunities, or practices of aes-

thetic behavior; they are nothing but examples for where and how aesthetic intuition or desisting from aesthetic intuition is *possible*. A historiography of aesthetic perception, which is not intended here, would be much concerned precisely with the historically and culturally diverse occasions for aesthetic states (be they peripheral or central).

12. On the semantics of the violence of aesthetic experience, see Chapter Five of this book.

13. As long as self-thrown things you catch, it's all
   mere virtuosity, a venial winning—:
   not till you find that you have caught the ball
   a constant fellow player, she, sent spinning
   at you, your centre, one of those throws
   precisely angled, mastered, such
   as God, the great bridge-builder, knows,
   will catching be a skill that counts for much,—
   not your skill, but a world's. And if at length
   you had the strength and courage for replying,
   no, better still, forgot your courage, strength
   and had *already* thrown . . . (as does the year,
   throwing the birds, a myriad migrant swarm
   which older warmth to newer warmth sends flying
   across the oceans—) only in that venture,
   a valid player, you'd be joining in.
   No longer would make it easy for yourself,
   no longer difficult. Launched from your hands
   into its spaces the meteor would spin . . .

   —Rainer Maria Rilke, *Poems 1912–1926*, selected, trans., and intro. Michael Hamburger (Redding Ridge, Conn.: Black Swan Books, 1981), p. 83.

14. I have attempted to show that this also holds for the aesthetics of an author who ostensibly disdains everything normative; see Seel, "Review of Niklas Luhmann, *Die Kunst der Gesellschaft*," *European Journal of Philosophy*, 1996, 4, 390–93.

15. Nor is it simply what a chemical or physical analysis that goes beyond sensuous perception could identify as its constitution, for this composition can change too.

16. Saul Kripke, *Naming and Necessity* (Cambridge, Mass.: Harvard University Press, 1980). I am relying here on Ursula Wolf's critical commentary on the status of singular terms, a discussion that stretches from Frege and Russell to Kripke and Putnam; see her "Einleitung," in *Eigennamen: Dokumentationen einer Kontroverse*, ed. Ursula Wolf (Frankfurt am Main: Suhrkamp, 1985), pp. 9–41.

17. This is why Robert Brandom writes "*Particularity is as much a conceptual*

matter as generality" (italics in the original) in *Making It Explicit: Reasoning, Representing, and Discursive Commitment* (Cambridge, Mass.: Harvard University Press, 1994), p. 620.

18. John McDowell, "Values and Secondary Qualities," in *Mind, Value, and Reality* (Cambridge, Mass.: Harvard University Press, 1998), pp. 131–50, at p. 136.

19. McDowell, "Aesthetic Value, Objectivity, and the Fabric of the World," in *Mind, Value, and Reality*, pp. 112–30, at p. 129. McDowell adds: "We should ask ourselves whether something's being independent of each particular experience might not be enough to secure as much truth as we want for the thesis that 'knowledge is of what is there anyway.'" As a consequence of this consideration, we have to distinguish *types of objectivity*, to which experience has access in different ways.

20. "Even in the case of colour experience, this integration [of objects into a wider reality as well as of concepts into a wide-ranging repertoire of world disclosure] allows us to understand an experience as *awareness of something independent of the experience itself*: something that is held in place by its linkage into the wider reality, so that we can make sense of the thought that it would be so even if it were not being experienced to be so" (italics added). McDowell, *Mind and World* (Cambridge, Mass.: Harvard University Press, 1994), p. 32.

21. The example comes from Hilary Putnam, "Replies," *Philosophical Topics*, 1992, *20*, 347–408, at 371.

22. For greater detail on this, see Seel, "Bestimmen und Bestimmenlassen."

23. Peter F. Strawson, "Perception and Its Objects," in *Perception and Identity*, ed. G. F. MacDonald (Ithaca, N.Y.: Cornell University Press, 1979), pp. 41–60, at p. 59. Regarding the scientific realist, Strawson adds: "If this means, as he must maintain it does, that our thought is condemned to incoherence, then we can only conclude that incoherence is something we can perfectly well live with and could not perfectly well live without."

24. Supra, *Phenomenal Individuality*, pp. 69–75.

25. If one follows an idea of John Haugeland's, which was inspired by Heidegger, the conceptual determination of objects can also be understood as a "letting be" of the objectivity of these objects; Haugeland, "Truth and Rule-Following," in *Having Thought: Essays in the Metaphysics of Mind* (Cambridge, Mass.: Harvard University Press, 1998), pp. 305–61, at pp. 325–27.

26. On the premises of the following observation, see Seel, "Bestimmen und Bestimmenlassen."

27. If the idea of a complete description (of the surface) of a ball is empty, this holds all the more for the idea of a complete description of the world. On the critique of this notion, see Putnam, *Renewing Philosophy* (Cambridge, Mass.: Harvard University Press, 1992), chapters five and six.

28. Supra, p. 4.

29. Even food—when savoring it—can be turned back and forth in the mouth.

30. Linking up with Wilhelm von Humboldt and Nietzsche, Günter Figal has determined this perception plausibly as a contest between "limitedness and limitlessness"; Figal, "Ästhetische Individualität: Erörterungen im Hinblick auf Ernst Jünger," in *Individuum: Probleme der Individualität in Kunst, Philosophie und Wissenschaft*, ed. Gottfried Boehm (Stuttgart: Klett-Cotta, 1994), pp. 151–71, at p. 158.

31. Supra, pp. 9–11 and 15.

32. This is also the case when the interpretations of an artwork point to knowledge that is *conveyed* by this work. It is therefore entirely legitimate to speak of "aesthetic knowledge" as long as it is not equated with knowledge *about* the work; I return to this in the section "Constellations of Art." No matter how one comprehends it, the concept of aesthetic knowledge can be explicated only in contrast to a concept of propositional knowledge, to which I confine myself here.

33. It is only when they are used like this that the corresponding predicates are "aesthetic predicates." It is therefore misleading to want to contrast aesthetic with other predicates of perception independently of their manner of use. In principle, *every* predicate of perception can be used in this way—when we describe a sculpture as "exceptionally light," a painting by Yves Klein as "exceptionally blue," or a piece of rock music as "exceptionally loud."

34. See Seel, "Bestimmen und Bestimmenlassen."

35. An aesthetics of "pure" appearing that is explicitly fundamentalist in this sense is developed by Armin Wildermuth, "Philosophie des Ästhetischen: Das erscheinungsphilosophische Denken Heinrich Barths," in *In Erscheinung treten: Heinrich Barths Philosophie des Ästhetischen*, eds. Günther Hauff, Hans Rudolf Schweizer, Armin Wildermuth (Basel: Schwabe, 1990), pp. 205–60.

36. "The reflective theory of the beautiful shows that acts of sensuous grasping and presenting, from now on called specifically 'aesthetic' acts, are not a different class of executions [of perception] *alongside* the standard acts of sensuous grasping and presenting. Rather, aesthetic acts are to be distinguished from nonaesthetic ones by the fact that, in executing the former, we become aware of the forces that operate in them. . . . The forces and their operation become evident in the medium of the beautiful because the forces operate differently here. In the medium of the beautiful, the forces operate 'freely'; this means they are not directed at a particular given end. This freedom is outwardly apparent as a heightened intensity: the free operation of forces in aesthetic executions [of perception] appears as an intensive operation of forces, as an operation of intensive forces." Christoph Menke, "Wahrnehmung, Tätigkeit, Selbstreflexion: Zur Genese und Dialektik der Ästhetik," in *Falsche Gegensätze: Zeitgenössische Positionen zur philosophischen Ästhetik*, eds. Andera Kern and Ruth Sonderegger (Frankfurt am Main: Suhrkamp, 2002), pp. 19–48, at pp. 45–46.

37. On the reconstruction of this history, see Rüdiger Bubner, "Über einige Bedingungen gegenwärtiger Ästhetik," in *Ästhetische Erfahrung* (Frankfurt am Main: Suhrkamp, 1989), pp. 9–51. It must, however, be emphasized that the contrast between an "aesthetics of being" and an "aesthetics of semblance" relates just to *figures of thought* whose conflict is *conducted* in almost all of the great theories of aesthetics, above all in Hegel and Adorno.

38. This type of perceiving (looks, sounds, feels, smells *like*) must of course be distinguished from a perception of mere similarities, which has nothing to do with sensuous semblance. The former, aesthetic perceiving, which is directed at a semblance we have seen through, is always a perceiving *as if.*

39. See the elaborate interpretations in Axel Müller, *Die ikonische Differenz: Das Kunstwerk als Augenblick* (Munich: Fink, 1997), chapter two; and Eva Schürmann, *Erscheinen und Wahrnehmen: Eine vergleichende Studie zur Kunst von James Turrell und der Philosophie Merleau-Pontys* (Munich: Fink, 2000).

40. *From Dusk Till Dawn* (USA 1995), directed by Robert Rodriguez.

41. Supra, pp. 13–14.

42. If at times it seems there were no presentation—as, for instance, in some of Marcel Duchamp's readymades, to which I return later in this chapter—then this is not due to a dramatic excess of semblance but because (of the semblance) of a dramatic absence of staging and semblance.

43. In Chapter Four I discuss why illusionist theories of the *picture* are not convincing. It is a different matter with cyberspace, different from pictures and films. The space of a virtually accessible library, for instance, is neither a representation space nor a represented space but a virtual bodily space that *seems* to encircle the location of its users (even though they know this is not the case). Accordingly, the books that can be read here are not representations of books but virtual books. But this semblance too is founded on electronically generated appearances. If there were to be a decidedly *artistic* construction of virtual worlds, there would also probably be a *presentation* of the particular spatiality of these spaces, which is not thematized in its pragmatic use. See Seel, "Vor dem Schein kommt das Erscheinen," in *Ethisch-ästhetische Studien*, pp. 104–25.

44. Something similar happens to children today when they see a 3D movie for the first time. They first have the impression that the airplane shown in three-dimensional representation is actually moving toward them; then after three minutes they *play-act* as if this were the case.

45. Moreover, it needs to be remembered that theater does not always stage narrative meaning occurrences but can also present nonfictional real events in a theatrical setting, as is the case currently in Heiner Goebbels's music theater.

46. Understood in a wide sense, the word "imagination" [*Vorstellung*] encompasses all kinds of mental states in which something is made present as something, irrespective of whether it is a ball that is there or not, or of evidence that is conclusive or inconclusive. I will not follow this wide use, however.

47. Accordingly, it is characteristic of objects of the imagination that they are "intuitive-absent, given to intuition as absent"; Jean-Paul Sartre, *The Psychology of the Imagination*, trans. anon. (London: Methuen, 1972), p. 13.

48. In reference to Husserl and Sartre, Wolfgang Iser determines the procedure of the imagination plausibly as one of "modification"; Iser, *Das Fiktive und das Imaginäre: Perspektiven literarischer Anthropologie* (Frankfurt am Main: Suhrkamp, 1991), pp. 393–96, cf. pp. 345–47.

49. An opposing position is defended by Richard Schanz, *Wahrheit, Referenz und Realismus: Eine Studie zur Sprachphilosophie und Metaphysik* (Berlin/New York: de Gruyter, 1996), pp. 364–75.

50. Raymond Chandler, *The Long Goodbye*, in *Later Novels and Other Writings* (New York: Library of America, 1995), pp. 417–734, at p. 515. Peter Handke, *Der Hausierer* (Frankfurt am Main: Suhrkamp, 1967).

51. Chandler, *The Long Goodbye*, p. 515.

52. That each reader develops *his or her* image of the empty pool is not relevant as long as all readers have *an* image in which meaninglessness and meaningfulness hold a portentous balance.

53. On this concept of artistic exemplification, see Nelson Goodman, *Languages of Art: An Approach to a Theory of Symbols* (Indianapolis: Bobbs-Merrill, 1968), chapter two.

54. Supra, pp. 58–59.

55. "I am not necessarily *captivated* by the text of pleasure; it can be an act that is slight, complex, tenuous, almost scatterbrained: a sudden movement of the head like a bird who understands nothing of what we hear, who hears what we do not understand"; Roland Barthes, *The Pleasure of the Text*, trans. Richard Miller, with a note on the text by Richard Howard (New York: Hill and Wang, 1975), pp. 24–25.

56. For greater detail on this topic, see Seel, "Natur als Schauplatz der Imagination" (Nature as an Arena of the Imagination), in *Eine Ästhetik der Natur*, pp. 135–84.

57. With minor changes, I adopt here my distinction among "contemplation," "correspondence," and "imagination" as the three standard dimensions of the aesthetic; see Seel, *Eine Ästhetik der Natur*, chapters one to three, and also the synopsis on pp. 235–46.

58. Gernot Böhme, *Atmosphäre: Essays zur neuen Ästhetik* (Frankfurt am Main: Suhrkamp, 1995); *Anmutungen: Über das Atmosphärische* (Ostfildern: Edition Tertium, 1998).

59. That landscapes, apartments, or cities permanently *have* a certain atmosphere means they *suggest* a certain tonality in their presence, when other interests and moods do not override sensitivity to the correspondences they release. They are in *proportion*—positive or negative, beautiful or sublime—to human life possibilities. I have elaborated this in Seel, *Eine Ästhetik der Natur*, pp. 240–44.

60. The subjunctive mood indicates that atmospheres can be experienced also

in the imaginative consciousness of how they would affect us if we were different from whom we are (today), or of how they affected us when we were different at one time.

61. On the concept of "life situation," see Seel, *Versuch über die Form des Glücks* (Frankfurt am Main: Suhrkamp, 1995), pp. 69–74.

62. I have discussed these relations in greater detail in *Eine Ästhetik der Natur*, pp. 257–66, and in "Zur ästhetischen Praxis der Kunst," in *Ethisch-ästhetische Studien*, pp. 126–44.

63. Arthur C. Danto, *The Transfiguration of the Commonplace: A Philosophy of Art* (Cambridge, Mass.: Harvard University Press, 1981).

64. Of course, in these symbolizations it is often the case that *some* sequences are precisely fixed, for instance the order of words in ritual utterances or the sequence of variously colored signals in a traffic light. Many other parameters—intonation, speed, color, and so on—can nonetheless be subject to a treatment that is arbitrary to a greater degree than is the case even in those artworks that operate with various random techniques (that is, in artworks in which it is always decisive that precisely *these* [kinds of] appearances are the outcome of a random operation).

65. Supra, pp. 32–33.

66. For the concept of presence, Heidegger's analysis of time in *Being and Time* (trans. John Macquarrie and Edward Robinson, Oxford: Blackwell, 1962, §§ 65–81, pp. 370–480) can be fruitfully drawn upon without having to adopt his general critique of the "ordinary conception of time."

67. To that extent, these reflections also have to do with "real presences"—not in the theological meaning that George Steiner imputes to all strong aesthetic experience; see his *Real Presences* (Chicago: University of Chicago Press, 1989).

68. "The scope of the dimension of a now varies; now in this hour, now in this second. This diversity of scope of dimension is possible only because the now is intrinsically dimensional" (a dovetailing of what endures and what passes away, of what has passed and what is to be expected) and is thus a "continuum of the flux of time"; Heidegger, *The Basic Problems of Phenomenology*, p. 249.

69. Heidegger, *Being and Time*, §§ 29–31, pp. 172–88.

70. This is why Sartre rightly says that the capacity for imagination is a constitutive component for all of the activities of consciousness; *The Psychology of the Imagination*, pp. 215–16, 218–19.

71. Angela Keppler, "Verschränkte Gegenwarten: Medien- und Kommunikationssoziologie als Untersuchung kultureller Transformationen," in *Soziologie 2000: Kritische Bestandsaufnahmen zu einer Soziologie für das 21. Jahrhundert* (*Soziologische Revue*, Sonderheft 5), eds. Richard Münch, Claudia Jauß, Carsten Stark (Munich: Oldenbourg, 2000), pp. 140–52.

72. Otherwise it would not be possible to make this life comprehensible to people as being joyful.

73. The *facultative* "objects of the imagination" discussed in the section "Appearing and Imagination" secure the possibility of a transition at any time to the perception of an *artistic* appearing.

74. I thus also oppose indirectly the understanding defended by Sartre, among others, that works of art are "unreal objects" (*The Psychology of the Imagination*, pp. 131–40). For an exemplary critique of this idea, see Wellmer, "Das musikalische Kunstwerk," in *Falsche Gegensätze: Zeitgenössische Positionen zur philosophischen Ästhetik*, eds. Andera Kern and Ruth Sonderegger (Frankfurt am Main: Suhrkamp, 2002), pp. 133–75.

75. I say "most of them" since there are arts that operate with nonsensuous— immaterial—materials, as with computer programs that acquire different sensuous forms of appearance only at the level of the artistic *operation*.

76. I have elaborated in greater detail the concept of medium that I rely on here and that goes back to G. Bateson and N. Luhmann, in Seel, "Medien der Realität und Realität der Medien," in *Medien—Computer—Realität*, ed. Sybille Krämer (Frankfurt am Main: Suhrkamp, 1998), pp. 244–68.

77. Adorno, "Die Kunst und die Künste," in *Ohne Leitbild* (Frankfurt am Main: Suhrkamp, 1967), pp. 168–92; "Über einige Relationen zwischen Musik und Malerei," in *Gesammelte Schriften*, vol. 16, ed. Rolf Tiedemann (Frankfurt am Main: Suhrkamp, 1978), pp. 628–42.

78. These concepts (merely alluded to here) of the medium of individual art forms—concepts open from the outset to the interwovenness of the arts—could be elaborated further, for instance in respect to the various spatiotemporal relations that are standard-setting in their perception. (On this see the discussions in Luhmann, *Art as a Social System*, trans. Eva M. Knodt [Stanford, Calif.: Stanford University Press, 2000], pp. 111–15.) Besides "inherent" relations, relations of "content" between art forms (the works of one art form relate to another—like the numerous architectural fantasies in painting and literature) could also be distinguished, as well as "inclusive" relations between them (one art form turns up in another one—such as, for instance, pictures in a church or an installation).

79. Philosophical aesthetics attempts to say what artworks *can do*; art criticism, by contrast, attempts to say *which ones* can do it. On the procedure of art criticism, which I do not go into here, see Seel, *Die Kunst der Entzweiung: Zum Begriff der ästhetischen Rationalität* (Frankfurt am Main: Suhrkamp, 1985), chapter three.

80. Adorno, *Aesthetic Theory*, p. 87.

81. Ibid. (italics added).

82. Ibid.

83. Here, the literal meaning of the Greek word *pháinestai* (shine, glow) leads Adorno to a far-reaching claim about the matter.

84. This view, which links up with Russian and Czech formalism, is also defended by Luhmann, *Art as a Social System*, esp. chapter three.

85. Wellmer, "Das musikalische Kunstwerk," unpublished manuscript, Berlin,

1999, p. 23 (this is an earlier version of the article cited in note 74 to this chapter); cf. Barthes, "Music's Body," in *The Responsibility of Forms: Critical Essays on Music, Art, and Representation*, trans. Richard Howard (Berkeley: University of California Press, 1985 [1982]), pp. 243–312.

86. On this, see Seel, "Art as Appearance: Two Comments on Danto's *After the End of Art*," *History and Theory*, 1998, theme issue 37, 102–14; and Danto's response to my critique, Danto, "The End of Art: A Philosophical Defense," *History and Theory, 1998*, theme issue 37, pp. 127–43, at 132–34. The topic of an overdue separation of art theory and aesthetics can also be found in Luhmann, *Art as a Social System*, p. 306.

87. Danto, *After the End of Art: Contemporary Art and the Pale of History* (Princeton: Princeton University Press, 1997), p. 13.

88. Ibid., p. 16.

89. Ibid., p. 25.

90. Ibid., p. 183.

91. Ibid., p. 84.

92. Ibid., p. 71 (italics added).

93. Adorno, *Aesthetic Theory*, p. 82 (italics in the original).

94. Joseph Kosuth, "Statement," *Flash Art* (Feb.–Mar. 1971), 2.

95. Kosuth, "Art After Philosophy" [1969], in *Conceptual Art*, ed. Ursula Meyer (New York: Dutton, 1972), pp. 155–70, at pp. 158 and 162.

96. Kosuth, "Three Answers by Joseph Kosuth to Four Questions by Pierre Restany," *Domus* (May 1971), 53–54, at 54.

97. Translator's note: unlike the comparatively free inversion of noun and adverb permissible in German, English can barely tolerate the word order of the latter sentence.

98. For de Maria, moreover, it is important to commemorate the earth, which supports the beholders as well as all the technical installations and constructions. This is what distinguishes this *land art* project from a conceivable *conceptualist* or *minimalist* realization that could even dispense with the rod extending into the depths of the earth.

99. Hegel, *Aesthetics: Lectures on Fine Art*, 2 vols., trans. T. M. Knox (Oxford: Clarendon Press, 1975), vol. 2, pp. 622–23 and 626–27. (Translator's note: because of the context, Knox translates "*Vorstellung*" as "ideas" on p. 622 and "imagination" on p. 626. When translating Seel's text, it is also rendered as "imagination" or "imaginative projection(s).")

100. Luhmann, *Art as a Social System*, pp. 25–26; cf. pp. 123–26.

101. On this distinction, see Paul de Man, "Reading (Proust)," in *Allegories of Reading: Figural Language in Rousseau, Nietzsche, Rilke, and Proust* (New Haven: Yale University Press, 1979), pp. 57–78. I criticize the thesis of a "disjunction" between the two types of reading in Seel, "Über die Arbeit des Schriftstellers," at pp. 184–87.

102. Honoré de Balzac, *Lost Illusions*, trans. and intro. Herbert J. Hunt (Harmondsworth: Penguin, 1971), p. 34.

103. The original French text makes this gulf clear with the help of a participle construction: "*En dessinant la position de la noblesse en France et lui donnant des espérances qui ne pouvaient se réaliser sans un bouleversement général, la Restauration entendit la distance morale qui séparait, encore plus fortement que la distance locale, Angoulême de l'Houmeau.*" Balzac, *Illusions perdues* (Paris: Garnier, 1961), p. 38.

104. Vladimir Nabokov, *Pnin* (London: Heinemann, 1957), p. 7.

105. Metaphors and other forms of figurative speech do not in themselves constitute literature since it is still characteristic of their language form to blur the *difference* between literal and figurative speech—as can be analyzed in an extreme form in Paul Celan's poetry, in which the literally seeming phrases are always brought into play metaphorically, and the metaphorical ones literally.

106. Illuminating observations on the relation between musical and literary scores are made by Wellmer in "Das musikalische Kunstwerk."

107. Supra, p. 119.

108. Supra, p. 97.

109. It is an analogous situation with paintings and movies: they change with the changes in the pictorial worlds in which they are exhibited and shown. A silent movie in the world of the sound movie and a black-and-white movie in the world of the technicolor movie are situated differently from when they were first perceived at the time of their premieres.

110. Stanislaw Jerzy Lec, *Unfrisierte Gedanken*, trans. Karl Dedecius (Munich: Hanser, 1959), p. 8.

111. Bertolt Brecht, *Stories of Mr. Keuner*, trans. Martin Chalmers (San Francisco: City Lights Books, 2001), p. 39 (translator's note: translation altered slightly).

112. I developed the concept of play relied on here in Seel, *Versuch über die Form des Glücks*, pp. 159–65. Ruth Sonderegger argues for a rehabilitation of the concept of play in the philosophy of art in *Für eine Ästhetik des Spiels: Hermeneutik, Dekonstruktion und der Eigensinn der Kunst* (Frankfurt am Main: Suhrkamp, 2000).

113. See the section "What Is Appearing."

114. Hans Ulrich Gumbrecht, "Die Schönheit des Mannschaftssports: American Football—im Stadion und im Fernsehen," in *Medien—Welten—Wirklichkeiten*, eds. Gianni Vattimo and Wolfgang Welsch (Munich: Fink, 1998), pp. 201–29, at p. 211; cf. Seel, "Die Zelebration des Unvermögens: Aspekte einer Ästhetik des Sports," in *Ethisch-ästhetische Studien*, pp. 188–200.

CHAPTER THREE

1. Kant, *Critique of Judgment*, §14, pp. 71–72. Kant does admittedly say of the aesthetic object that it could be "either play of shapes (in space, namely, mimetic art and dance) or mere play of sensations (in time)," here thinking of music and

painting. Since, however, the "play of sensations" also follows an interaction of shapes (of music or the picture), a "play of shapes" has to be accepted as a correlate here too, which moreover should not be reduced to a play of *formal* aspects of the object, as in Kant, but ought to be grasped as a play of its *appearances* (in the manner elaborated in the preceding chapter, in the sections "What Is Appearing" and "Being-so and Appearing").

2. Nietzsche, *The Birth of Tragedy*, pp. 16–17.

3. Nietzsche, "Attempt at a Self-Criticism," in *The Birth of Tragedy*, pp. 3–12, at p. 8.

4. To be mentioned here are Bohrer, *Suddenness*, and Menke, *Die Souveränität der Kunst*.

5. (Translator's note: I retain in the heading for this subsection the German terms for "resonating" [*Rauschen*] and "intoxication" [*Rausch*] because of their striking character as a pair.)

6. The intoxication generated by movement, as can be had in certain types of sport or at funfairs, is something else. Paul Virilio took this as his starting point in *The Aesthetics of Disappearance*, trans. Philip Beitchman (New York: Semiotext, 1991). In these instances, intoxication can arise at best as an attendant phenomenon; the intoxication itself (here it has the form of a body tumble) remains objectless. Its activation is not tied to the perception of external objects; rather, it lies in eccentric movement that jumbles space-time coordinates. The perception of *artistic* resonating does indeed have—as Nietzsche also saw—moments of literal or metaphorical tumbling (to which I return shortly); in terms of this alone, however, resonating cannot be understood.

7. Here lies the significant difference vis-à-vis the information-theoretic concept of resonating as a state in which more information cannot be transmitted; this negative concept, which is moreover restricted to failing communication, is not sufficient for aesthetic considerations. (Translator's note: the term *static*, in the sense of a crackling noise that interferes with electronically sent signals, would be a more idiomatic rendering of *Rauschen* here.)

8. To call "mere" resonating simply "natural" resonating would be wrong; the difference between the two kinds lies generally not in what is natural in contrast to what is artificial but rather in whether it is part of an *artistic* construction or not.

9. Hegel writes that "one may still hear the German language praised for its wealth—that wealth consisting in its special expression for special sounds— *Rauschen, Sausen, Knarren*, etc.;. . . . Such superabundance in the realm of sense and of triviality contributes nothing to form the real wealth of a cultivated language." Hegel, *Philosophy of Mind: Being Part Three of the Encyclopaedia of the Philosophical Sciences (1830)*, trans. William Wallace, *Zusätze*, trans. A. V. Miller, Foreword by J. N. Findlay (Oxford: Clarendon Press, 1977), p. 214.

10. The other senses are not receptive to resonating; states of resonating are sensed here necessarily as ranging from uncomfortable to abhorrent since the in-

determinable engages here in direct contact with the sensing body, touches it, or pierces it. From this there follows an interesting justification for the traditional distinction ascribed to the two "theoretical" senses: only seeing and hearing are receptive to resonating.

11. To the eye, the calm sea is much more a resonating one than the sea moved by waves; in respect of resonating, the eye and the ear perceive differently. To the eye *and* the ear, the sea is resonating only when it is extremely stirred—when it is a "roaring" sea.

12. "Emptiness" and "fullness" as varieties of resonating can be distinguished as underdetermination that becomes overdetermination, and overdetermination that becomes underdetermination. On emptiness and fullness, see the pertinent reflections of Hans Thies Lehmann, "Ästhetik: Eine Kolumne: Fülle, Leere," *Merkur*, 1995, *49*, 432–38.

13. This determinacy of the character of a resonating, despite the indeterminacy of its characteristics, is important especially for artistic resonating. Just as there is little determinable to be recognized *in* resonating, there can be a lot to recognize in an artwork that *is resonating*: its type, power, position in the oeuvre, relation to other "resonating" works, and so on.

14. Nietzsche, *The Birth of Tragedy*, pp. 18, 21–22, 35.

15. The aesthetic act required here is thus essentially an omission. One could speak of an aesthetic lethargy; but this cannot survive without a certain degree of aesthetic energy—the energy that is expended in forgetting for a while one's own knowledge and will.

16. In recollection of Freud's *Beyond the Pleasure Principle*, it could be said that here the pleasure principle has found a way not to be an agent of the death instinct. In resonating, the pleasure principle has found an *experienceable* state of perception on the boundaries of all perception (the capacity to perceive, which for Aristotle is the criterion for all living beings); it has found a state of rest that satisfies the organism's need for stillness—should this need exist—without being an anticipation of death. Sigmund Freud, *Beyond the Pleasure Principle*, trans. and ed. by James Strachey, intro. Gregory Zilboorg (New York: Norton, 1975), esp. parts five and seven.

17. Adorno, "In Memory of Eichendorff," p. 65.

18. Moreover, this mystic execution can, of course, be charged substantively. This is not a necessary component of the experience, nor therefore of the theory of resonating. How a substantive mystics of resonating can be ideologically charged is shown by Gerhard Kurz, "Graue Romantik: Zu Walter Flex' *Wildgänse rauschen durch die Nacht*," in *Hermenautik—Hermeneutik: Literarische und geisteswissenschaftliche Beiträge zu Ehren von Peter Horst Neumann*, eds. Holger Helbig, Bettina Knauer, and Gunnar Och (Würzburg: Könighausen and Neumann, 1996), pp. 133–52.

19. To characterize the acoustic tapestry oscillating between extreme pitch lev-

els, volume levels, and sound modulations in *Volumina* for organ (1961/1962), Ligeti himself employs a metaphor of formlessness: "From all of this there arises an empty form, so to speak, shapes develop without features . . . , immense expanses and distances, an architecture consisting merely of scaffolding and without any tangible building"; leaflet accompanying the CD, György Ligeti, *Continuum/ Zehn Stücke für Bläserquintett/Artikulation/Glissandi/Etüden für Orgel/Volumina*, Wergo (B000025R93), 1988, p. 18. Thanks are due to Bodil von Thülen for the reference to Ligeti.

20. Sabine Sanio, "Das Rauschen, Paradoxien eines hintergründigen Phänomens," in *Das Rauschen*, eds. Sabine Sanio and Christian Scheib (Hofheim: Wolke, 1995), pp. 50–66.

21. See Lehmann, "Ästhetik."

22. Four possible forms of resonating can be distinguished in the language of literature: (1) phonetic resonating, in which the sound of speech drowns out its meaning (as, for example, frequently in C. Brentano's or R. D. Brinkmann's poems); (2) rhythmic resonating, where the continuous form of the sentences overruns every clear utterance (as, for instance, in Thomas Bernhard's *Correction*); (3) logical resonating, where the logical construction of sentences undermines their consistent meaning (as at the beginning of Hölderlin's "Bread and Wine"); and (4) referential resonating, in which the complexity of the semantic references of a text renders what it speaks of opaque (as in H. M. Enzensberger's *The Sinking of the Titanic: A Poem*). A literary "language of resonating," one could say, is given when some or all phenomena of this resonating are central to the composition of the text, that is, when they repeatedly gain prevalence or push to the fore. In the state of resonating, texts become opaque in various ways. Of course, this loss of reference on the part of literary speech has strong meaning within the construction of the works in question themselves—for example, that of being an indication of the general or special limits of (commensurable or communicable) meaning.

23. Johann Wolfgang von Goethe, *Faust*, part one, trans. Anna Swanwick (Project Gutenberg Etext, posted in Internet Public Library, www.ipl.org).

24. Adorno, "In Memory of Eichendorff," p. 69. (Translator's note: unlike in other places in Adorno's essay where *Rauschen* is translated variously as "rushing," "rustling," or "murmuring," the German word is left untranslated in this passage.)

25. Thus Nietzsche says of the person who experiences resonating: "Man is no longer an artist, he has become a work of art: the artistic power of the whole of nature reveals itself to the supreme gratification of the primal Oneness amidst the paroxysms of intoxication"; *The Birth of Tragedy*, p. 18. Of music, we read that it "symbolizes a sphere beyond and prior to appearance" (p. 35). (Translator's note: "*Erscheinung*" is rendered here as "appearance" and not as "phenomena," as in the Whiteside translation.)

26. Gilles Deleuze, *Francis Bacon—Logik der Sensation*, vol. 1, trans. Joseph Vogl (Munich: Fink, 1995), p. 39.

27. It would also be incorrect to interpret artistic resonating generally as an asemantic process, as a departure from a work's meaning constellation, as Nietzsche suggests when he understands the Dionysian state as a transcending of "Apollonian semblance." Steve Reich, for example, says of his composition from 1965 *It's Gonna Rain*, in which he applied for the first time the method of phase shifts with recordings of the voice of a black preacher: "Finally the process moves to eight voices and the effect is a kind of controlled chaos, which may be appropriate to the subject matter—the end of the world"; CD leaflet accompanying Steve Reich, *Early Works*, Elektra Nonesuch, 1987. Resonating is an extreme state of artistic articulation, *up to and including* phases of pure—meaningless—appearing, which belong for their part to the operative strategy of the artwork. For a differentiated view of the semantics of resonating in the case of modern music, see Günter Mayer, "Das 'Rauschen' des Irrealen: Zur Kritik des radikalen Konstruktivismus im Bereich der Ästhetik und Musikästhetik," *Das Argument*, 1977, *39*, 351–66.

28. There is another mystical side to the work of art, not addressed here: entering into and becoming one with the *world* of the work (one need only think of the example of reading crime novels).

29. Other recent examples are the movies *Twister* by Jan de Bont (USA 1996) and *Volcano* by Mick Jackson (USA 1997).

30. Elfriede Jelinek, *Die Kinder der Toten* (Reinbek bei Hamburg: Rowohlt, 1995), pp. 12–13.

CHAPTER FOUR

1. Clement Greenberg, "Avant-Garde and Kitsch," in *The Collected Essays and Criticism*, vol. 1: *Perceptions and Judgments, 1939–1944*, ed. John O'Brian (Chicago: University of Chicago Press, 1986–1993), pp. 5–22; idem., "Modernist Painting," in *The Collected Essays and Criticism*, vol. 4: *Modernism with a Vengeance, 1957–1969*, pp. 85–93; Danto, *The Transfiguration of the Commonplace*; idem., *After the End of Art: Contemporary Art and the Pale of History*, esp. chapters one and two.

2. Maurice Henri Pirenne, *Optics, Painting and Photography* (London: Cambridge University Press, 1970); Michael Polanyi, "What Is a Painting?" *British Journal of Aesthetics*, 1970, *10*, 225–36.

3. On this, see Oliver R. Scholz, *Bild, Darstellung, Zeichen: Philosophische Theorien bildhafter Darstellung* (Freiburg/Munich: Alber, 1991).

4. Goodman, *Languages of Art*, esp. chapter four.

5. With this distinction Neil McDonell augments the instruments developed by Goodman; McDonell, "Are Pictures Unavoidably Specific?" *Synthese*, 1983, *57*, 83–98; on this, see Scholz, *Bild, Darstellung, Zeichen*, pp. 105–8.

6. Goodman, *Languages of Art*, chapter two.

7. Cf. Hans Jonas, "Homo Pictor: Von der Freiheit des Bildens," in *Was ist ein Bild?* ed. Gottfried Boehm (Munich: Fink, 1994), pp. 105–24.

8. Klaus Sachs-Hombach, "Was ist ein Bildalphabet?" in *Bildgrammatik: Interdisziplinäre Forschungen zur Syntax bildlicher Darstellungsformen*, eds. Klaus Sachs-Hombach and Klaus Rehkämper (Magdeburg: Scriptum-Verlag, 1999), pp. 57–66, at p. 63.

9. Another conspicuous case of the individual picture is the early works of children; in viewing them, it is important to pay attention to exactly *the* line and coloring that the amazing Jane Doe produced at the age of three (before kindergarten and school laid her hands in chains).

10. Following Scholz, *Bild, Darstellung, Zeichen*, p. 107.

11. On this too, see Scholz, *Bild, Darstellung, Zeichen*, pp. 70–74. Singular pictures do not have to be individual pictures. There can be a number of phenomenally identical prints of a picture that is understood as the picture of an excellent specimen of a lion (hence understood singularly) such that the picture is not bound to a single realization—as is the case with an individual sign.

12. I say "frequently" because artists can experiment with subsidiary pictorial forms (one need only think of painters such as Sigmar Polke, A. R. Penck, or Keith Haring). Here, individual pictures are indeed again produced. But, first, it is not to be ruled out that an artistic picture denies the usual art status in a manner similar to that of some of Duchamp's readymades; and second, artistic pictures do not have to be strictly individual pictures, as mentioned in the commentary to the third statement, even those that are not are understood—at least until today—as occasionally ingenious metamorphoses of the classic composition of the picture.

13. Gottfried Boehm, "Die Wiederkehr der Bilder," in *Was ist ein Bild?* pp. 11–38. On Boehm's position and that of the authors in his anthology, see also Lambert Wiesing, "Bilder im Geiste und an der Wand," *Philosophische Rundschau*, 1999, *46*, 56–71.

14. I discussed this procedure, which Kosuth uses frequently, in greater detail in Chapter Two under "Constellations of Art."

15. *Which* pictures we classify as artistic and *which* as nonartistic (for instance, to what extent do we include or exclude the images of advertising?) is not relevant to this reflection.

16. The exceptions are the works, mentioned in note 1, by Greenberg and Danto, but also Goodman's theory of (metaphorical) "exemplification" in *Languages of Art*, chapter two.

17. Wiesing, *Die Sichtbarkeit des Bildes: Geschichte und Perspektiven der formalen Ästhetik* (Reinbek bei Hamburg: Rowohlt, 1997), esp. 160–64; Reinhard Brandt, *Die Wirklichkeit des Bildes: Sehen und Erkennen—vom Spiegel zum Kunstbild* (Munich: Hanser, 1999).

18. "After the gray paintings, after the dogma of 'fundamentalist painting,' whose puritan, moral aspect fascinated me to the point of self-denial, the only option left to me was a completely new beginning. Then the first color sketches in indeterminacy and openness emerged, on the premise of 'multicolor and complex,'

that is, the opposite of anti-painting and painting that doubts its own legitimacy." *Gerhard Richter*, ed. Kunst- und Ausstellungshalle der Bundesrepublik Deutschland (Stuttgart: Kunst- und Ausstellungshalle der Bundesrepublik Deutschland, 1993), vol. 2, p. 61.

19. On the difference between literal and metaphorical presentation, see Goodman, *Languages of Art*, chapter two.

20. "I began by dropping the picture theory of language and ended by adopting the language theory of pictures." Goodman, "The Way the World Is," in *Problems and Projects* (Indianapolis: Bobbs-Merrill, 1972), pp. 24–32, at p. 31. The objection I raise is also advanced by Reinhard Brandt, *Die Wirklichkeit des Bildes*, p. 201.

21. Sartre, *The Psychology of the Imagination*; Maurice Merleau-Ponty, "Eye and Mind," in *The Primacy of Perception, and Other Essays on Phenomenological Psychology, the Philosophy of Art, History, and Politics*, trans. Carleton Dallery, ed. and intro. James M. Edie (Evanston, Ill.: Northwestern University Press, 1964), pp. 159–78; idem., "Cézanne's Doubt," in *Sense and Non-Sense*, trans. Hubert L. Dreyfus and Patricia A. Dreyfus (Evanston, Ill.: Northwestern University Press, 1964), pp. 9–25; Michael Polanyi, "What Is a Painting?"; Richard Wollheim, *Art and Its Objects: With Six Supplementary Essays* (Cambridge: Cambridge University Press, 1980).

22. Boehm, "Die Wiederkehr der Bilder," pp. 29–30. See also in the same volume idem., "Die Bilderfrage," pp. 325–43.

23. Boehm, "Die Wiederkehr der Bilder," p. 30.

24. Ibid.

25. With respect to Newman's *Who's Afraid of Red, Yellow and Blue IV*, it could be such an advertising placard in a DIY store; it would then function not as a picture but merely as a sample.

26. This is also argued by Klaus Sachs-Hombach and Klaus Rehkämper, "Aspekte und Probleme der bildwissenschaftlichen Forschung: Eine Standortbestimmung," in *Bildgrammatik*, pp. 9–20, at p. 13. By contrast, Lambert Wiesing argues for the superiority of a phenomenological interpretation over a semiotic one, in *Die Sichtbarkeit des Bildes*; for a critique of Wiesing, see Georg W. Bertram and Jasper Liptow, "Lambert Wiesing: Die Sichtbarkeit des Bildes: Geschichte und Perspektiven der formalen Ästhetik," *Zeitschrift für Ästhetik und allgemeine Kunstwissenschaft*, 1998, 43, 295–303.

27. Wollheim, "Seeing-as, Seeing-in, and Pictorial Representation," in *Art and Its Objects*, pp. 205–26.

28. See Wolfgang Künne, "Sehen: Eine sprachanalytische Betrachtung," *Logos* (new series), 1995, 2, 103–21.

29. This is contrary to Danto, "Animals as Art Historians: Reflections on the Innocent Eye," in *Beyond the Brillo Box: The Visual Arts in Post-Historical Perspective* (Berkeley: University of California Press, 1998), pp. 15–31.

30. It is a borderline case when we grasp something that is (according to our own understanding) not a picture *as* a pictorial presentation. This projective pic-

ture seeing can nevertheless be understood only from the perspective of genuine picture seeing. On this, see Seel, *Eine Ästhetik der Natur*, chapter three, "*Natur als Imagination der Kunst.*"

31. Max Imdahl, "Ikonik: Bilder und ihre Anschauung," in *Was ist ein Bild?* pp. 300–25.

32. It is a further characteristic of the art picture that here the pictorial ground calls for far greater attentiveness than in other cases of picture use.

33. I employ the concept of cyberspace here in the narrow sense of a mechanically produced spatial state that changes its vistas in coordination with the bodily movements of beholders (equipped with data helmets or suits). Understood in this strict sense, the Internet still does not by any means constitute a cyberspace.

34. Walter Benjamin, "Surrealism: The Last Snapshot of the European Intelligentsia," in *Reflections: Essays, Aphorisms, Autobiographical Writings*, trans. Edmund Jephcott, ed. and intro. by Peter Demetz (New York: Harcourt Brace Jovanovich, 1978), pp. 177–92, at pp. 191–92. (Translator's note: translation altered.)

35. Wiesing, *Die Sichtbarkeit des Bildes*, esp. 168–92.

36. Siegfried Kracauer, *Theory of Film: The Redemption of Physical Reality*, intro. Miriam Bratu Hansen (Princeton: Princeton University Press, 1997), esp. pp. xlix and 27–40.

37. Barthes, *The Responsibility of Forms: Critical Essays on Music, Art, and Representation*, trans. Richard Howard (Berkeley: University of California Press, 1985); Deleuze, *Cinema 1: The Movement-Image*, trans. Hugh Tomlinson and Barbara Haberjam (Minneapolis: University of Minnesota Press, 1986); idem., *Cinema 2: The Time-Image*, trans. Hugh Tomlinson and Robert Galeta (Minneapolis: University of Minnesota Press, 1989).

38. Erwin Panofsky, "Style and Medium in the Motion Pictures," in *Three Essays on Style*, ed. Irving Lavin (Cambridge, Mass.: MIT Press, 1995), pp. 91–125; cf. Kracauer, *Theory of Film*, p. 309.

39. On this—and also on the difference between film and theater—see the astute reflections of Noël Carroll, "Towards an Ontology of the Moving Image," in *Philosophy and Film*, eds. Cynthia A. Freeland and Thomas E. Wartenberg (New York: Routledge, 1995), pp. 68–85.

40. See Seel, "Fotografien sind wie Namen," in *Ethisch-ästhetische Studien*, pp. 82–103, esp. pp. 100–103.

41. To vary the example given in the eleventh statement, we can imagine a cyberspace in which pictures and films are visible side by side.

CHAPTER FIVE

1. Keppler, "Über einige Formen der medialen Wahrnehmung von Gewalt," *Kölner Zeitschrift für Soziologie und Sozialpsychologie*, 1997, Sonderheft 37, 380–400, at 380.

2. Ibid.

3. Joan Simon, "Breaking the Silence: An Interview with Bruce Nauman," *Art in America*, Sept 1988, 76(9), 140–49, at p. 142.

4. If at least the ingredients of a "resonating" are a part of every successful artwork and this artistic resonating generates at least moments of a disoriented reception, then the argument is valid even without granting any exaggeration. On this, see Chapter Three.

5. *Arbeit macht frei*, 1958, Mr. and Mrs. Graham Gund Collection; *"Die Fahne hoch!"* 1959, Whitney Museum of American Art, New York.

6. Cormac McCarthy, *Blood Meridian, or, The Evening Redness in the West* (New York: Vintage Books, 1992), pp. 53–54.

7. Peter Weiss, *Die Ästhetik des Widerstands*, vol. 2 (Frankfurt am Main: Suhrkamp, 1983), pp. 119–20.

8. Bohrer, "Gewalt und Ästhetik als Bedingungsverhältnis," *Merkur*, 1998, 52, 281–93; see also idem., "Stil ist frappierend: Über Gewalt als ästhetisches Verfahren," in *Kunst—Macht—Gewalt: Der ästhetische Ort der Aggressivität*, ed. Rolf Grimminger (Munich: Fink, 2000), pp. 25–42.

9. David Sylvester, *Interviews with Francis Bacon, 1962–1979* (London: Thames and Hudson, 1980), p. 65.

10. Bohrer, "Gewalt und Ästhetik als Bedingungsverhältnis," p. 291 (italics added).

11. On this, see Keppler, "Über einige Formen der medialen Wahrnehmung von Gewalt."

Bibliography

Adorno, Theodor W. "Die Kunst und die Künste." In *Ohne Leitbild*. Frankfurt am Main: Suhrkamp, 1967, pp. 168–92.

———. *Negative Dialectics*. Translated by E. B. Ashton. London: Routledge & Kegan Paul, 1973.

———. "Über einige Relationen zwischen Musik und Malerei." In *Gesammelte Schriften*. Vol. 16. Edited by Rolf Tiedemann. Frankfurt am Main: Suhrkamp, 1978, pp. 628–42.

———. "In Memory of Eichendorff." In *Notes to Literature*. Vol. 1. Translated by Shierry Weber Nicholsen, edited by Rolf Tiedemann. New York: Columbia University Press, 1991, pp. 55–79.

———. "Valéry's Deviations." In *Notes to Literature*. Vol. 1, pp. 137–73.

———. *Aesthetic Theory*. Edited by G. Adorno and Rolf Tiedemann, translated by Robert Hullot-Kentor. Minneapolis: University of Minnesota Press, 1997.

Adorno, Theodor W., and Max Horkheimer. *Dialectic of Enlightenment*. Translated by John Cumming. London: Verso, 1979.

Balzac, Honoré de. *Illusions perdues*. Paris: Garnier, 1961.

———. *Lost Illusions*. Translated and introduced by Herbert J. Hunt. Harmondsworth: Penguin, 1971.

Barthes, Roland. *The Pleasure of the Text*. Translated by Richard Miller, with a note on the text by Richard Howard. New York: Hill and Wang, 1975.

———. "Music's Body." In *The Responsibility of Forms: Critical Essays on Music, Art, and Representation*. Translated by Richard Howard. Berkeley: University of California Press, 1985 [1982], pp. 243–312.

Baumgarten, Alexander Gottlieb. *Theoretische Ästhetik*. Translated and edited by Hans Rudolf Schweizer. Hamburg: Meiner, 1983.

Benjamin, Walter. "Surrealism: The Last Snapshot of the European Intelligentsia." In *Reflections: Essays, Aphorisms, Autobiographical Writings*. Translated by Edmund Jephcott, edited by and intro. by Peter Demetz. New York: Harcourt Brace Jovanovich, 1978, pp. 177–92.

Bernhard, Thomas. *Correction*. Translated by Sophie Wilkins. New York: Vintage, 1983.

Bertram, Georg W., and Jasper Liptow. "Lambert Wiesing: Die Sichtbarkeit des Bildes—Geschichte und Perspektiven der formalen Ästhetik." *Zeitschrift für Ästhetik und allgemeine Kunstwissenschaft,* 1998, *43,* 295–303.

Blumenberg, Hans. "Sokrates und das 'objet ambigu': Paul Valérys Auseinandersetzung mit der Tradition der Ontologie des ästhetischen Gegenstandes." In *Epimeleia: Die Sorge der Philosophie um den Menschen.* Edited by Franz Wiedmann. Munich: Pustet, 1964, pp. 285–323.

Boehm, Gottfried. "Die Wiederkehr der Bilder." In *Was ist ein Bild?* Edited by Gottfried Boehm. Munich: Fink, 1994, pp. 11–38.

———. "Die Bilderfrage." In *Was ist ein Bild?* pp. 325–43.

Böhme, Gernot. *Atmosphäre: Essays zur neuen Ästhetik.* Frankfurt am Main: Suhrkamp, 1995.

———. *Anmutungen: Über das Atmosphärische.* Ostfildern, Germany: Edition Tertium, 1998.

Bohrer, Karl Heinz. *Suddenness: On the Moment of Aesthetic Appearance.* Translated by Ruth Crowley. New York: Columbia University Press, 1994.

———. "Aesthetics and Historicism: Nietzsche's Concept of 'Appearance.'" In *Suddenness,* pp. 113–47.

———. *Das absolute Präsens: Die Semantik ästhetischer Zeit.* Frankfurt am Main: Suhrkamp, 1994.

———. "Gewalt und Ästhetik als Bedingungsverhältnis." *Merkur,* 1998, *52,* 281–93.

———. "Stil ist frappierend: Über Gewalt als ästhetisches Verfahren." In *Kunst—Macht—Gewalt: Der ästhetische Ort der Aggressivität.* Edited by Rolf Grimminger. Munich: Fink, 2000, pp. 25–42.

Brandom, Robert B. *Making It Explicit: Reasoning, Representing, and Discursive Commitment.* Cambridge, Mass.: Harvard University Press, 1994.

Brandt, Reinhard. *Die Wirklichkeit des Bildes: Sehen und Erkennen—vom Spiegel zum Kunstbild.* Munich: Hanser, 1999.

Brecht, Bertolt. *Stories of Mr. Keuner.* Translated with an afterword by Martin Chalmers. San Francisco: City Lights Books, 2001.

Bubner, Rüdiger. *Ästhetische Erfahrung.* Frankfurt am Main: Suhrkamp, 1989.

———. "Über einige Bedingungen gegenwärtiger Ästhetik." In *Ästhetische Erfahrung,* pp. 9–51.

Carroll, Noël. "Towards an Ontology of the Moving Image." In *Philosophy and Film.* Edited by Cynthia A. Freeland and Thomas E. Wartenberg. New York: Routledge, 1995, pp. 68–85.

Chandler, Raymond. *The Long Goodbye.* In *Later Novels and Other Writings.* New York: Library of America, 1995, pp. 417–734.

Danto, Arthur C. *The Transfiguration of the Commonplace: A Philosophy of Art.* Cambridge, Mass.: Harvard University Press, 1981.

————. *After the End of Art: Contemporary Art and the Pale of History.* Princeton: Princeton University Press, 1997.

————. "Animals as Art Historians: Reflections on the Innocent Eye." In *Beyond the Brillo Box: The Visual Arts in Post-Historical Perspective.* Berkeley: University of California Press, 1998, pp. 15–31.

————. "The End of Art: A Philosophical Defense." *History and Theory,* 1998, Theme Issue 37, 127–43.

Deleuze, Gilles. *Cinema 1: The Movement-Image.* Translated by Hugh Tomlinson and Barbara Haberjam. Minneapolis: University of Minnesota Press, 1986.

————. *Cinema 2: The Time-Image.* Translated by Hugh Tomlinson and Robert Galeta. Minneapolis: University of Minnesota Press, 1989.

————. *Francis Bacon—Logik der Sensation.* Vol. 1. Translated by Joseph Vogl. Munich: Fink, 1995.

Enzensberger, Hans Magnus. *The Sinking of the Titanic: A Poem.* Translated by the author. Boston: Houghton Mifflin, 1980.

Figal, Günter. "Ästhetische Individualität: Erörterungen im Hinblick auf Ernst Jünger." In *Individuum: Probleme der Individualität in Kunst, Philosophie und Wissenschaft.* Edited by Gottfried Boehm. Stuttgart: Klett-Cotta, 1994, pp. 151–71.

Freud, Sigmund. *Beyond the Pleasure Principle.* Translated and newly edited by James Strachey. Introduced by Gregory Zilboorg. New York: Norton, 1975.

Gabriel, Gottfried. *Zwischen Logik und Literatur: Erkenntnisformen von Dichtung, Philosophie und Wissenschaft.* Stuttgart: Metzler, 1991.

Goodman, Nelson. *Languages of Art: An Approach to a Theory of Symbols.* Indianapolis: Bobbs-Merrill, 1968.

————. "The Way the World Is." In *Problems and Projects.* Indianapolis: Bobbs-Merrill, 1972, pp. 24–32.

Greenberg, Clement. "Avant-Garde and Kitsch." In *The Collected Essays and Criticism.* Vol. 1: *Perceptions and Judgments, 1939–1944.* Edited by John O'Brian. Chicago: University of Chicago Press, 1986–1993, pp. 5–22.

————. "Modernist Painting." In *The Collected Essays and Criticism.* Vol. 4: *Modernism with a Vengeance, 1957–1969.* Edited by John O'Brian. Chicago: University of Chicago Press, 1986–1993, pp. 85–93.

Gumbrecht, Hans Ulrich. "Die Schönheit des Mannschaftssports: American Football—im Stadion und im Fernsehen." In *Medien—Welten—Wirklichkeiten.* Edited by Gianni Vattimo and Wolfgang Welsch. Munich: Fink, 1998, pp. 201–29.

Handke, Peter. *Der Hausierer.* Frankfurt am Main: Suhrkamp, 1967.

Haugeland, John. "Truth and Rule-Following." In *Having Thought: Essays in the Metaphysics of Mind.* Cambridge, Mass.: Harvard University Press, 1998, pp. 305–61.

Hegel, Georg Wilhelm Friedrich. *Aesthetics: Lectures on Fine Art.* 2 vols. Translated by T. M. Knox. Oxford: Clarendon University Press, 1975.

————. *Philosophy of Mind: Being Part Three of the Encyclopaedia of the Philosophical Sciences (1830).* Translated by William Wallace. *Zusätze* translated by A. V. Miller. Foreword by J. N. Findlay. Oxford: Clarendon Press, 1977.

————. *Hegel's Introduction to Aesthetics.* Translated by T. M. Knox, introduced by Charles Karelis. Oxford: Oxford University Press, 1979.

Heidegger, Martin. *Being and Time.* Translated by John Macquarrie and Edward Robinson. Oxford: Blackwell, 1962.

————. "The Origin of the Work of Art." In *Poetry, Language, Thought.* Translated by Albert Hofstadter. New York: Harper & Row, 1971, pp. 15–87.

————. *The Basic Problems of Phenomenology.* Translated by Albert Hofstadter. Bloomington: Indiana University Press, 1982.

Henrich, Dieter. "Kunst und Kunstphilosophie der Gegenwart." In *Immanente Ästhetik und ästhetische Reflexion.* Edited by Wolfgang Iser. Munich: Fink, 1966, pp. 11–32.

Hölderlin, Friedrich. "Bread and Wine." In *Poems and Fragments.* 3rd ed. Translated by Michael Hamburger. London: Anvil Press Poetry, 1994, pp. 263–73.

Imdahl, Max. "Ikonik: Bilder und ihre Anschauung." In *Was ist ein Bild?* Edited by Gottfried Boehm. Munich: Fink, 1994, pp. 300–325.

Iser, Wolfgang. *Das Fiktive und das Imaginäre: Perspektiven literarischer Anthropologie.* Frankfurt am Main: Suhrkamp, 1991.

Jelinek, Elfriede. *Die Kinder der Toten.* Reinbek bei Hamburg: Rowohlt, 1995.

Jonas, Hans. "Homo Pictor: Von der Freiheit des Bildens." In *Was ist ein Bild?* Edited by Gottfried Boehm. Munich: Fink, 1994, pp. 105–24.

Kafka, Franz. "In the Penal Colony." In *The Best Short Stories.* Edited and translated by Stanley Appelbaum. New York: Dover, 1997, pp. 140–67.

Kant, Immanuel. *Critique of Judgment.* Including the First Introduction. Translated by Werner S. Pluhar. Indianapolis: Hackett, 1987.

Keppler, Angela. "Über einige Formen der medialen Wahrnehmung von Gewalt." *Kölner Zeitschrift für Soziologie und Sozialpsychologie,* 1997, Sonderheft 37, 380–400.

————. "Verschränkte Gegenwarten: Medien- und Kommunikationssoziologie als Untersuchung kultureller Transformationen." In *Soziologie 2000: Kritische Bestandsaufnahmen zu einer Soziologie für das 21. Jahrhundert. Soziologische Revue,* Sonderheft 5. Edited by Richard Münch, Claudia Jauß, Carsten Stark. Munich: Oldenbourg, 2000, pp. 140–52.

Kosuth, Joseph. "Statement." *Flash Art,* Feb.–Mar. 1971, 2.

————. "Three Answers by Joseph Kosuth to Four Questions by Pierre Restany." *Domus,* May 1971, 53–54.

————. "Art After Philosophy." In *Conceptual Art.* Edited by Ursula Meyer. New York: Dutton, [1969] 1972, pp. 155–70.

Kracauer, Siegfried. *Theory of Film: The Redemption of Physical Reality.* Introduced by Miriam Bratu Hansen. Princeton: Princeton University Press, 1997.

Kripke, Saul A. *Naming and Necessity.* Cambridge, Mass.: Harvard University Press, 1980.

Künne, Wolfgang. "Sehen: Eine sprachanalytische Betrachtung." *Logos* (new series), 1995, 2, 103–21.

Kunst- und Ausstellungshalle der Bundesrepublik Deutschland, editor. *Gerhard Richter.* Vol. 2. Stuttgart: Kunst- und Ausstellungshalle der Bundesrepublik Deutschland, 1993.

Kurz, Gerhard. "Graue Romantik: Zu Walter Flex' *Wildgänse rauschen durch die Nacht.*" In *Hermenautik—Hermeneutik: Literarische und geisteswissenschaftliche Beiträge zu Ehren von Peter Horst Neumann.* Edited by Holger Helbig, Bettina Knauer, and Gunnar Och. Würzburg: Königshausen & Neumann, 1996, pp. 133–52.

Lec, Stanislaw Jerzy. *Unfrisierte Gedanken.* Translated by Karl Dedecius. Munich: Hanser, 1959.

Lehmann, Hans Thies. "Ästhetik: Eine Kolumne—Fülle, Leere." *Merkur,* 1995, 49, 432–38.

Luhmann, Niklas. *Art as a Social System.* Translated by Eva M. Knodt. Stanford: Stanford University Press, 2000.

McCarthy, Cormac. *Blood Meridian, or, The Evening Redness in the West.* New York: Vintage Books, 1992.

McDonell, Neil. "Are Pictures Unavoidably Specific?" *Synthese,* 1983, 57, 83–98.

McDowell, John. *Mind and World.* Cambridge, Mass.: Harvard University Press, 1994.

———. *Mind, Value, and Reality.* Cambridge, Mass.: Harvard University Press, 1998.

Man, Paul de. "Reading (Proust)." In *Allegories of Reading: Figural Language in Rousseau, Nietzsche, Rilke, and Proust.* New Haven: Yale University Press, 1979, pp. 57–78.

Mayer, Günter. "Das 'Rauschen' des Irrealen: Zur Kritik des radikalen Konstruktivismus im Bereich der Ästhetik und Musikästhetik." *Das Argument,* 1977, 39, 351–66.

Menke, Christoph. *Die Souveränität der Kunst: Ästhetische Erfahrung nach Adorno und Derrida.* Frankfurt am Main: Suhrkamp, 1988.

———. "Wahrnehmung, Tätigkeit, Selbstreflexion: Zur Genese und Dialektik der Ästhetik." In *Falsche Gegensätze: Zeitgenössische Positionen zur philosophischen Ästhetik.* Edited by Andera Kern and Ruth Sonderegger. Frankfurt am Main: Suhrkamp, 2002, pp. 19–48.

Merleau-Ponty, Maurice. "Cézanne's Doubt." In *Sense and Non-Sense.* Translated by Hubert L. Dreyfus and Patricia A. Dreyfus. Evanston, Ill.: Northwestern University Press, 1964, pp. 9–25.

————. "Eye and Mind." In *The Primacy of Perception, and Other Essays on Phe-nomenological Psychology, the Philosophy of Art, History, and Politics.* Translated by Carleton Dallery, edited and introduced by James M. Edie. Evanston, Ill.: Northwestern University Press, 1964, pp. 159–78.

Müller, Axel. *Die ikonische Differenz: Das Kunstwerk als Augenblick.* Munich: Fink, 1997.

Nabokov, Vladimir. *Pnin.* London: Heinemann, 1957.

Nietzsche, Friedrich. *The Birth of Tragedy out of the Spirit of Music.* Translated by Shaun Whiteside, edited by Michael Tanner. Harmondsworth: Penguin, 1993.

Panofsky, Erwin. "Style and Medium in the Motion Pictures." In *Three Essays on Style.* Edited by Irving Lavin. Cambridge, Mass.: MIT Press, 1995, pp. 91–125.

Pirenne, Maurice Henri. *Optics, Painting and Photography.* London: Cambridge University Press, 1970.

Polanyi, Michael. "What Is a Painting?" *British Journal of Aesthetics,* 1970, *10,* 225–36.

Pothast, Ulrich. "Bereitschaft zum Anderssein: Über Spürenswirklichkeit und Kunst." In *Im Rausch der Sinne: Kunst zwischen Animation und Askese.* Edited by Konrad Paul Liessmann. Vienna: Zsolnay, 1999, pp. 258–82.

Putnam, Hilary. *Renewing Philosophy.* Cambridge, Mass.: Harvard University Press, 1992.

————. "Replies." *Philosophical Topics,* 1992, *20,* 347–408.

Rilke, Rainer Maria. "As long as self-thrown things you catch . . . " In *Poems 1912–1926.* Selected, translated, and introduced by Michael Hamburger. Red-ding Ridge, Conn.: Black Swan Books, 1981, p. 83.

Sachs-Hombach, Klaus. "Was ist ein Bildalphabet?" In *Bildgrammatik: Interdiszi-plinäre Forschungen zur Syntax bildlicher Darstellungsformen.* Edited by Klaus Sachs-Hombach and Klaus Rehkämper. Magdeburg: Scriptum-Verlag, 1999, pp. 57–66.

Sachs-Hombach, Klaus, and Klaus Rehkämper. "Aspekte und Probleme der bild-wissenschaftlichen Forschung: Eine Standortbestimmung." In *Bildgrammatik,* pp. 9–20.

Sanio, Sabine. "Das Rauschen, Paradoxien eines hintergründigen Phänomens." In *Das Rauschen.* Edited by Sabine Sanio and Christian Scheib. Hofheim: Wolke, 1995, pp. 50–66.

Sartre, Jean-Paul. *The Psychology of the Imagination.* Translated by anon. London: Methuen, 1972.

Schanz, Richard. *Wahrheit, Referenz und Realismus: Eine Studie zur Sprachphiloso-phie und Metaphysik.* Berlin/New York: de Gruyter, 1996.

Scheer, Brigitte. *Einführung in die philosophische Ästhetik.* Darmstadt: Wissen-schaftliche Buchgesellschaft, 1997.

Scholz, Oliver R. *Bild, Darstellung, Zeichen: Philosophische Theorien bildhafter Darstellung.* Freiburg/Munich: Alber, 1991.

Schopenhauer, Arthur. *The World as Will and Representation.* Vol. 1. Translated by E.F.J. Payne. New York: Dover, 1969.

Schürmann, Eva. *Erscheinen und Wahrnehmen: Eine vergleichende Studie zur Kunst von James Turrell und der Philosophie Merleau-Pontys.* Munich: Fink, 2000.

Schweizer, Hans Rudolf, and Armin Wildermuth. *Die Entdeckung der Phänomene.* Basel: Schwabe, 1981.

Seel, Martin. *Die Kunst der Entzweiung: Zum Begriff der ästhetischen Rationalität.* Frankfurt am Main: Suhrkamp, 1985.

———. *Eine Ästhetik der Natur.* Frankfurt am Main: Suhrkamp, 1991.

———. *Versuch über die Form des Glücks.* Frankfurt am Main: Suhrkamp, 1995.

———. *Ethisch-ästhetische Studien.* Frankfurt am Main: Suhrkamp, 1996.

———. "Review of Niklas Luhmann, *Die Kunst der Gesellschaft.*" *European Journal of Philosophy,* 1996, 4, 390–93.

———. "Art as Appearance: Two Comments on Arthur C. Danto's *After the End of Art.*" *History and Theory, 1998,* Theme Issue 37, 102–14.

———. "Bestimmen und Bestimmenlassen: Anfänge einer medialen Erkenntnistheorie." *Zeitschrift für Philosophie,* 1998, *46,* 351–65.

———. "Die Macht des Erscheinens: Nietzsches ästhetische Marginalisierung des Seins." *du,* 1998, *6,* 26–28.

———. "Medien der Realität und Realität der Medien." In *Medien—Computer—Realität.* Edited by Sybille Krämer. Frankfurt am Main: Suhrkamp, 1998, pp. 244–68.

Simon, Joan. "Breaking the Silence: An Interview with Bruce Nauman." *Art in America,* Sept. 1988, *76*(9), 140–49.

Sonderegger, Ruth. *Für eine Ästhetik des Spiels: Hermeneutik, Dekonstruktion und der Eigensinn der Kunst.* Frankfurt am Main: Suhrkamp, 2000.

Steiner, George. *Real Presences.* Chicago: Chicago University Press, 1989.

Strawson, Peter F. "Perception and Its Objects." In *Perception and Identity.* Edited by G. F. MacDonald. Ithaca, N.Y.: Cornell University Press, 1979, pp. 41–60.

Sylvester, David. *Interviews with Francis Bacon, 1962–1979.* London: Thames and Hudson, 1980.

Theunissen, Michael. "Freiheit von der Zeit: Ästhetisches Anschauen als Verweilen." In *Negative Theologie der Zeit.* Frankfurt am Main: Suhrkamp, 1991, pp. 285–98.

Valéry, Paul. *Eupalinos; ou l'architecte, précédé de l'âme et la danse.* Paris: Gallimard, 1924.

———. *Autres Rhumbs.* In *Tel Quel II.* Paris: Gallimard, 1943, pp. 103–97.

———. *Eupalinos, or The Architect.* In *Dialogues: The Collected Works of Paul Valéry.* Vol. 4. Translated by William McCausland Stewart. Princeton: Princeton University Press, 1977, pp. 65–150.

Virilio, Paul. *The Aesthetics of Disappearance.* Translated by Philip Beitchman. New York: Semiotext(e), 1991.

Weiss, Peter. *Die Ästhetik des Widerstands.* Vol. 2. Frankfurt am Main: Suhrkamp, 1983.

Wellmer, Albrecht. *The Persistence of Modernity: Aesthetics, Ethics and Postmodernism.* Translated by David Midgley. Cambridge, Mass.: MIT Press, 1991.

———. "Das musikalische Kunstwerk." Unpublished manuscript, Berlin, 1999.

———. "Das musikalische Kunstwerk." In *Falsche Gegensätze: Zeitgenössische Positionen zur philosophischen Ästhetik.* Edited by Andera Kern and Ruth Sonderegger. Frankfurt am Main: Suhrkamp, 2002, pp. 133–75.

Wiesing, Lambert. *Die Sichtbarkeit des Bildes: Geschichte und Perspektiven der formalen Ästhetik.* Reinbek bei Hamburg: Rowohlt, 1997.

———. "Bilder im Geiste und an der Wand." *Philosophische Rundschau,* 1999, *46,* 56–71.

Wildermuth, Armin. "Philosophie des Ästhetischen: Das erscheinungsphilosophische Denken Heinrich Barths." In *In Erscheinung treten: Heinrich Barths Philosophie des Ästhetischen.* Edited by Günther Hauff, Hans Rudolf Schweizer, Armin Wildermuth. Basel: Schwabe, 1990, pp. 205–60.

Wolf, Ursula. "Einleitung." In *Eigennamen: Dokumentationen einer Kontroverse.* Edited by Ursula Wolf. Frankfurt am Main: Suhrkamp, 1985, pp. 9–41.

Wollheim, Richard. *Art and Its Objects: With Six Supplementary Essays.* Cambridge: Cambridge University Press, 1980.

———. "Seeing-as, Seeing-in, and Pictorial Representation." In *Art and Its Objects,* pp. 205–26.

Cultural Memory | *in the Present*

Samuel Weber, *Institution and Interpretation: Expanded Edition*

Jeffrey S. Librett, *The Rhetoric of Cultural Dialogue: Jews and Germans in the Epoch of Emancipation*

Ulrich Baer, *Remnants of Song: Trauma and the Experience of Modernity in Charles Baudelaire and Paul Celan*

Samuel C. Wheeler III, *Deconstruction as Analytic Philosophy*

David S. Ferris, *Silent Urns: Romanticism, Hellenism, Modernity*

Rodolphe Gasché, *Of Minimal Things: Studies on the Notion of Relation*

Sarah Winter, *Freud and the Institution of Psychoanalytic Knowledge*

Samuel Weber, *The Legend of Freud: Expanded Edition*

Aris Fioretos, ed., *The Solid Letter: Readings of Friedrich Hölderlin*

J. Hillis Miller/Manuel Asensi, *Black Holes/J. Hillis Miller; or, Boustrophedonic Reading*

Miryam Sas, *Fault Lines: Cultural Memory and Japanese Surrealism*

Peter Schwenger, *Fantasm and Fiction: On Textual Envisioning*

Didier Maleuvre, *Museum Memories: History, Technology, Art*

Jacques Derrida, *Monolingualism of the Other; or, The Prosthesis of Origin*

Andrew Baruch Wachtel, *Making a Nation, Breaking a Nation: Literature and Cultural Politics in Yugoslavia*

Niklas Luhmann, *Love as Passion: The Codification of Intimacy*

Mieke Bal, ed., *The Practice of Cultural Analysis: Exposing Interdisciplinary Interpretation*

Jacques Derrida and Gianni Vattimo, eds., *Religion*